Meade and Lee After Gettysburg

The Forgotten Final Stage of the Gettysburg Campaign
from Falling Waters to Culpeper Court House,
July 14 - 31, 1863

Jeffrey Wm Hunt

Savas Beatie
California

Library of Congress Cataloging-in-Publication Data

Names: Hunt, Jeffrey Wm. (Jeffrey William), 1962- author.
Title: Meade and Lee After Gettysburg: The Forgotten Final Stage of the Gettysburg Campaign from Falling Waters to Culpeper Court House, July 14 - 31, 1863 / Jeffrey Wm Hunt.
Description: El Dorado Hills, California : Savas Beatie LLC, 2017. | Includes bibliographical references and index.
Identifiers: LCCN 2017014058| ISBN 9781611213430 (alk. paper) | ISBN 9781611213447 (ebk.) | ISBN 9781611214451 (pbk)
Subjects: LCSH: Gettysburg Campaign, 1863. | Virginia—History—Civil War, 1861-1865—Campaigns. | United States—History—Civil War, 1861-1865—Campaigns.
Classification: LCC E475.51 .H86 2017 | DDC 973.7/349—dc23
LC record available at https://lccn.loc.gov/2017014058

First Edition, First Printing

SB

Published by
Savas Beatie LLC
989 Governor Drive, Suite 102
El Dorado Hills, CA 95762

Phone: 916-941-6896
(web) www.savasbeatie.com
(E-mail) sales@savasbeatie.com

Savas Beatie titles are available at special discounts for bulk purchases in the United States by corporations, institutions, and other organizations. For more details, please contact Savas Beatie, P.O. Box 4527, El Dorado Hills, CA 95762, or you may e-mail us at sales@savasbeatie.com, or visit our website at www.savasbeatie.com for additional information.

Proudly published, printed, and warehoused in the United States of America.

For

Dr. George Forgie,
University of Texas at Austin

The epitome of the word "Professor,"
a friend and inspiration,
with great admiration and gratitude

Table of Contents

Table of Contents (continued)

Maps

(All maps courtesy of Chris Hunt)

Illustrations

ACCORDING to a broad and deep historical consensus, the Gettysburg campaign came to close when Robert E. Lee's Army of Northern Virginia successfully slipped back across the swollen Potomac River into Virginia on the night of July 13-14, 1863. Some accounts discuss in broad terms the ten days that followed, but students of the war have long been led to believe the campaign ended once Lee was across the Potomac. Until I read Jeff Hunt's *Meade and Lee After Gettysburg* manuscript, I thought so as well.

Meade and Lee After Gettysburg is the first entry in a proposed series of books that study what happened in the Virginia Theater during the five months after Lee's army crossed the Potomac River in mid-July and the onset of the winter encampment in December 1863. That extensive period surely had an impact on the course of the war and has much of value worth studying, but historians have breezily skipped past it to get to the main event that kicked off in the Wilderness in early May 1864, and did not end until General U. S. Grant accepted Lee's surrender in the McLean parlor at Appomattox the following April.

This first installment (which might be subtitled "The Lost weeks of the Gettysburg Campaign") covers the second half of July 1863 and the eyebrow-raising events that transpired during that tight time frame. The major topics that fill out the balance of these months include Bristoe Station, Rappahannock Station, and the Mine Run campaign.

I was introduced to Jeff Hunt three years ago by Theodore P. Savas, the managing director of Savas Beatie. At the time, Jeff was already well along the path of producing a landmark study of what is surely the most under-reported period of the Civil War in the Eastern Theater. As it turned out, Jeff produced a very large single volume. Ted convinced him to split the mammoth effort into three separate books. Throughout I have followed with great interest Jeff's shaping and reshaping of his study in general, and this manuscript in particular.

Meade and Lee After Gettysburg touches on the battle itself lightly, eases Lee and his Virginia army across the river, and then, when the curtain is fully raised, delves deeply into the ten or so days that follow. To my knowledge, no previous scholar has attempted to examine, at this depth, the operations in the northern reaches of Virginia (Lee's men west of the Blue Ridge Mountains, and Meade's army mostly on the eastern side in Loudoun Valley). Other than the very occasional article, a passing mention in biographies and works on the larger conflict, or very specialized topics, this period has been utterly neglected.

Lee's goal, which began the moment Pickett's Charge failed, was to escape back into Virginia and reach a safe position to rest and reorganize his battered army. That location was the Rappahannock River line, the area from which he had begun the campaign in early June. Meade's goal was to cut off Lee's retreat and inflict a decisive defeat, something he failed to achieve at Falling Waters. Once back in Virginia, his immediate objective was to block the Blue Ridge passes and trap the Confederates in the Lower (northern) Shenandoah Valley, force a battle on unfavorable terms for Lee (or one or more of his corps commanders), and destroy or disperse the Virginia army.

The remarkable cat and mouse game that ensued during those lost weeks brimmed with strategic decisions pregnant with import on not just the course of the war in Virginia, but perhaps the war itself. It may come as a surprise to many students that Lee had a fully functioning and still very dangerous army. Many engagements ensued, most of the smaller variety, but some were surprisingly large with game-changing outcomes dangling by a thread. Once this time period is understood, it becomes obvious the Gettysburg campaign in no way ended when Lee crossed the Potomac river, and only came to a conclusion when the armies resumed their positions along the Rappahannock line. The Potomac offers a clean, easy demarcation line; research and deep thinking and allowing the evidence to take you where it leads, is much harder and very rare.

The more involved I became with Jeff's manuscript, the more excited I was by its fresh research and keen insights. Jeff's work offers an interesting interpretation of the war in the Eastern Theater while breaking new ground—a difficult and rare combination in an era that, more often than not, churns out cut-and-paste history by the numbers.

Something that must not be overlooked is that Jeff's study is also the first (and long overdue) examination of the generalship of George Gordon Meade as an independent commander. There was a gap in the Meade scholarship yearning to be filled. The Gettysburg campaign was well underway and the main battle just three days off when Meade was plucked from V Corps command to lead the Army of the Potomac. Some scholars, Edwin Coddington, Stephen Sears, and Harry Pfanz among them, take pains to (mostly) laud Meade for his generalship before, during, and immediately after Gettysburg—perhaps partially in response to those who blame Meade for not being more aggressive in the three-day battle or during the pursuit of Lee to the Potomac River. Gordon Rhea, the author of the monumentally important multi-volume Overland Campaign series, thinks highly of General Grant and implies that his plans in 1864 failed to defeat Lee's army sooner mostly because of the timidity of Meade and his Army of the Potomac generals. Keith Poulter, the former editor of *North & South Magazine*, takes it one step further by claiming the Army of the Potomac was a second-rate organization, and Grant's Army of the Tennessee was the only truly great Union army in the Civil War.

The gulf between these two interpretations of Meade and his army is significant. Meade cannot be the same man described in these conflicting views. The only place left to seek out an accurate assessment of Meade's generalship is during the period after Lee crossed back into Virginia (July 13-14, 1863) and the nearly five months that followed until December, when the armies went into winter quarters and before Grant arrived in the Eastern Theater to assume supreme command and take up residence in the field. It was during this period that Meade was the master of his domain and in charge of the Army of the Potomac. This book, and the two installments that will follow, offers the first full opportunity to fairly judge General Meade in independent command.

The portrait of Lee is less incomplete, but gaps remain. The Southern commander is often castigated for his decision to invade the North rather than send troops to save Vicksburg, and for his failure to properly oversee his subordinates during the Gettysburg campaign. In stark contrast, his conduct during the Overland fighting is usually (though of course not always) commended as tactically extraordinary. There is distance between the Lee of Gettysburg and the Lee of the Overland Campaign—and the comparison is not unlike the Meade we have come to know through the pens of historians. What has been missing is a bridge between these campaigns that can help us develop the sense of continuity necessary to fully appreciate the generalship of each man and the performance of their armies. The period from mid-July 1863 through the end of the year offers precisely that.

Therefore, it gives me tremendous pleasure to help introduce this work to the reading public, and to introduce Jeff Hunt as both my friend and as a historian and writer I greatly respect.

Bryce Suderow
Washington, D. C.

THE genesis of this book occurred nearly thirty years ago. I was an undergraduate at the University of Texas in Austin taking Professor George Forgie's course on the Civil War. The best part of that semester was engaging in frequent after-class discussions with Dr. Forgie. One afternoon, when our conversation turned to the Gettysburg campaign, we discussed Lee's goals during the Pennsylvania invasion and the importance of the campaign. Dr. Forgie's suggestion that Gettysburg may not have been as critical to the outcome of the war as many historians postulate left me intrigued. I decided to explore the issue.

There were many variables involved, and I decided to first determine the impact of Gettysburg by examining the military situation in Virginia from the conclusion of the campaign through the end of 1863. That investigation turned into a two-decade exploration of the operations conducted by the Army of the Potomac and the Army of Northern Virginia during the last six months of 1863. The first thing that struck me was how little these critical months had been seriously studied. War coverage mostly ended with Lee's return to Virginia in mid-July and did not resume until the elevation of General U. S. Grant the following March 1864. What happened in between?

My research, first with the *Official Records* and then with newspapers, journals, regimental histories, and other sources, convinced me that not only was this time frame filled with important events, but that this fascinating period was vital to understanding the course of the war that followed. My initial purpose of studying this period morphed into my determination to write about the fall campaigns of 1863. Naturally, the chronological boundaries of my study would begin with the end of the Gettysburg campaign and conclude with the onset of winter and the end of active military operations. As it turned out, it wasn't quite that simple.

Historians and students of the war almost exclusively agree that the Gettysburg campaign ended when the Confederate army escaped across the Potomac River on night of July 13-14, 1863. I, too, had long held that opinion. The more closely I studied this period, however, the more I came to believe this was simply not so.

The letters and diaries penned by the soldiers who marched and fought through those days, coupled with the reports and correspondence that make up the war's official record, tell a very different story. They were well aware that another major battle was very likely during the final weeks of July 1863 as General Lee endeavored to push his battered army through the Blue Ridge Mountains toward the Rappahannock line, and the more cautious General Meade did his best to foil that attempt. The strategic chess match produced a flurry of activity and several severe clashes as Meade did his best to trap Lee in the northern reaches of the Shenandoah Valley.

The soldiers and commanders who experienced the hardships of those weeks, as well as the newspaper correspondents who covered them, left behind an enormous amount of primary material. Their accounts, largely neglected by historians and virtually unknown to general readers of the Civil War, offer a story ripe with drama and import that nearly changed the entire course of the war in the Eastern Theater.

These documents leave no doubt that the saga of Gettysburg did not conclude until the rival armies came to rest along the Rappahannock River near Culpeper Court House, Virginia, on July 28, 1863. Indeed, in one of the many ironies of this campaign, its final engagement was a sharp cavalry action around Brandy Station on August 1—a combat waged in same general area and by the same military arm that fought the much larger Battle of Brandy Station on June 9 in what many believe was the opening fight of the campaign.

Meade's pursuit south of the Potomac and his efforts to block Lee and bring him to battle was as potentially dangerous to the Virginia army as the actions in Maryland following the July 1-3 fighting. In other words, the Gettysburg campaign ended along the banks of the Rappahannock and not the Potomac, and it ended two weeks later than most people believe.

As best as I could tell, no one had researched and written a book-length account of those two weeks. For readers, it is important to understand that my original manuscript (more than 800 pages long), included the entire period from mid-July to the end of the Mine Run Campaign. On the advice of my editor, we divided this into three separate books, so the one you hold in your hand includes only the last two weeks of July. The footnotes and the bibliography reflect that reality.

*   *   *

This book represents the latest chapter in my lifelong passion for military history. That fascination began before I started school. Where this interest consumed me is hard to say. Perhaps it is because my father was serving in the US Army when I was born. My mother swears the first word I ever said was "combat," apparently learned while watching the old World War II themed TV series of the same name. Certainly a love of history and military history in particular, has always been a large part of who I am. Also courtesy of Dr. Forgie I met fellow students who introduced me to historical reenacting—a hobby I have enjoyed for more than three decades. When I chose to become a professional historian, my parents greeted the decision with supportive skepticism.

Fortunately I had mentors and friends who helped me turn passion into a vocation. Once I earned my Master's degree I secured a position as an adjunct professor of history at Austin Community College, and I have had the pleasure of teaching there part-time for more than 28 years. My full-time employment is in the museum field. From 1994 until 2006 I was the curator of collections and the director of the living history program at the National Museum of the Pacific War in Fredericksburg, Texas (the hometown of Fleet Admiral Chester W. Nimitz). In 2007, I became the director of the Texas Military Forces Museum—the official museum of the Texas National Guard—at Camp Mabry in Austin. Throughout my career I've had the honor of working alongside service men and woman from every branch of the armed forces and the inestimable privilege of interacting with many hundreds of veterans.

Although my interests and work encompass the entire sweep of United States history, the Civil War has always been my primary passion. All of my published works, including my first book, *The Last Battle of the Civil War: Palmetto Ranch* (2002) and contributions to *The Revised Handbook of*

Texas, The Essential Civil War Curriculum, and the *Gale Library of Daily Life: Civil War*, focus on the great struggle between the North and the South. My three decades of participation in Civil War reenacting and living history programs has helped me acquire a helpful understanding of how the veterans of that conflict lived, marched, and fought, as much as such a thing is possible today. More importantly, my hope is that decades of teaching about and studying the Civil War have given me the ability to do justice to the remarkable men whose incredible story I try to tell in these pages.

Acknowledgments

The publication of this book is the culmination of a long and fascinating journey. It was not a trip I took alone. There were many along the way who lent assistance, encouragement, enthusiasm, support and a critical eye to my efforts. One of the greatest joys connected to bringing these volumes to print is the opportunity to say thank you to my companions on this particular voyage of inquiry and discovery.

The genesis of this project was a conversation with my mentor, Dr. George Forgie of the University of Texas at Austin, during a question-and-answer session following one of his outstanding lectures on the Civil War. As a young college student I had already learned a great deal about the war, courtesy of a life-long fascination with the subject that began in fourth grade. But as is typical of youth, I thought I knew a good deal more than I really did, and my grasp of the conflict (I now know) was sometimes narrow, simplistic and too utterly accepting of the conventional wisdom constructed by historians up to the early 1980's.

Dr. Forgie's remarkable and charismatic intellect was much too sharp and nimble to accept the idea that all there was to know about the war had been uncovered already. Like every great professor, he taught not only by answering questions, but by asking questions of his students. In this way he encouraged me to ponder my own certitude regarding the course of the war and its many battles. In particular he challenged my assumption that Gettysburg was the turning point of the Civil War by helping me realize I could not defend such an assertion with the certainty I assumed. Thus, he not only prompted me to try to find the answers to questions he had helped me articulate, he also convinced me to make history my profession as well as my avocation.

The search for evidence to prove or refute the idea that Gettysburg was the war's turning point led me to the examine the final weeks of the Gettysburg campaign as well as the Bristoe Station and Mine Run campaigns. That pursuit ultimately led to these volumes. The joy of discussing history with George Forgie, the encouragement he gave me as a student and the honor of studying under his instruction are treasures for which there is no true recompense, and for which my heartfelt thanks seem a paltry repayment for what has been given.

Throughout the research and writing of this work, I have been actively involved in Civil War reenacting. The knowledge I have gained of the life of the common soldier as well as the way he marched, maneuvered and fought as a result of my reenacting experiences have been invaluable to my ability to understand the campaigns I have written about.

Too often, reading historians' accounts of military action leaves me with the inescapable feeling that the author is casually waving their hand over the map when describing or explaining the movements of military units. As any real soldier will tell you, the map is not the territory. War is a simple thing when reduced to crisp arrows drawn on maps that give an unobstructed, birds-eye view to their beholder. Real campaigns and real combat are very different, plagued as they are by uncertainty, terrain, weather, confusion, contradictory or nonexistent intelligence, and the foibles of human nature.

Obligatory references to the "fog of war" aside, it is one to thing to question why such and such a general did not hurl his men into an attack as soon as they reached the battlefield, and another to understand what soldiers feel and are capable of after a 20-mile march, with little rest or food. Likewise the complexities of moving Civil War units through the evolutions of the line to deploy them on the battlefield, the time it takes to form a line of battle or a column of march, the rigors of moving down dusty roads and suffering the accordion-like motion of a column slowed by a creek, the noise and confusion of a smoke-covered battlefield, and the inertia that can grip troops in action against a foe of unknown strength, are things critical to truly understanding the letters, diaries, memoirs and official reports of the men who fought the war. To be sure, a reenacted march or "battle" is a far cry from the real thing, but it is as close as modern man can get, and the insights created by taking part in quality events have proved enlightening beyond measure.

Therefore I want to thank the reenacting community and especially those men I have soldiered alongside over many decades for everything they have done to help me better understand the realities experienced by the common soldier and field officer. Just as importantly, the camaraderie so lovingly recalled in memoirs and reunions after the war, are every bit as real for the reenactor as for the veteran. The power of those emotions and the impact they have on unit cohesion and the ability to endure suffering is something that has to be experienced to be understood. The comrades, with whom I have marched, camped, cooked, froze, sweltered, dug, worked, planned and "fought" are as dear to me as those of any veteran's. So I will indulge myself by taking this opportunity to say thank you to the men of the Confederate Guard, the Texas Rifles, the Tom Green Rifles, the 1st Trans-

Mississippi Battalion and the Red River Battalion. It has been a pleasure to serve and learn with you.

No author can write about history without standing on the shoulders of the chroniclers who have traveled the road before him: the curators who have diligently collected the letters, diaries, reports, memoirs, newspaper articles and other first-person accounts of the war, and archivists who have painstakingly cataloged and preserved them. Being a museum professional, I understand the enormous amount of work and care that go into such endeavors.

I would like to thank Corinne Nordin (Indiana Historical Society), Christine Beauregard, (New York State Library), Linda Thornton (Auburn University), Janet Bloom (William Clements Library–University of Michigan), Leah Weinryb Grohsgal, Teresa Burk and Kathy Shoemaker (Robert Woodruff Library–Emory University), Joan Wood (Stewart Bell, Jr. Archives, Handley Regional Library, Winchester-Frederick County Historical Society), Blaine Knupp and Theresa McDevitt (Indiana University of Pennsylvania), Helen Conger (Case Western Reserve University Archives), Katherine Wilkins (Virginia Historical Society), Peiling LI and Alyson Barrett (Gilder Lehrman Institute of American History), Matthew Turi (Southern Historical Collection, University of North Carolina), Vicki Catozza (Western Reserve Historical Society Library and Archives), Jennifer Coleman (Navarro College), Shannon Schwaller (United States Military History Institute), Emilie Hardman (Houghton Library, Harvard University), the Research & Instructional Services Staff of the Wilson Library (University of North Carolina), and the staff of the Museum of the Civil War (formerly the Museum of the Confederacy).

I would also like to extend my sincere appreciation to Amanda Shields, Associate Registrar at Brandywine River Museum of Art, for her very kind assistance in securing permission to use the fabulous painting by N.C. Wyeth which graces the dust jacket of this volume. Additionally, my sincere gratitude goes to Mr. Jonathon T. Mann, Jane Faulkner Wiltshire Snyder (great granddaughter to Senator Charles James Faulkner II), Mr. Ben Ritter, of Winchester, Virginia and Mr. Jim Heflin, Archivist at the Warren Heritage Society in Front Royal, Virginia, Sharon Bradley, Special Collections Librarian at the University of Georgia School of Law, Mr. Ed Jackson and Ms. Marie Mize for assisting me in obtaining some of the rare photographs used in this work.

It was also my pleasure to have a pair of excellent researchers assisting my efforts by doing the hard work of tracking down and photographing materials in archives I could not get to in a timely fashion. Mark Ragan did outstanding work on my behalf at the National Archives and Library of Congress while Jonathan Wiley did the same at the North Carolina State Archives and University of North Carolina. I cannot thank them enough for their professionalism, patience and perseverance.

No book makes it into print without a publisher. Theodore P. Savas, managing director of Savas Beatie, saw merit in my study and believed in it from the start. He was an encouraging and honest critic throughout. When he found ways to make my original manuscript better, he let me know and firmly pushed me to undertake additional work to make this as good as possible. It was his idea to divide my original manuscript into three books. Ted assigned Steven Smith, Savas Beatie's new editorial director, as my development editor. Steve was fantastic to work with, and his enthusiasm for this story and skill in fine-tuning my manuscript were remarkable. He is the kind of editor every writer dreams of working with. Marketing director Sarah Keeney and all the other great folks at Savas Beatie who have played a part in bringing this volume to print, also have my utmost respect and gratitude.

As I was developing my manuscript I was honored to pick the brain of Civil War scholar Bryce Suderow. He was an intellectual joy to chat with and an insightful commentator on this period of the war and my approach to it. This work is much the better because of the contributions he made to it. I also owe a debt of gratitude to Dr. Gary Gallagher and Kent Masterson Brown, two of the war's preeminent historians, for their encouragement and support of this endeavor.

There is, of course, no substitute for walking the ground where a battle was fought or campaign unfolded. Bill and Austin McMeans and Gill Eastland accompanied me on my initial sojourn to the historic fields written about in these pages. They were not only enjoyable companions and fellow enthusiasts for Civil War and military history, but also endured my sometimes barely constrained excitement at seeing the ground for the first time.

Last but certainly not least, my wife Chris deserves special commendation. She is not only my rock and partner, but is always ready with encouragement and understanding. Chris drafted the outstanding maps for this book (an endeavor that requires incredible talent and patience), proofread the initial manuscript, listened sympathetically as I talked through events and questions aloud, and never muttered a complaint about the weekends and long nights spent working on this project or the small fortune in books and research materials I purchased. She is remarkable.

I do not pretend that this volume and the ones I hope will follow comprise the last word on war in Virginia between mid-July and the end of December 1863. My hope is that they bring long-deserved attention to these campaigns and the experiences of the men and women who lived through them. My humble wish is for these pages to contribute to the scholarship and our understanding of America's seminal conflict, and do justice to those men of both sides who lived this chapter in our history.

Jeffrey Wm Hunt
Austin, Texas

Chapter 1

"The War Will Be Prolonged Indefinitely"

The Retreat from Gettysburg—Meade's Hesitation—Lee's Escape—President Lincoln's Disappointment—Meade Retains Command—the War Continues

T HE battle of Gettysburg was the largest fought in the war thus far. For three bloody days, Union and Confederate armies contested the hills and woods near that little Pennsylvania town. The Rebels came close to winning the struggle, but in the end the advantage rested with the Federals. General Robert E. Lee's Army of Northern Virginia, forced into a rare admission of defeat, abandoned the field of battle and withdrew toward Virginia. As the Rebels retreated from Pennsylvania, the last Confederate bastions on the Mississippi River—Vicksburg and Port Hudson—surrendered, giving the North complete control over the great waterway and cutting the Southern Confederacy in two.

Such Union victories in the Western Theater were not uncommon, although they had been few and far between since the beginning of 1863. In the Eastern Theater, however, it had been a long time since the Army of the Potomac had bested the Rebels. In fact, many questioned whether the Federals in Virginia had ever really beaten the Confederates. First Bull Run, the Peninsula campaign and Seven Days, Cedar Mountain, Second Bull Run, Fredericksburg, Chancellorsville, and Second Winchester were among the more prominent names on the list of Union disasters. Only Antietam had provided relief from the procession of defeats. Unfortunately, its long casualty list and Major General George B. McClellan's failure to follow up on General Lee's subsequent withdrawal lessened the public impact of what was a strategic achievement.

Gettysburg, on the other hand, was an unquestioned tactical and strategic triumph. The Army of the Potomac, seemingly poorly led and chronically unlucky, often derided in the press, had finally, decisively, whipped the Army of Northern Virginia. Accustomed to the defeat of their Eastern army, Northerners were overjoyed, and perhaps a bit surprised, by Major General George Meade's upset victory. Headlines announcing the Confederate defeat proclaimed the battle the greatest military success in history. Relief and glee over Lee's defeat morphed into euphoria when the news from Vicksburg multiplied Northern joy.

Captain William T. Lusk, stationed in Wilmington, Delaware, personified the depth of Yankee ecstasy. Feeling the Union had survived its "dark hour," Lusk exclaimed, "the dawn is broken, and the collapsed confederacy has no place where it can hide its head." Amid the "patriotic clamor" of ringing church bells and celebratory cannon fire, people were grinning "at one another with fairly idiotic delight," he wrote, explaining that the news from Gettysburg and Vicksburg combined was "a little too much happiness for poor mortal men."[1]

In Pennsylvania, the men who made up the Army of the Potomac were justly proud of their triumph. Letters penned soon after the battle were full of proclamations about the nature of the Federal victory. The triumph was gratifying in many ways, not least in that it provided a ready answer to critics of the Eastern army and those who compared its disappointing record to victories won by Union forces under Major Generals Ulysses S. Grant and William S. Rosecrans.[2]

More importantly, the Pennsylvania victory allowed many to believe the end of the war might be in sight. Thomas Carpenter, a clerk at army

---

1 Lusk, William Thompson, *War Letters of William Thompson Lusk* (New York, NY, 1911), 184-185.

2 Frederick Winkler letter of July 4, 1863 www.russscott.com/~rscott/25thwis/ 26pgwk63. htm; Lawrence F. Kohl and Margaret C. Richard, ed., *Irish Green and Union Blue: The Civil War Letters of Peter Welsh: Color Sergeant 28th Massachusetts Volunteers* (New York, NY, 1986), 113; Oliver Norton, *Army Letters 1861-1865* (Chicago, IL, 1903), 161; Raymond G. Barber and Gary E. Swinson, ed., *The Civil War Letters of Charles Barber, Private, 104th New York Volunteer Infantry* (Torrance, CA, 1991), 136; James Robertson, ed., "An Indiana Solider in Love and War: the Civil War Letters of John V. Hadley," *Indiana Magazine of History*, 59, No. 3, Sept. 1963.

headquarters, thought the "fourth of July morning that saw Lee's shattered army retreat and Vicksburg surrender . . . will date as the downfall of the Rebellion." Carpenter's sentiments were echoed in hundreds, perhaps thousands of letters written by Union troops after the battle. Joy and optimism seem to pervade every piece of correspondence. "I really begin to think now that we are soon to see the end of the war," wrote one Federal, while another admitted he was "in great hopes of the war coming to a close soon." Samuel Cormany, a sergeant in the 16th Pennsylvania Cavalry, thought likewise, telling his diary the Confederacy was a "waning cause tottering on its last legs."[3]

The Northern press agreed. Anticipating the complete and rapid destruction of the rebellion, it heaped scorn on the retreating Confederates. Noting that Southern papers never tired of proclaiming the military genius of Robert E. Lee, *Harper's Weekly* admitted "it has not been unfashionable, even among loyal men," to believe the Confederate general far superior to his Union counterparts. The triumph in Pennsylvania, however, spelled the end of the Rebel's supposed dominance. Lee's reputation as a great general, *Harper's Weekly* assured its readers, "begins and ends at Gettysburg."[4]

While denigrating Lee, Northern papers were quick to praise the leadership of General Meade, who had been appointed to the thankless task of leading the Army of the Potomac just days before the Pennsylvania victory. Even in far-off London, the Federal general received plaudits for his handling of the battle. Everywhere editors proclaimed Meade the best general to have ever led the Army of the Potomac, and the man apt to end the war by destroying Lee's Army of Northern Virginia.[5]

Many of Meade's troops cautiously concurred with that appraisal. Thomas Carpenter felt Meade had "shown a skill and judgment in the Gettysburg battle that cannot be too highly commended." The victory created hope that the North had found the man capable of crushing Lee and his army. "If Meade holds out as well as he has begun," Carpenter continued,

---

3   Thomas Carpenter, letter of July 7, Missouri Historical Society; Stephen M Weld, *War Diary and Letters of Stephen M. Weld 1861-1865* (Boston, MA, 1979), 239-240; George Bolton, letter of July 18, 1863; James C. Mohr, ed., *The Cormany Diaries: A Northern Family in the Civil War* (Pittsburg, PA, 1982), 345.

4   *Harper's Weekly*, August 8, 1863.

5   *Illustrated London News*, August 1, 1863.

"he will make his name famous and beloved for more than one generation." After seeing so many generals show much early promise, only to disappoint in the end, however, Carpenter hedged his bet on Meade: "I would not *swear* by him because he has won one battle, yet I think he will do."[6]

Major Henry L. Abbott of the 20th Massachusetts was also uncertain how much faith to put in the army's new commander. Describing the general as "tall, thin, lantern-jawed, [and] respectable," Abbott thought Meade's spectacles made him look the part of a good "family doctor" more than a triumphant warrior. Appearances notwithstanding, he felt the general was "an extremely good officer, with no vanity or nonsense of any kind," and applauded his leadership at Gettysburg where Meade had seemed to know "exactly what he could do & what he couldn't."[7]

Nonetheless, Abbot, like Carpenter and many others, could not quite bring himself to wholeheartedly invest faith in Meade. He wondered whether the determination of Union troops and the fact that they had occupied eminently defensible terrain on their own soil, meant that the common soldiers "deserve fully as much credit as the generalship of Meade" for Gettysburg. For now he felt "great confidence" in the general, "though no enthusiasm."[8]

One reason George Meade failed to incite passion was that he was virtually unknown outside the V Corps until his appointment as commander of the Army of the Potomac on June 28, 1863. His relative anonymity wasn't because he had not been in the thick of the fighting. Meade established a solid reputation leading a brigade on the Virginia Peninsula until he was wounded in the hip and arm at White Oak Swamp on June 30, 1862. He remained on the field until loss of blood and pain forced him to seek medical attention. After a brief convalesce, Meade returned to duty in time to take part in the battles of Second Bull Run, and then lead a division at South Mountain, Antietam (where he held temporary corps command), and Fredericksburg, where his division turned in what was arguably the best performance on a disastrous day. In each engagement he received plaudits for his coolness and courage under fire as well as his aggressiveness—all of

---

6   Thomas Carpenter Diary, Missouri Historical Society.

7   Robert G. Scott, ed., *Fallen Leaves: The Civil War Letters of Major Henry Livermore Abbott* (Kent, OH, 1992), 189.

8   Ibid, 189.

Major General George Gordon Meade

Library of Congress

which helped propel him from brigadier to major general, to date from November 29, 1862. He led the V Corps in the Chancellorsville campaign, during which he expressed dismay at Major General Joseph Hooker's decision to abandon the battle and retreat across the Rapidan.[9]

The 47-year-old Meade was highly regarded by his peers. Lieutenant Colonel Horace Porter, who would get to know the general well during the last year of the war, described him as "a most accomplished officer [who had] a complete knowledge of both the science and the art of war." Porter also wrote that that Meade "was well read, possessed of a vast amount of interesting information, had cultivated his mind as a linguist, and spoke French with fluency." When foreign military observers visited the army, explained Porter, "they were invariably charmed."[10]

A London reporter interviewed the general during the summer of 1863 and came away quite flattered. "He is a very remarkable looking man—tall, spare, of a commanding figure and presence, his manner pleasant and easy but having much dignity," explained the foreign writer. "His head is partially bald and is small and compact, but the forehead is high. He has the late Duke of Wellington class of nose, and his eyes, which have a serious and almost sad expression, are rather sunken, or appear so from the prominence of the curved nasal development. He has a decidedly patrician and distinguished appearance."[11]

When he wasn't entertaining the foreign press, however, Meade looked anything but distinguished. One officer quipped that "his habitual personal appearance is quite careless, and it would be rather difficult to make him look well dressed." That appraisal was accentuated by the general's tall cavalry boots and well-weathered "slouched hat with a conical crown and a turned-down rim" that gave him the kind of rough and ready look that soldiers approved.[12]

---

9 Patricia L. Faust, ed. *Historical Times Illustrated Encyclopedia of the Civil War* (New York, NY, 1986), 482-483.

10 Horace Porter, *Campaigning with Grant* (New York, NY, 1897), 247. Porter met Meade while serving as Lieutenant General Ulysses S. Grant's aide-de-camp in April 1864. Porter was promoted to Brevet Brigadier General in 1866.

11 www.thelatinlibrary.com/chron/civilwarnotes/meade.html.

12 Porter, *Campaigning with Grant*, 28, 247.

Although everyone seemed to admire his bravery and patriotism, the impression Meade made on his equals and the press did not translate easily to junior officers or the rank and file. Meade "was a disciplinarian to the point of severity," thought Colonel Porter, and "in his intercourse with his officers the bluntness of the soldier was always conspicuous, and he never took pains to smooth anyone's ruffled feelings." Indeed, Meade's most remarked-upon trait was his volatile temper. The 1835 West Point graduate, veteran of the Seminole Wars, and father of seven did not suffer fools gladly or incompetence lightly, and during active operations throughout the Civil War was quick to snap at anyone who failed to meet his exacting standard of performance or duty. The harshness with which the general lashed out was extraordinary, and often made him seem heartless, demeaning, or cruel. His soldiers called him "a damned old goggle-eyed snapping turtle"—an unflattering description of which Meade was fully aware. But if his temper could erupt suddenly and violently, it also relieved some of the general's frustrations and tension. On occasion he softened his outbursts with kind words or humor. "Meade does not mean to be ugly," wrote Colonel Charles S. Wainwright, commander of the I Corps' artillery, "but he cannot control his infernal temper."[13]

Whether or not Meade was *the* man who would win the war, there was no mistaking that "the tide of success" seemed to be flowing in favor of the Federals, as the *Illustrated London News* put it. The paper was also quick to point out, however, that the Union victory in Pennsylvania was, as yet, incomplete. The *Philadelphia Inquirer's* announcement that Gettysburg had eclipsed Waterloo was, to say the least, premature. Waterloo had brought about the final downfall of Napoleon's France. Gettysburg was a long way from achieving similar results against the Southern Confederacy.[14]

Even as the North hailed Gettysburg as a great victory, more thoughtful people in and out of the army realized it was only a beginning. Perhaps the end of the war might well be in sight, but it would take much more than the defensive success of the first three days of July to accomplish the destruction of the rebellion. Major Frederick C. Winkler of the 26th Wisconsin was among the many who understood the need to capitalize on Gettysburg before

13 Porter, *Campaigning with Grant*, 247; Allan Nevins, ed., *Diary of Battle: The Personal Journals of Colonel Charles S. Wainwright* (New York, NY, 1962), 116.

14 Freeman Cleaves, *Meade of Gettysburg* (Norman, OK, 1960), 170.

final victory could be won. In a letter home he expressed hope another battle could be fought north of the Potomac River, where the Union might "give the rebels a blow which will go far to end the war."[15]

In order to complete that task, Meade needed to quickly pursue the retreating Confederate army and destroy it before it could re-cross the Potomac. Just about everyone saw this, and one who saw it with unmistakable clarity was President Abraham Lincoln. After hearing the news from Gettysburg, Lincoln wrote Union General-in-Chief Henry W. Halleck, "If General Meade can complete his work, so gloriously prosecuted thus far, by the literal or substantial destruction of Lee's army, the rebellion will be over." Most people thought Meade would do just that. The general's own son, serving with his father as an aide, wrote his mother: "Papa will end the war."[16]

From a distance, the chances of Meade finishing off the Rebels looked very good. Recent heavy rains had swollen the Potomac to flood stage, making it unfordable. Lee had left a pontoon bridge over the river at Williamsport, Maryland, but it had been destroyed by a detachment of Union cavalry on July 3. As a result, when Lee's battered army reached the Potomac along with some 10,000 wounded men and enormous quantities of captured supplies, there was no ready way to get across the angry waters and back to relative safety in Virginia.[17]

While his engineers undertook the construction of a new bridge, Lee was forced to turn and face Meade. The Rebels dug in with speed and skill and were waiting for the Yankees when they began to arrive in strength on July 12. The Army of the Potomac's appearance no doubt came too early for Lee's taste, but as far as the administration in Washington was concerned, Meade was moving with agonizing slowness.

Lincoln, in particular, was worried. Indeed, his concerns about Meade had begun just two days after Gettysburg when he read the general's congratulatory order to his troops for their victory. After thanking his men for producing the "glorious result of the recent operations," Meade went on to tell his soldiers, "our task is not yet accomplished and the commanding

---

15 Frederick Winkler letters of July 4 and 8, 1863.

16 Cleaves, *Meade of Gettysburg*, 307.

17 Francis Walker, *History of the Second Army Corps* (New York, NY, 1887), 308.

general looks to the army for greater efforts to drive from our soil every vestige of the presence of the invader."[18]

Although the prose read well, it drove the president to heights of discontent. In a war being waged to prove the supremacy of the national government and the indivisible nature of the Federal Union, it did no good to imply the Southern Confederacy was a legitimate nation in its own right. Meade's order did just that. If there was an "our soil" that meant there must be a "their soil." Of course this was the reality of the moment, but it was a reality Federal armies were charged with changing. "Will our generals never get that idea out of their heads?" asked a frustrated Lincoln. "The whole country is our soil."[19]

Some Northern troops were equally unimpressed with Meade's pronouncement. Colonel James Gwyn, commanding the 118th Pennsylvania, had Meade's congratulatory order read before his regiment. Riding out in front of his men at the end of the address, Gwyn exhorted three cheers for General Meade. The soldiers, however, refused to utter a sound. They had seen commanders come and go with great rapidity. Each had promised victory. None had delivered, leaving the troops wary and more than a bit cynical. There would be "no more cheering" for any general.[20]

Whether they liked George Meade or not, few outside the army seemed to recognize the serious difficulties with which he contended. It was easier to focus on the equally difficult (or worse) problems Lee suffered—a reality those in Washington felt Meade was ignoring. Indeed, many in Lincoln's administration were uneasy about the apparent lack of killer instinct in the Union army's pursuit. Meade, naturally, felt differently.

The fact that the battle of Gettysburg had badly damaged Lee's Rebel army was vigorously reported by Northern newspapers. What most overlooked, however, was that the Army of the Potomac was as seriously damaged by its victory as the Army of Northern Virginia was by its defeat. Meade had taken upwards of 88,000 men into the battle. Of that number,

---

18 *War of the Rebellion: A Compilation of the Official Records of the Union and Confederate Armies*, 128 vols. (Washington, D.C., 1880-1901) Series 1, vol. 27, pt. 3, 519. Hereafter cited as *OR*. All references are to Series 1 unless otherwise noted.

19 Herman Hattaway and Archer Jones, *How the North Won* (Chicago, IL, 1983), 468.

20 J. Gregory Acken, ed., *Inside the Army of the Potomac: The Civil War Experience of Captain Francis Adams Donaldson* (Mechanicsburg, PA, 1998), 113.

3,155 men were killed, 14,529 wounded, and another 5,365 taken prisoner. Among the Union wounded were two division and two corps commanders. The head of the I Corps, Major General John Reynolds, had been killed and seven brigade commanders killed or mortally wounded. Several more brigadiers were wounded and unable to lead their men. In total, more than 300 Union officers of all ranks were lost during the battle.[21]

A roll call on the morning of July 5, 1863, for example, showed only 47,087 men present for duty. In addition, more than 5,000 unwounded Southern prisoners had to be dealt with, and many thousands more lying in makeshift hospitals. To state the matter plainly, almost the entire Army of the Potomac was exhausted and badly disorganized. The XI and I Corps, severely mauled during the first day of the battle, would never regain their former strength or élan. The III Corps suffered an equal fate on July 2. The cavalry had been heavily engaged and its horses, as well as those in the rest of the army, were in bad shape. Only the VI Corps came out of the battle in fairly good condition, having taken only a small part in the fighting.[22]

The entire army had undergone a very tough campaign, making forced marches of up to 36 miles a day through the June heat in an effort to catch up with Lee during his invasion. Meade's supply lines were in disarray. Slow-moving quartermaster trains had barely managed to keep up with the army, and hence the issue of rations, clothing, footwear, and essentials other than ammunition had been spotty. Some units were as bad off for shoes and clothing as the Rebels. One Pennsylvanian noted that many men in his brigade were "actually marching in their undershirt and drawers," while more were "barefoot or with only an apology for a shoe."[23]

In view of these facts, Meade did not feel he could simply hurl his army at the retreating Confederates. Lee's men had been beaten, not routed. His troops, accustomed to victory, would be eager to even the score at the earliest possible moment. The Army of Northern Virginia was a wounded panther

---

21 Mark Boatner III, *The Civil War Dictionary* (New York, NY, 1959), 339; Cleaves, *Meade of Gettysburg*, 173.

22 Andrew Humphreys, *From Gettysburg to the Rapidan: The Army of the Potomac July, 1863 to April, 1864* (New York, NY, 1883), 6.

23 Joseph R. C. Ward, *History of the One Hundred Sixth Regiment Pennsylvania Volunteers 2nd Brigade, 2nd Division, 2nd Corps* (Philadelphia, PA, 1883), 179.

and any careless step might cost the Union all it had won so dearly at Gettysburg.

Lee's withdraw ran through mountain passes back toward the Potomac. The gaps in these heights were easily defended, and it seemed fruitless to pursue Lee on his direct line of retreat. Instead, Meade sent his strongest corps, the VI, to follow the Rebels while the rest of the army made a wide swing to the east in an effort to get around the Southern flank. This allowed Meade to stay connected to his supply line while keeping his army between Lee and Washington, D.C. Meade hoped he could cut the Southern army off before it reached the Potomac. The same rains that made the river impassable, however, turned the roads into seas of mud. Forced to take a longer route and slog through ever-deepening mire, the exhausted Union army stood no real chance of catching the Confederates on the move to the Potomac, and it didn't.

As soon as Lee's troops reached the river, they turned to face their pursuers. Throwing up stout earthworks, the Rebels soon had a battle line firmly anchored on both flanks by the swollen river. Meanwhile, Lee's quartermasters employed makeshift ferries to transport wagon loads of badly injured men back to Virginia and transfer fresh stocks of ammunition to Maryland. As the Rebel infantry dug and the wounded slowly trickled across the Potomac, Southern engineers worked furiously to build a pontoon bridge to carry the rest of the army to safety.

By the time Meade got most of his men into line facing the entrenchments surrounding Lee's position, the Confederates had yet to complete their bridge and remained stuck north of the Potomac. With its back to an unfordable river, Lee's army looked ripe for destruction. If the Federals could break the Southern line, they would drive the Rebel force back to the Potomac and trap and destroy it there. A fight was eagerly anticipated. *Harper's Weekly*, confusing a clash of cavalry with the start of a general engagement, actually reported that Meade had attacked Lee at Williamsport, and that a great battle was in "active progress"[24]

*   *   *

---

24 *Illustrated London News*, July 25, 1863; *Harper's Weekly*, July 18, 1863.

Robert E. Lee certainly anticipated just such an attack. Although his army was in a formidable position, with solid and well-manned entrenchments to help thwart a Federal assault, he sought to stiffen the resolve of his troops with an order of the day issued on July 11.

Commending them for enduring with typical fortitude the "long and trying marches" made during the invasion, he reminded his men that they had forced the enemy out of the South and back onto his own soil. Although the "fierce and sanguinary battle" they had fought at Gettysburg had not been "attended with the success" that had "hitherto crowned [their] efforts," they could be proud of exhibiting the same "heroic spirit that has commanded the respect of your enemies, the gratitude of your country, and the admiration of mankind." Now, continued Lee, they must once more meet the enemy from whom they had "won on so many fields a name that will never die." Evoking everything for which Southern soldiers fought—family, home, honor, independence—and calling on the assistance of "that benign Power" which had "so signally blessed" their former efforts, Lee exhorted "each heart [to] grow strong in the remembrance of [the army's] glorious past" and "go forth in confidence to secure the peace and safety" of the Confederacy. The order ended with a ringing appeal: "Soldiers, your old enemy is before you. Win from him honor worthy of your right cause, worthy of your comrades dead on so many illustrious fields."[25]

By all accounts the general's message stirred the emotions of his soldiers. The fact that General Lee felt the need to issue such a moving address to his veteran troops while still on campaign emphasizes just how dire he believed was their predicament. Lee's concern was justified for Meade certainly intended to attack the cornered Rebels.

To be sure, Meade was getting plenty of urging from Washington to do so. General Halleck was fully aware of Lincoln's desire that Lee not escape, and he sent his army commander an imperative order to "push forward and fight Lee before he can cross the Potomac." When Meade and his commanders got a good look at the Confederate position around Williamsport, however, they were not inclined to make any rapid strikes.[26]

The Army of the Potomac's chief of staff, Major General Andrew A. Humphreys, was well known for his battlefield aggressiveness. An

---

25 *Harper's Weekly*, July 25, 1863.

26 Camp Clark, *Gettysburg: The Confederate High Tide* (Alexandria, VA, 1985), 153.

examination of the Rebel position, however, gave him pause. Much of the enemy line was concealed from view, but what could be seen "was naturally strong and . . . strongly entrenched." Humphreys could discern "no vulnerable points," while noting Lee's "flanks were secure and could not be turned." Meade reached the same conclusion and decided against an immediate attack. Instead, he determined to launch a reconnaissance in force, supported by his entire army, to seek a weak spot in the Southern line. If such a spot were found, then a proper assault could be organized to exploit it.[27]

The reconnaissance was scheduled for the morning of July 13. On the evening preceding the planned advance, Meade held a council of war with his corps commanders. During it, he discovered that nearly all of them were "adverse to the proposed operation." Faced with their doubts, and his own, Meade cancelled the movement pending further examination of the ground.[28]

On the morning of the 13th, rain pelted Federal troops busy throwing up earthworks instead of attacking the Rebel line. In the 118th Pennsylvania, Captain Francis Donaldson, among others, was frustrated the army had yet to assail Lee. He saw no reason for digging in. "Certainly it cannot be possible that Lee will again assume the offensive," Donaldson opined to his journal. Fearing building breastworks "just now" would make his troops "timid," the captain wondered what Meade was about. Everywhere along the line, Union troops fidgeted in anticipation and uncertainty. Most wondered "why the ball does not open," complained the adjutant of the 10th New York. Feeling the army was "full of spirit and eager to finish the war there and then," he couldn't understand why the order to attack had not already been given.[29]

Thomas Carpenter expressed the instinct of many Federal soldiers. "If our generals, now that they have the Rebellion on the downhill track, will but *push* it along, they may soon send it to destruction on the double quick," he wrote. Unworried by assertions that Meade lacked the strength to break

27 Humphreys, *From Gettysburg to the Rapidan*, 6

28 Ibid.

29 Acken, *Inside the Army of the Potomac*, 315; Charles W. Cowtan, *Services of the Tenth New York Volunteers* (New York, NY, 1882), 214-215.

Edwin Forbes painted this scene based on a sketch he drew of Lee's Williamsport defenses from within the Rebel works on July 14, 1863. The fields of fire and strength of the positions are obvious. *Library of Congress*

Lee's line, Carpenter believed "there are soldiers enough in the army *now* if they are only put to *work right off* to finish this job all up."[30]

Among the officer corps, however, there was no such certainty. Colonel Charles S. Wainwright, commanding the I Corps artillery, thought the odds of a battle very good if Lee did not slip across the Potomac first. Whether the impending engagement was to be desired, however, was an entirely different question. "It would nearly end the rebellion if we could actually bag" Lee's

30 Carpenter letters, Missouri Historical Society, letter of July 9, 1863.

army, he wrote. "But on the other hand, a severe repulse" would make up for all the damage done to the Rebels at Gettysburg and injure the morale of the North "greatly." Facing a decision of such monumental consequences, the colonel only hoped Meade would not hazard a battle unless his chances of success were "at least four out of five." Exactly how such a calculation could be made was left unstated.[31]

No similar doubts existed in the White House or in the War Department. Whatever his troops thought, Meade was very aware of the pressure to attack being exerted upon him by Washington. Seeking to reassure Lincoln, he

---

31 Allan Nevins, ed. *A Diary of Battle: The Personal Journals of Colonel Charles S. Wainwright, 1861-1865* (New York, NY, 1998), 239.

telegraphed Halleck a promise that the "decisive battle of the war will be fought in a few days."[32]

This message did not go over well in the Federal capital. The administration wanted an attack launched at once, lest Lee escape first. Halleck replied with an angry message to Meade telling him to "act upon your own judgment and make your generals execute your orders. Call no council of war. It is proverbial that councils of war never fight. Do not let the enemy escape." Meade had no doubt what he was expected to do, and he issued new orders accordingly. The reconnaissance-in-force would commence on the morning of July 14.[33]

Shortly after daybreak, skirmishers along Meade's entire front climbed over their earthworks and moved toward the Rebel fortifications. The entire army seemed to hold its breath as they advanced "rapidly across the intervening space," expecting "every moment to receive the fire of the enemy." Braced for the worst, the Northern skirmishers drew nearer the Confederate line. "When their formidable works loomed up before us," recalled a soldier in the 140th Pennsylvania, "a rush was made to occupy them." Racing the last handful of yards toward the ugly wall of dirt marking the enemy's position, the Federals quickly found themselves atop and then inside the fortifications. "To our great surprise and also to our *great relief*," admitted the Pennsylvanian, "we found them almost deserted."[34]

The Rebels Were Gone

As was so often the case, the Army of the Potomac acted too late. On the night of July 13, with his bridge finished and the waters of the Potomac just fordable, Lee managed to get his army back into Virginia. Well before Federal skirmishers moved forward to probe abandoned earthworks, the last Confederate formations were crossing the river, leaving only a modest rearguard to slow down any Union troops.

32 Camp Clark, *Gettysburg: The Confederate High Tide*, 156.

33 Ibid.

34 Robert L. Stewart, *History of the One Hundred Fortieth Regiment Pennsylvania Volunteers* (The Regimental Association, 1912), 147; Levi Fritz diary, Southern Historical Collection, University of North Carolina (SHC, UNC).

The Federals picked up 1,000 or so stragglers, but the Rebels managed to slip away virtually untouched. They even found time to destroy the bridge they had built, preventing the Yankees from using it for any attempt at pursuit. Despite the expectations of many, plus the orders of the general-in-chief and the express wishes of the president, Lee escaped.

When Union generals and soldiers got a good look at Lee's fortifications from the inside, many found reason to be glad Meade delayed his assault. What looked like a formidable position from the Union lines appeared to be impregnable from within the Southern works. General Humphreys put it concisely when he wrote that an assault on Lee's entrenchments "would have resulted disastrously."[35]

Henry Abbott thought Meade's wisdom at Williamsport equal to his generalship at Gettysburg. "It would have been madness to attack," the major wrote home, "as besides the entrenchments, the positions of Gettysburg would have been precisely reversed." Meade might yet prove to be a great general, or he might not, but for now Abbott was impressed.[36]

Private Edwin B. Weist of the 20th Indiana had a different take on the matter. He concurred in the common appraisal of Lee's fortifications, but not in the results. "The enemy's position was a very strong one and well entrenched," he confided to his diary. "We would have probably lost 10,000 men in taking it." Weist, however, did not share the belief of officers like Humphreys and Abbott that such loss would have been to no avail. Among he and his comrades there were "no doubts" the Rebel line would have been carried.[37]

There, in a nutshell, was the problem. Both generals and privates agreed the Rebel works at Williamsport were strong and that casualties in an attack would have been significant. The high command, doubting the line could be taken and uncertain the cost was worth the risk, hesitated, and afterward felt vindicated for not attacking. Privates like Weist thought the attack would have prevailed and, given the probable impact of a successful assault on the course of the war, believed the effort worth the risk and regretted the attempt was not made. All opinions on the issue were now moot. Lee and his army

---

35 Humphreys, *From Gettysburg to the Rapidan*, 7.

36 Scott, *Fallen Leaves*, 192.

37 Weist Diary, July 14.

were gone. The potentially decisive, war-winning fruits of Gettysburg left unpicked.

News that the Rebels had gotten away was a bitter blow in and out of the Union army. Many Federals could scarcely credit that "the golden opportunity of crushing Lee's army was lost." Observant officers admitted their men were "very much depressed" by Lee's escape. Rufus Ricksecker, commissary sergeant of the 126th Ohio, was furious at the news. "It looks as if *somebody* did not care about having this war finished very soon," he wrote in a letter two weeks later, his obvious frustration still in evidence.[38]

Not a few Union soldiers considered the failure to strike the Rebels gross incompetence. "Great dissatisfaction exists among the troops," one bemoaned to his diary. "We were all aware that we only needed the word to advance in order to have scattered the remains of Lee's army to the winds." That those orders were never given didn't fully surprise, however. "The army has got so used to bungles that it almost seems a matter of course."[39]

Eseck G. Wilber in the 120th New York thought Meade had handled the battle at Gettysburg "first rate," though word of Lee's escape confirmed an earlier prediction. "It is just as I expected," he wrote home. "Meade was very afraid of a little rain and laid over 24 hours too long and they slipped away." The effect on his fellow infantrymen was easy to see. "Every soljer is growling . . . because we might just as well had him as not."[40]

Headquarters clerk Thomas Carpenter thought Meade should have "caught Lee before he left Maryland, or knocked his army to fragments." With no little sarcasm, he wrote his parents, "But, perhaps you are not aware that *I* was not in command of the Army of the Poke-em-Back. Neither did the commander of that army consult me in regard to his operations. If he had," Carpenter continued, "and listened to my counsels, we should have tried it on, whatever the result might have been."[41]

Some troops tried to give Meade and his generals the benefit of doubt. The fact that the Rebels had made a "very clean and apparently orderly

38 Clapp Diary, July 13, 1863; Ricksecker letter, July 28.

39 Edward Cassedy, ed., *Dear Friends at Home: The Civil War Letters and Diaries of Sergeant Charles T. Bowen, Twelfth United States Infantry, First Battalion, 1861-1864* (Baltimore, MD, 2001), 296; Levi Fritz Diary, SHC/UNC.

40 Wilber letters July 12 , July 15, 1863, Fondren Library, Rice University.

41 Carpenter diary, July 20.

retrograde movement" refuted the idea that Lee's army was demoralized and on the verge of dissolution. Major Henry Winkler heard similar opinions. Writing home to his wife, he confided that many officers in whose military judgment he had "great confidence" were saying the army had "every reason to congratulate" itself on Lee's withdrawal across the Potomac. They assured Winkler any attack upon the Rebel earthworks would have been "doubtful of success." True or not, the major was certain events would be seen differently back home. "The public, I suppose, will be greatly disappointed," he predicted. The blame for their distress Winkler placed squarely on the press for giving "very exaggerated accounts of the effect of the late battle on the Rebel army," and making "great promises of its entire annihilation."[42]

Backing off his claim of just a week earlier, Winkler no longer believed it within the power of the Army of the Potomac to "give the rebels a blow which will go far to end the war." The army, he asserted, was in no condition to finish off Lee's host. Reinforcements and reorganization would be needed before Meade's command could be "reliably effective," and capable of another campaign.[43]

*   *   *

Whatever the rationale or justification within the army for the Rebel escape, the failure to assail Lee at Williamsport won Meade no friends in the Federal capital or the Northern press. Lincoln in particular was sullenly disappointed. The president could not shake the sinking feeling that his generals had failed to do all they could have done to turn Gettysburg into a war-winning triumph. On the evening of July 14, with Lee safely across the Potomac, the president received a message that poured salt into the wound of his despair. The correspondence was a telegram sent by Simon Cameron—a noted, some would say notorious, Pennsylvania politician—who had been Lincoln's secretary of war until January 1862, when the president had deftly eased him out of office for incompetence, corruption, and political maneuvering.

42 Winkler letters, July 12; Levi Fritz diary, SHC/UNC.

43 Ibid.

Visiting the Army of the Potomac the day before, Cameron had learned of Meade's council of war that had resulted in the postponement of the attack on Lee's bridgehead. Declaring the Union army in "fine spirits and eager for battle," Cameron assured Lincoln it would win a victory if given the chance. The former secretary feared, however, that Meade would allow the Rebels to get across the Potomac. He urged the president to use all his authority to urge every Federal commander within marching distance to reinforce Meade and leave that general "no reason for delay in giving battle."[44]

Lincoln did not receive this telegram until 10:00 p.m., by which time the realization of Cameron's fear was many hours old. Responding to the Pennsylvanian early the next morning, the president fully revealed the angst weighing on his soul. After informing his fellow Republican that the Confederates had already made good their withdrawal, Lincoln went on to confess he "would give much to be relieved of the impression that Meade" and other Union generals, had "striven only to get Lee over the river, without another fight."[45]

As the president saw it, his commanders had let slip through their fingers the great chance to end the war. Lincoln was so distressed by this fact that he wrote Meade a reproachful letter. "I do not believe you appreciate the magnitude of the misfortune involved in Lee's escape," he explained. Lee, continued the president, "was within your easy grasp, and to have closed upon him would, in connection with our other late successes, have ended the war. As it is, the war will be prolonged indefinitely."[46]

Whether Lincoln was correct in supposing Lee had been in Meade's easy grasp is open to debate, but it is nearly impossible to argue that the destruction of the Army of Northern Virginia would not have brought about the end of the war. The president was correct in his view that the struggle would now be prolonged indefinitely. Perhaps, in light of that fact, Meade should have assumed the significant risk of attacking at Williamsport. Trapped against the flooded river and 130 miles away from his nearest railhead at Staunton, Lee had never before been so vulnerable. A Union victory there could have had monumental consequences, whereas a repulse

44 *OR* 27 pt. 3, 700.

45 Ibid.

46 Cleaves, *Meade of Gettysburg*, 185.

would hardly have dissuaded the Rebel army from still retreating back into Virginia. Even a failed effort to destroy Lee would have left Meade in better graces with his superiors and the press than no effort at all.

Precisely because the war was going to continue, however, Lincoln— ever the pragmatist—had second thoughts about sending his letter. In the end, he put the document away and decided to leave well enough alone. Lee had escaped to fight another day, but Meade had indeed won a great and undeniable victory, which was more than could be said of every previous commander of the Army of the Potomac. It would not be politic to remove him or provoke his resignation. Besides, if the administration were to dismiss Meade, with whom would it replace him?

Even though Lincoln did not send his letter, evidence of the President's disappointment managed to find its way to Meade. After being informed Lee was across the Potomac, Halleck sent Meade a telegram clearly indicating Lincoln's view toward Lee's escape. "The enemy should be pursued and cut up, wherever he may have gone. . . . I need hardly say to you that the escape of Lee's army without another battle has created great dissatisfaction in the mind of the president," wrote Halleck, "and it will require an active and energetic pursuit on your part to remove the impression that it has not been sufficiently active heretofore."[47]

General Meade, whose short temper was well known, did not take Halleck's message well. He had been reluctant to assume command of the army from the start, and had done so because he was a soldier who obeyed orders. Meade had long felt Washington interfered too much with the army's operations and dictated strategy on the basis of politics rather than sound military science. A handful of weeks before the battle, he had written his wife Margaret that "the command of this army is not to be desired or sought . . . it is more likely to destroy one's reputation than to add to it." Margaret Meade, the daughter of a prominent Philadelphia politician and savvy in the ways of politics herself, concurred. She warned her husband that command of the army "would only be your ruin." Indeed, on June 27 when Colonel James A. Hardie arrived at Meade's headquarters with orders for him to take control of the army, Meade protested and tried to beg off the appointment. When Hardie informed him the instructions were "unquestionable and peremptory," the general was left with no choice but to comply. In a

47 *OR* 27, pt. 1, 92.

half-joking tone he told Hardie, "Well, I've been tried and condemned without a hearing, and I suppose I shall have to go to the execution."[48]

Meade, then, had taken command of the army just three days prior to the battle at Gettysburg. Now, in middle July, worn out from the physical and mental strain of fighting a large pitched battle and conducting a difficult pursuit, he was in no mood to be chastised by Henry Halleck. Within 90 minutes of receiving notice of the president's dissatisfaction, Meade sent a dispatch of his own: "Having performed my duty conscientiously and to the best of my ability, the censure of the President conveyed in your dispatch of 1 p.m. this day, is, in my judgment, so undeserved that I feel compelled most respectfully to ask to be immediately relieved from the command of this army."[49]

Halleck was smart enough to know that losing Meade was bad for the Union, and thus quick to respond. Before the afternoon ended he replied to the prideful general that his "telegram, stating the disappointment of the President . . . was not intended as a censure, but as a stimulus to an active pursuit. It is not deemed a sufficient cause for your application to be relieved."[50]

After receiving Halleck's second telegram, Meade let the matter drop. The Northern press, however, did not. When newspapers began to voice public distress over the successful Confederate retreat, Major General Oliver Otis Howard, commander of the Army of the Potomac's XI Corps, became concerned about the way the army and its new commanding general were being thought of in Washington. Howard took it upon himself to send a letter directly to the president.

The general told Lincoln that he was writing because he "noticed in the newspapers certain statements bearing upon the battle of Gettysburg and subsequent operations" he thought "calculated to convey a wrong impression" to the president. In the face of some of the charges being made, Howard wished to "submit a few statements" for Lincoln's consideration. He believed Meade deserved tremendous credit for winning the battle of

---

48 Cleaves, *Meade of Gettysburg*, 118; Charles F. Benjamin, "Hookers Appointment and Removal," *Battles and Leaders of the Civil War*, Vol. 3 (New York, NY 1956), 2341-2343.

49 *OR* 27, pt. 1, 92.

50 Ibid., 93-94.

Gettysburg, had handled the army well, and had thrown in the reserves at just the right time and place to produce the triumph.[51]

Regarding the failure to assault Lee's bridgehead at Williamsport, Howard assured Lincoln "it is by no means certain that the repulse of Gettysburg might not have been turned upon us. At any rate, the commanding general was in favor of an immediate attack, but with the evident difficulties in our way, the uncertainty of a success and the strong conviction of our best military minds against the risk, I must say that I think the general acted wisely."[52]

By this time Lincoln was putting as bright a face as possible on his lingering disappointment. The war would continue, and Meade would stay in command of the Union's Eastern army. Lincoln responded to Howard that he was "profoundly grateful" for what Meade had done "without criticism for what was not done." Lincoln went on to tell Howard that Meade had his "confidence as a brave and skillful officer and a true man."[53]

This was all well and good, but it was hardly enthusiastic praise. The fact of the matter is that Meade was not quite what Lincoln was looking for in an army commander. He was better than anyone else the Potomac army had produced, but Meade's view of how the war should be conducted did not quite fit with that of the president. This difference in opinion would create more difficulties before the year was over.

Whether Meade had been right not to strike at Williamsport, or whether he had blundered there, was now beyond knowing. But this much the president and the men of the Army of the Potomac did know: the failure to destroy Lee's army meant the promise of Gettysburg had yet to be reaped. More blood, perhaps much more, would be shed in Virginia before a similar chance was likely to come again.[54]

---

51 Ibid., 700.

52 Ibid.

53 Cleaves, *Meade of Gettysburg*, 188.

54 For a thorough tactical examination and expert analysis of the operations of both armies north of the Potomac River, see Eric J. Wittenberg, J. David Petruzzi, and Michael F. Nugent, *One Continuous Fight: The Retreat from Gettysburg and the Pursuit of Lee's Army of Northern Virginia, July 4-14, 1863* (New York, NY, 2008).

CHAPTER 2

"The Maryland Campaign is Ended"

Robert E. Lee—Battle at Gettysburg—The Confederates Pause to Regroup—Lee Receives Reinforcements—Federals Occupy Harper's Ferry—Meade's Decides to Cross the Potomac—Union Engineers Prepare to Bridge the River—Cavalry Fight at Halltown—Colonel Harmon Captured

ROBERT E. Lee was not accustomed to failure. Most of his life was a procession of accomplishments. The son of Revolutionary War hero "Light Horse" Harry Lee received an appointment to West Point in 1825 and graduated four years later second in his class—and without a single demerit—holding the title of corps adjutant, the highest post of honor for a cadet. A commission in the elite Corps of Engineers followed, as did his marriage in 1831 to Mary Custis, the great granddaughter of Martha Washington. Throughout the 1830s and first half of the 1840s, Lee enjoyed a distinguished career as a military engineer.[1]

And then war came. Lee gained national prominence serving as a captain on the staff of Lieutenant General Winfield Scott in Mexico. He laid out the US batteries that pummeled Veracruz into surrender in March 1847, and carried out a daring reconnaissance during Scott's advance on Mexico City. Lee's efforts proved crucial to the American victory at Cerro Gordo on April 18, 1847, and resulted in a promotion to brevet major. Similar performances

---

1 Patricia Faust, ed., *Historical Times Illustrated Encyclopedia of the Civil War* (New York, NY, 1986), 429-430.

during the rest of the campaign, and especially in the September 13, 1847 assault on Chapultepec, led to the capture of the Mexican capital and Lee's promotion to brevet lieutenant colonel.[2]

Following the Mexican War and more engineering projects, Lee served as Commandant of West Point from 1852-55. When Secretary of War Jefferson Davis created two elite cavalry regiments to serve on the Indian Frontier, Lee was appointed lieutenant colonel in the 2nd US Cavalry—his first line command—and stationed in central Texas. As the political divisions between North and South deepened, Lee fortuitously found himself in Washington, DC, where he assumed command of the troops who put down abolitionist zealot John Brown's October 1859 raid on the Federal arsenal at Harpers Ferry.[3]

Lee loved the United States and felt that every constitutional option should be exhausted before the remedy of secession—which he believed to be revolution—was taken up. When Virginia left the Union on April 17, 1861, Lee declined an exploratory offer from the Lincoln administration to assume command of the Federal army and instead resigned his commission and offered his services to his native state. As a major general and commander of Virginia's military forces he did much to prepare the Old Dominion for war. Once Virginia formally joined the Confederacy, Lee was made a full general in the Confederate Army, and saw his first field service in the mountains of western Virginia, where he was defeated in the Cheat Mountain Campaign. Lee was condemned in some circles for his failure to redeem a hopeless military situation. He was appointed to command the Department of South Carolina, Georgia and Florida on November 5, 1861, where his insistence on building defensive fortifications along the coasts won him the derisive nicknames "King of Spades" and "Granny Lee."[4]

The Confederate president, however, recognized Lee's skills and tapped the general as his military advisor. Lee was serving in that capacity when General Joseph E. Johnston was seriously wounded just outside Richmond at Seven Pines on May 31, 1862. Davis elevated Lee to command of the army defending the Southern capital. Many openly questioned his

2   Ibid.

3   Ibid; Tony Horwitz, *Midnight Rising: John Brown and the Raid That Sparked the Civil War* (New York, NY, 2011), 174-178.

4   Faust, *Encyclopedia of the Civil War*, 429-430.

appointment. Major Edward Porter Alexander, who would go on to become one of Lee's most trusted artillerists, asked Colonel Joseph Ives, a member of Jefferson Davis' staff, whether Lee had sufficient audacity to meet the challenge. "If there is one man in either army, Confederate or Federal, head and shoulders above every other in audacity," declared Ives, "it is General Lee! His name might be Audacity. He will take more desperate chances, and take them quicker than any other general in this country, North or South."[5]

Events soon bore out that assessment. At the head of the Army of Northern Virginia, Lee quickly demonstrated his considerable military talents by launching a bloody week-long offensive against Major General George McClellan's Army of the Potomac that drove the Federals away from Richmond. The victory was followed up by a more spectacular operational campaign that ended with the defeat of John Pope's Army of Virginia at Second Manassas and a raid north into Maryland. At Sharpsburg on September 17, 1862, Lee warded off McClellan's attacks but had no viable choice other than retreating back into Virginia. His record of victories resumed with a strong defensive victory at Fredericksburg that December, where a Federal division led by George Meade was the only one to reach and break through his line. The following spring of 1863, the heavily outnumbered Lee boldly divided his army into several parts and, with a grand flanking operation against the exposed Federal right flank led by Lieutenant General Thomas "Stonewall" Jackson, defeated Joe Hooker's Army of the Potomac at Chancellorsville and sent it back over the Rappahannock River. The Federal V Corps under George Meade saw but little combat because it anchored the left flank of Hooker's army. Unfortunately for Lee and the South, victory arrived at the unbearably high price of the death of Jackson, who succumbed to pneumonia after being wounded by friendly fire on the evening of May 2.[6]

In the aftermath of Jackson's death Lee reorganized his army into three corps. The First Corps continued to be led by the reliable Lieutenant General James Longstreet. Jackson's Second Corps was handed to the newly promoted Lieutenant General Richard S. Ewell. The new Third Corps, which included troops from the other corps and outside the army, was given

---

5 Gary W. Gallahger, *Fighting for the Confederacy: The Personal Recollections of General Edward Porter Alexander* (Chapel Hill, NC, 1989), 90-91.

6 Ibid.

to A. P. Hill, who was also elevated from major general to lead it. A cavalry division led by Major General James Ewell Brown (Jeb) Stuart completed the restructured Army of Northern Virginia.

This makeover came at a time of crisis for the Confederacy. Major General Ulysses S. Grant's Army of the Tennessee was laying siege to Vicksburg, Mississippi, and another Union force was besieging Port Hudson, Louisiana farther south. The loss of both strongholds, which seemed likely, would give the North control of the Mississippi River from its headwaters to the Gulf of Mexico. When President Davis proposed that Lee send part of his army to help save Vicksburg, the general convinced Davis that the best way to help the embattled Mississippi bastion was for him to invade the North. This bold move, argued Lee, was the most likely method of pulling Union forces away from the Mississippi River Valley and helping lift the sieges. The move would also draw the Federals out of war-torn Virginia, allow Lee's army to gather enormous quantities of supplies in Maryland and Pennsylvania, and—if the circumstances were right—meet and defeat the Army of the Potomac on Northern soil.[7]

The campaign began on June 3, 1863, when the first of Lee's infantry corps began leaving the Rappahannock River line around Fredericksburg for the Shenandoah Valley. The move went well during the early stages of the campaign until, as a result of a series of events, Stuart's cavalry lost contact with Lee's army. Without his regular intelligence reports from his trusted cavalryman, Lee crossed the Potomac River and moved through Maryland and into Pennsylvania with less information than he would have liked.

When he learned from a spy that Hooker had been replaced by General Meade and the Army of the Potomac was moving above the Potomac river chasing after him, Lee ordered his corps to concentrate east of the South Mountain range around Cashtown and the crossroads village of Gettysburg. On June 30, just outside Gettysburg and before that battle began, Lee met Lieutenant Colonel Arthur L. Fremantle of the British Army's Coldstream Guards. Fremantle was touring the Confederacy as a military observer. Lee impressed the Englishman, who described him as "almost without exception, the handsomest man of his age I ever saw." The 56-year-old Lee,

---

7 Douglas Southall Freeman, *R.E. Lee: A Biography* (New York, NY, 1946), Vol. 3, 8-17. Lee has been the subject of many biographies and examinations of his generalship. Freeman's work remains the standard by which all others are judged.

General Robert E. Lee *Library of Congress*

continued Fremantle, was "tall, broad-shouldered, very well made, well set up—a thorough soldier in appearance" who carried no side arms and sported "a well-worn, long, gray jacket, a high, black felt hat, and blue trousers tucked into his Wellington boots." His only insignia was that of a colonel—three stars on his collar—indicating his last rank in the US military.[8]

Appearances and courtly manner aside, the attribute that most distinguished Lee was his aggressiveness. Because of the industrial and manpower disparity between the North and South, he was convinced that only bold action triggering a string of Union defeats could win the war by convincing the United States to abandon the effort and make peace.[9]

On the morning of July 1, advance elements of Hill's corps met cavalry under Brigadier General John Buford west of Gettysburg. Soon thereafter, Major General John Reynolds' I Corps of infantry arrived, more Confederate troops were fed into the action, Reynolds was killed, and a major meeting engagement erupted.

Ewell's troops fortuitously arrived from the north on the flank of the I Corps. Their arrival made the Federal position untenable—including the line of Major General Oliver Howard's XI Corps, which had taken up a poor position north of town. Outflanked to the north and pressed from the west, the Union troops collapsed and fell back through town to the high ground beyond Gettysburg. The confusion of the chaotic victory, moderate losses, poor reconnaissance, and a lack of cavalry to protect his exposed left flank convinced Ewell that a further advance that evening was unwise. Darkness put an end to the fighting. Meade, who arrived on the field late in the day, was apprised that the ground was good for defensive operations. He ordered his army to concentrate and prepared to receive Lee's assault the following day.

With most of his army on the field by dawn on July 2, Lee determined to continue his offensive. Longstreet disagreed. He argued for a move around Meade's left to find a good defensive position between the Federal army and Washington, DC, and force Meade to attack them there. Lee rejected the plan and ordered Longstreet to take two divisions and assault the enemy left

---

8 Arthur L. Fremantle, *Three Months in the Southern States* (New York, NY, 1864), 248-49.

9 Gallahger, ed., *Fighting for the Confederacy*, 90-91.

flank, with troops from Hill's corps joining in the attack as it rolled north up Cemetery Ridge. Ewell, meanwhile, would attack Culp's Hill on the enemy far right. For a variety of reasons the assault did not begin until late that afternoon. Although Longstreet carried several positions, including the Peach Orchard, Devil's Den, and large stretches of the Emmitsburg Road, the bloody fighting failed to achieve the result Lee desired. Some of Hill's troops managed to break through lower Cemetery Ridge, but were driven back at dusk. Coordination broke down on Hill's front, with the corps commander noticeably disengaged from the action. Ewell's troops failed to take Culp's Hill, and a proposed joint attack at dusk against Cemetery Hill also failed.

Having tried to collapse both Federal flanks, Lee decided on the morning of July 3 to break Meade's center on Cemetery Ridge with an infantry attack, preceded by a massive artillery bombardment. Pickett's fresh division had arrived to spearhead the attack. Two other shot-torn divisions from Hill's Third Corps, one under Johnston Pettigrew and the other under Isaac Trimble, where tapped to join the effort. Longstreet, who was put in charge of the assault, vehemently disagreed with the plan and argued to no avail once more that the army move around Meade's left (something the Federal commander also feared Lee might do). After a long artillery bombardment by some 150 guns that failed to drive away the enemy or silence Federal tubes, the infantry stepped out of the woods and crossed the open fields. The casualties were horrific, and only a few hundred Rebels managed to reach and breach the Union line. The attack melted away. The battle of Gettysburg was over.[10]

Despite the sharp repulse, the Army of Northern Virginia had not lost faith in its commander, although some men blamed Lee for launching the desperate July 3 attack. Colonel Fremantle recalled Confederate artillery-men declaring that they still believed in Lee. "We've not lost confidence in the old man," they assured the Englishman, "This day's work will do him no harm. Uncle Robert will get us into Washington yet; you bet he will." Nor had the army lost confidence in itself. Its discipline and skill remained intact. On the night of July 4, after waiting an entire day to meet an enemy

<hr/>

10 Faust, *Encyclopedia of the Civil War*, 305-308, 584. There are several excellent books on Pickett's Charge. The latest and perhaps best is James Hessler and Wayne Motts, *Pickett's Charge at Gettysburg: The Most Famous Attack in American History* (Savas Beatie, 2015).

counterattack that never came, and giving his long supply and ambulance trains a head start, Lee withdrew his army from the blood soaked fields of Gettysburg. Under Lee's leadership, and with his principle subordinates performing much better during the retreat than they had during the battle, the Confederate commander shepherded his men to the swollen Potomac River and boldly held Meade at bay there until his engineers could bridge the river. On the night of July 13 the Rebels crossed the Potomac.[11]

The successful return to Virginia soil allowed Lee some time to regroup, but he was not out of danger. Just as the withdrawal of General McCellan's army below the Chickahominy River outside Richmond in June 1862 had not ended the Seven Day's Battles, the crossing of the Potomac had not ended the Gettysburg Campaign. So long as Meade remained determined to continue the fighting, another large-scale battle remained a very real possibility. For the time being, however, there would be a brief interval to rest and refit after the bloodletting at Gettysburg.

The successful withdrawal below the Potomac had both allowed Lee to avoid an unwanted battle and afforded him the ability to fully reopen his line of communication back to Richmond. The latter benefit enabled the army to be resupplied and reinforced for the first time since entering Pennsylvania. It also meant the fruits and consequences of the Gettysburg campaign could flow south.

As the Rebels paused to rest and reorganize, more than 4,500 Union prisoners kept trudging toward the railhead at Staunton. From there, railway cars would carry them to prison camps around the Confederate capital. Traveling in the same direction were 26,000 head of cattle and 22,000 sheep confiscated in Pennsylvania—a bounty that would feed Lee's soldiers for months to come. Making up an infinitely more melancholy procession was a long line of wagons carrying some 8,000 wounded and sick to Staunton's overflowing complex of hospitals.[12]

Securing the invasion's booty while clearing wounded and prisoners from the lower Shenandoah Valley was only a necessary first step in preparing for the hardships certain to follow. An equally important task was putting the army into condition for a continuance of the campaign and the

11 Fremantle, *Three Months in the Southern States*, 270-271.

12 Kent Masterson Brown, *Retreat from Gettysburg: Lee, Logistics, and the Pennsylvania Campaign* (Chapel Hill, NC, 2005), 378.

likelihood of another major engagement. This required time to rest weary bodies, tend overworked animals, and refit worn-out commands. Unfortunately, how long—or more aptly, how brief—the period of rest and recovery might last would depend on Meade intentions, not Lee's wishes or ability to meet his foe again in the field.

Advance warning of the next Federal move could only be provided by cavalry, and this meant Southern troopers would find little of the respite enjoyed by most of their infantry brethren. The commander of Lee's mounted arm, Major General Jeb Stuart, was under something of a cloud because of his recent performance. Many in the army believed he had failed in his mission to screen the army and keep Lee informed of Federal movements, riding off instead in search of glory and press plaudits. Regardless, Stuart's reputation as an excellent and aggressive officer whose intelligence reports could be trusted was well earned. Lee knew this better than most, and although he had let Stuart feel the sting of his disappointment over recent errors, the commanding general still trusted and relied upon the 30-year old cavalier.[13]

The two Virginians had first met when Stuart was attending West Point and Lee was the school's commandant. For a time, Cadet Stuart (who graduated in 1854) courted Lee's daughter Mary. Lee and Stuart served together in October 1859 when both were in Washington, DC when John Brown raided Harpers Ferry. Stuart carried news of the insurrection from the War Department to Lieutenant Colonel Lee, who was home on leave at his Arlington estate just across the Potomac. Stuart accompanied Lee to Harpers Ferry, where he personally transmitted the colonel's surrender demand to Brown. When that ultimatum was refused, it was Stuart who gave the signal to storm the holdout.[14]

Like Lee, after the secession of Virginia Stuart resigned his commission in the US Army and offered his services to his state. As the commander of the state's military, Lee issued Stuart his first wartime orders: report to Harpers Ferry as colonel of the 1st Virginia Cavalry. Their path's intersected

---

13 For a detailed account of Stuart's role in the Gettysburg Campaign, including substantial new information that casts the event in a different light, see *Plenty of Blame to Go Around: Jeb Stuart's Controversial Ride to Gettysburg*, by Eric J. Wittenberg and J. David Petruzzi (Savas Beatie, 2011).

14 Horwitz, *Midnight Rising*, 174-178.

again, this time permanently, when Lee assumed command of the Army of Northern Virginia, by which time Stuart was a brigadier general.[15]

Stuart's performance during the Peninsula Campaign impressed Lee, who recommended him for promotion to major general and command of the army's mounted arm. Since that time Lee had come to rely on the Virginia cavalier's fighting skills and outstanding talent at gathering accurate intelligence. Despite severe critiques of Stuart's operations during the invasion of Pennsylvania (one of Lee's staff officers suggested Stuart be shot), Lee saw Gettysburg as an aberration in Stuart's otherwise stellar career.[16]

Cognizant of the criticisms leveled against him and anxious to redeem himself, Stuart carefully deployed his horsemen to keep a watchful eye on the enemy. Brigadier General William E. "Grumble" Jones' four Virginia regiments spread out to cover Winchester from the direction of Harpers Ferry. Wade Hampton's brigade, led by Colonel Lawrence A. Baker, picketed the Potomac River from Falling Waters to Hedgesville. Brigadier General Beverly Robertson's brigade, reduced by detachments to just 300 men in two regiments, covered the west bank of the Shenandoah River. East of that watercourse, "strong pickets" from Jones' and Robertson's commands—left behind at the start of the Gettysburg campaign—guarded Snickers' and Ashby's gaps in the Blue Ridge Mountains.[17]

The remaining three brigades of Stuart's division under Fitzhugh Lee, William H. F. "Rooney" Lee, and Albert G. Jenkins, moved to Leetown. The latter two brigades were directed by temporary leaders due to earlier misfortunes. Colonel John R. Chambliss led Rooney Lee's regiments because Lee had been wounded and captured in June, while Colonel Milton J. Ferguson had assumed command of Jenkins' brigade when its commander fell wounded at Gettysburg. These brigades would convalesce as best they could while standing ready to respond to any threat on short notice.[18]

With Stuart's troopers providing a protective screen, Lee ordered his infantry and artillery into camp along the Valley Turnpike midway between

---

15 Faust, *Encyclopedia of the Civil War*, 728, 430.

16 Ibid.

17 Walter Clark, ed., *Histories of the Several Regiments and Battalions from North Carolina in the Great War 1861-1865*, 5 Volumes (Goldsboro, NC, 1901), vol. 3, 464.

18 *OR* 27, pt. 2, 705; *OR*, 27, pt. 3, 1006.

Martinsburg and Winchester. The First Corps, under Longstreet—the longest serving and most reliable of Lee's principle subordinates—bivouacked along Mill Creek east of the village of Bunker Hill. A. P. Hill's Third Corps was posted west of town along the same watercourse. Richard Ewell's Second Corps, meanwhile, made its camps in the vicinity of Darkesville some ten miles south of Martinsburg.[19]

In these bivouacs the Army of Northern Virginia prepared for the next phase of the campaign. Over the last six weeks the troops had endured heat, dust, rain, mud, rapid long-distance marches, a brutal battle, dozens of smaller engagements, and the emotional and physical strain that went along with such endeavors. Since Gettysburg, rations had been short and time to properly prepare them shorter still, which only compounded their monotony and lack of nutritional value. The effect of this on the health of the men was obvious, not only in terms of exhaustion but in terms of widespread sickness.

The 43rd North Carolina Infantry of Brigadier General Junius Daniel's brigade (Rodes' division, Ewell's corps), offers a case in point. The ranks of the 43rd, already depleted by combat, were hobbled further by illness. Shortly after reaching Darkesville, 150 men from the regiment had reported for sick call, all of them suffering from chronic diarrhea. Luckily, the command discovered a large field of blackberry vines near its camp—an occurrence that would become commonplace for soldiers in both armies during the coming week. The North Carolinians attacked the fruit with the enthusiasm of hungry men and ate it by the hatful. The act did far more than fill empty stomachs. Blackberries are rich in vitamins C and B as well as antioxidants, and within a day or so almost everyone's diarrhea was cured and the next morning just 15 men reported for sick call.[20]

In addition to an improvement in health and a chance to rest, the army also began to regain some strength. The return of stragglers to their units helped bolster, to a modest degree, the numbers in some commands. More rifled-muskets were added to the ranks as men recovered from disease or wounds and returned to their regiments. The most substantial reinforcement, however, came in the form of a 1,200-man brigade belonging to Major General George E. Pickett's hard-hit division.

19 Ibid., 27, pt. 3, 1006.

20 Leonidas L Polk, "The 43rd North Carolina Regiment during the War: Whiffs from My Old Camp Pipe," in *Weekly Ansonian* (Polkton, NC), 1876.

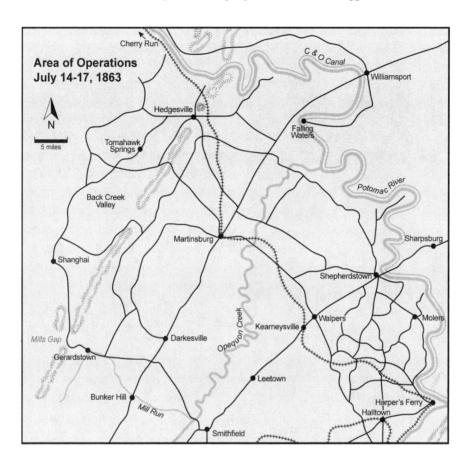

Brigadier General Montgomery D. Corse was an experienced and capable soldier and Mexican War veteran who had spent years prospecting in California before returning to his native Virginia to become a banker. He commanded a militia battalion before the Civil War. Appointed colonel of the 17th Virginia in 1861, he led the regiment at First Manassas, on the Peninsula, and at Second Manassas where he was wounded. Corse was injured again near Boonsborough, Maryland in September 1862. Although the 17th Virginia mustered just 56 men at Sharpsburg, Corse led it in a valiant attack that captured two enemy flags. When the smoke cleared and the fighting ended, only he and seven others remained.[21]

21 Faust, ed., *Encyclopedia of the Civil War*, 186; Ezra Warner, *General in Gray: The Lives of Confederate Commanders* (Baton Rouge, LA, 1965), 63.

Brigadier General Montgomery Dent Corse
Generals in Gray (1959 LSU edition by Ezra J. Warner)

The Virginian was promoted to brigadier on November 1, 1862 and given command of a brigade of five regiments (including the 17th Virginia) in George Pickett's division. Corse's troops were but lightly engaged at Fredericksburg and missed Chancellorsville entirely because most of Longstreet's corps was operating around Suffolk when Hooker crossed the river to engage Lee. To Corse's dismay, when the Army of Northern Virginia launched its invasion of the North in June 1863, his brigade was one of two left behind to guard the Virginia Central Railroad. When news of the Gettysburg defeat reached Richmond, Corse was ordered to march north and rejoin Lee's weakened army. Breaking camp at Gordonsville on July 9, his Virginia regiments moved to rejoin Pickett's mauled command in the northern reaches of the Shenandoah Valley. They reached Winchester five days later during a driving rainstorm on the evening of July 13.[22]

Once he sent word of his arrival to Pickett, Corse put his footsore, cold, wet and muddy men into camp. Having covered nearly 100 miles in less than a week, the Virginians were relieved when Pickett left them at Winchester rather than make them march another 12 miles to Bunker Hill. Regardless of where the men of the arriving command slept, the return of Corse's brigade was encouraging. So too was word that Brigadier General Samuel Jones was bringing two brigades and a pair of batteries from his Department of Southwest Virginia to strengthen Lee's reduced army. Although these additional units would do but little to offset the enormous losses suffered at

22 Faust, *Encyclopedia of the Civil War*, 186; *OR* Vol. 27, part 3, Cooper to Corse, July,7, 1863, 979; Corse's strength from *OR* Vol. 27, part 3, 893; George Wise, *History of the Seventeenth Virginia, C.S.A.* (Baltimore: Kelly, Piet & Co., 1870), 156-159.

Gettysburg, they were at least a start toward increasing the army's strength and morale.[23]

For the Union forces north of the Potomac, an extended pause to rest or receive reinforcements was out of the question. The Lincoln administration and the Northern public expected—one might say demanded—that Meade's victorious army move to force a final showdown with Lee's Rebels. Meade was hardly blind to that reality, so even as he fumed about Halleck's telegrams and Lincoln's disappointment, he puzzled over how best to continue his pursuit.

Strategically speaking, there was little to be gained by simply following the Rebels into the Shenandoah Valley. Such a course would give Lee absolute freedom of maneuver and in no way compel him to turn and fight until he was ready to do so on a field of his choosing. Logistically speaking, the deplorable state of the Baltimore & Ohio (B&O) and Winchester & Potomac (W&P) railroads, both extensively damaged and useless as supply arteries, argued against taking the army into the Valley. In view of these factors Meade rejected as impracticable chasing the Confederates along their direct line of retreat. Instead, the Army of the Potomac would sidle east and cross the river at Harpers Ferry, Virginia and Berlin, Maryland.[24]

Once he made this decision, Meade wasted no time implementing it. Early the next morning, July 15, his army began to move. Four infantry corps—the I, II, V and VI—along with the Reserve Artillery and the 1st and 3rd cavalry divisions, marched for Berlin, while the 2nd Cavalry Division, and three infantry corps—the XI, XII and III—moved on Harpers Ferry. Ahead of these formations engineers scrambled to lay the groundwork necessary for crossing the Potomac, which was no easy task since the sudden shift from supporting an anticipated battle around Williamsport to facilitating a change in the army's axis of advance caught most such units out of position, if not entirely by surprise. Fortunately for Meade, his engineers and logisticians would prove equal to the task.[25]

23 Montgomery Dent Corse Letters, Special Collections Branch Alexandria Library, Alexandria, VA; Edgar Warfield, *A Confederate Soldier's Memoirs* (Richmond, VA, 1936), 150; *OR* 27, pt. 3, 978; 981-982.

24 *OR* 27, pt. 1, 93. Berlin is modern-day Brunswick.

25 Ibid., pt. 3, 695.

The Shenandoah Valley as seen from Maryland Heights, drawn by Alfred Waud. Harper's Ferry is in the left foreground *Library of Congress*

One of those who would rise to the challenge was Brigadier General Gouverneur K. Warren. As chief engineer of the Army of the Potomac, Warren had performed yeoman's service at Gettysburg, where his keen foresight had helped save the Union position at Little Round Top on July 2. Within the next few days, Meade would recommend his promotion to major general and appointment to command the II Corps in the absence of the wounded Winfield Hancock. Until then, Warren continued in his current engineering capacity, charged with anticipating Meade's next moves and making sure the roads the army would travel were capable of carrying the heavy load about to be thrust onto them.

Cognizant that the upcoming movement into Virginia meant the Maryland portion of the Gettysburg campaign had ended, Warren telegraphed the War Department and asked its chief topographical engineer to send him maps covering a huge swath of Northern Virginia. Specifically, Warren wanted charts embracing a square framed by the Potomac River to the north, Gordonsville to the south, the entire Shenandoah Valley to the

west and the Blue Ridge Mountains to the east. Once these were at hand, the brigadier could make a careful examination of the region's roads and topography. When Meade inevitably asked questions about potential routes of advance, Warren would be ready to answer.[26]

The news that Lee had successfully withdrawn into Virginia also spurred Brigadier General Herman Haupt into action. The self-styled Chief of Construction and Transportation, U.S. Military Railroads, Haupt was not surprised by Lee's escape. Well aware of the pitiable condition of the B&O and W&P, he also foresaw Meade's decision to move east. This meant that the Orange & Alexandria Railroad, which ran southwest from Washington toward Culpeper Courthouse, would soon become the army's principle line of communication.

A fair portion of the O&A had been neglected and unused for some time and many of its bridges and culverts had been destroyed in earlier campaigns. Certain it would take enormous effort to put the road into operation, Haupt planned to throw his entire work force south of the

26 Ibid., pt. 1, 96, and pt. 3, 691.

Army of the Potomac Corps Commanders
July 13 to July 31, 1863

I Corps
Major General John Newton*

II Corps
Brigadier General William Hays*

III Corps
Major General William H. French*

V Corps
Major General George Sykes

VI Corps
Major General John Sedgwick

XI Corps
Major General Oliver Otis Howard

XII Corps
Major General Henry W. Slocum

Cavalry Corps
Major General Alfred Pleasonton

* Replacement for Gettysburg casualty.

Potomac as soon as practicable. Not one to dally once his mind was made up, the general directed all railroad construction crews in Pennsylvania to abandon whatever they were doing, concentrate at Alexandria, Virginia, and be ready to go to work as soon as Meade's troops moved south.[27]

Like Haupt's repair gangs, the army's few engineer units were also hurriedly put in motion toward the river. Orders to advance on Harpers Ferry and lay down a pontoon bridge reached Lieutenant Colonel Ira Spaulding's 50th New York Engineers at 11:00 p.m. on July 14, even as a torrential downpour swept through his bivouac. Fortunately, the regiment was only a few miles from its destination. However, that did nothing to ease the job of

27 Ibid., pt. 3, 696.

hitching teams amid what one soldier called the "darkest of Egyptian nights" and getting ponderous pontoon wagons out onto the muddy road. It was 2:00 a.m. before the New Yorkers began their march and nearly dawn before they found themselves on the banks of the Potomac.[28]

They waited there, along the banks of the swollen muddy river, for the arrival of troops under the command of Brigadier General Henry M. Naglee. His 3,400-man force was a hastily assembled milieu of independent companies and separate battalions that had been guarding the B&O, reinforced by parts and pieces of regiments still forming and emergency militia. For the last few days this odd assortment of soldiers had peered down at Harpers Ferry from the entrenchments on Maryland Heights, which loomed over the town from the Potomac's north bank. After making the steep and difficult descent from their post, they would become the first men in blue to pursue Lee over the river.[29]

By the time Naglee arrived, the engineers had pontoon boats in the water and were waiting to ferry his infantry to the opposite shore. As soon as troops could be loaded into the boats the Federals began paddling toward the historic town. Seeing the enemy coming, an outpost comprised of troopers from the 12th Virginia Cavalry emptied their revolvers toward the pontoons before evacuating their position. The Rebels left, "scampering . . . away as fast as horses could carry them," observed one Union soldier. Once the far bank was under Federal control, the 50th New York Engineers commenced work on its bridge and just three hours later completed the span. Naglee promptly moved across the river and soon had possession of the town as well as its surrounding entrenchments.[30]

Shortly afterward, the first clash of arms south of the Potomac occurred when Naglee ordered Major Charles Farnsworth to picket the roads radiating out of Harpers Ferry and scout for Rebel horsemen lurking nearby. Farnsworth was an aggressive officer who had brought three companies of the 1st Connecticut Cavalry to Maryland Heights on July 6. Since arriving near the Potomac, he had complained regularly about having to conduct

28 Ed Malles, ed., *Bridge Building in Wartime: Colonel Wesley Brainerd's Memoir of the 50th New York Volunteer Engineers* (Knoxville, TN 1997), 167.

29 *OR* 27, pt. 1, 154; Edwin B. Coddington, *The Gettysburg Campaign: A Study in Command* (New York, NY, 1968), 560-61; Malles, *Bridge Building*, 167.

30 Malles, *Bridge Building*, 167; *OR* 27, pt. 2, 204.

fruitless patrols instead of fighting. The major's thirst for action was about to be slaked.[31]

With a contingent of 53 men, Farnsworth advanced down the tracks of the W&P toward the village of Halltown about two miles southwest of Harpers Ferry. Unbeknownst to the Connecticut major, Colonel Asher W. Harman of the 12th Virginia Cavalry was moving in the same direction and the two commands were on a collision course.

Harman, who had been wounded in the large cavalry battle of Brandy Station in early June, had just resumed command of his regiment. On the afternoon of July 14 he left his camp near Charles Town determined to find out what the Federals were up to at Harpers Ferry. Accompanied by Captain George Grandstaff's 50-man strong Company B, Harman rode east until he reached Halltown. Finding the reserve picket post of Company K in the village, Harman ordered Grandstaff to dismount his men and wait in the town while he and six troopers rode toward Bolivar Heights on a scouting expedition.[32]

Just minutes later, the small patrol was spotted by Captain Erastus Blakeslee, who was leading an advance guard of 18 men from Farnsworth's Union force. Sensing easy prey, the captain ordered a charge to capture the surprised Confederate troopers. In the ensuing flurry of movement, Colonel Harman's horse fell, leaving its rider stunned and unconscious on the ground. Most of the six men accompanying Harman were captured, but a couple fled toward Halltown with Blaskeslee's New Englanders in hot pursuit.[33]

Back in the village, meanwhile, Captain Grandstaff heard the gunfire from Harman's unlucky encounter and immediately ordered his company into the saddle. Hurrying eastward, the Confederates had just crossed the tracks of the W&P Railroad outside of town when they spied Blaskeslee's Federals. Without too much hesitation Grandstaff ordered a bold charge. At almost the same instant, Farnsworth, who had been closely following

31 *OR* 27, pt. 2, 204; Charles E. Farnsworth, *Whirlwind and Storm: A Connecticut Cavalry Officer in the Civil War and Reconstruction* (Bloomington, IN, 2014), 42. Farnsworth's strength was 184 men.

32 *OR* 27, pt. 2, 204-205; Farnsworth, *Whirlwind and Storm*, 42; George Baylor, *From Bull Run to Bull Run; or, Four Years in the Army of Northern Virginia* (Richmond, VA, 1900), 151.

33 *OR* 27, pt. 2, 766.

Blakeslee with the rest of his troopers, saw the onrushing Rebels and charged as well.[34]

What happened next was as confusing as it was violent. It appears as though Blaskeslee's surprised men attempted to turn and make a run for it, only to be caught between the colliding forces of Farnsworth and Grandstaff. The opposing sides smashed into one another in the midst of a small stream called Flowing Springs Run. The collision triggered a brief but wild fight. Horses reared and kicked while their riders tried mightily to kill one another. Above the swirl of men and animals rose a cacophony of pistol shots, splashing water, and snorting horses, mixed with the excited angry yells of men.

Although each side thought itself seriously outnumbered, the odds were almost exactly even. The Rebels, however, held an advantage. The Federals entered the fight after a prolonged chase at high speed, their horses spent, while those of the Virginians were fresh. Moreover, the Confederates attacked all together, while one group of Federals paused in uncertainty, unsure whether to run or fight, even as another contingent rushed to come to grips with the enemy.

In the melee, Farnsworth's horse was shot out from under him and his men were overpowered. Blakeslee either ordered or led a spontaneous retreat, managing to escape with 28 troopers—just over half Farnsworth's total force—and three prisoners. The dismounted major and 24 of his men fell into Rebel hands along with 31 horses. Both sides claimed to have killed or wounded a number of their opponents, but neither reported any loss to itself other than prisoners.[35]

Shortly after the repulse of the 1st Connecticut Cavalry, the leading elements of Brigadier General David M. Gregg's 2nd Cavalry Division crossed the Potomac River. Their orders, which had been issued the evening before by the commander of the Army of the Potomac's Cavalry Corps, Major General Alfred Pleasonton, were to disrupt General Lee's important line of communications stretching between Williamsport and Winchester. As yet unaware that the Confederates had crossed the river, General Gregg

---

34 Ibid.

35 Ibid.

began pushing his troopers outward from Harpers Ferry not long after Farnsworth's discomfiture.[36]

Soon enough, the Union advance brushed up against the 12th Virginia Cavalry operating near Halltown. It also swept past the spot where Colonel Harman had been unhorsed and was lying unnoticed in the tall grass, where he was probably waiting for nightfall and a chance to slip back into his own lines. Unfortunately for the Virginia colonel his adjutant (who was also his nephew) became so disturbed by reports that his uncle was missing that he and a few members of the 12th Virginia Cavalry's regimental staff rode forward under a flag of truce to inquire as to Harman's whereabout and potential fate.[37]

The Confederate search party encountered skirmishers from the 1st New Jersey Cavalry, who summoned their commander, Major Hugh H. Janeway, to the front. Word of a missing Confederate officer was news to the Federals, and Major Janeway immediately ordered a search that quickly discovered Colonel Harman. Manhandled to his feet by a Union sergeant, the Virginian was declared a prisoner of war and brought forward to his well-meaning comrades to prove their commander was unhurt. The fact that their solicitude had led to his captivity did not sit well with the colonel, who lashed out with "very forcible language" at the men who had unwittingly placed him in enemy hands.[38]

While this small affair was playing out, Federal engineers were busy wrestling with a serious challenge six miles east of Harpers Ferry. Colonel Spaulding of the 50th New York Engineers had been warned on the afternoon of the 14th that in the near future a bridge would be needed at Berlin. Taking into account the flood stage of the Potomac River, the New Yorker had immediately telegraphed his superiors in Washington to ask for an additional 600 feet of pontoons and all the bridging material he would need to accomplish his task.[39]

Because the Rebels had broken an aqueduct at the mouth of the Monocacy River that fed water into the Chesapeake & Ohio canal, however,

36 Ibid ., 27, pt. 3, 676.

37 Ibid., pt. 1, 959.

38 Henry Pyne, *History of the First New Jersey Cavalry (Sixteenth Regiment, New Jersey Volunteers)* (Trenton, NJ, 1871), 167.

39 *OR* 27, pt. 3, 691.

a significant stretch of the channel east of Berlin was dry. Therefore, floating additional pontoons to the needed location—which would have been the fastest method of getting them there—was impossible. The superintendent of the canal was attempting to make repairs, but was seriously hamstrung by a shortage of wheelbarrows, having a mere seven on hand. Without those mundane implements his workers could make only slow progress, and Spaulding predicted it would require two full days to complete repairs. In view of these facts the lieutenant colonel recommended sending the extra bridging by railroad.[40]

Remarkably, the condition of the canal was unknown in the Federal capital. On July 15, when General Warren inquired by telegraph if the extra pontoons had been dispatched, the reply came back that one group of 52 boats had already been sent via canal and another 32 were about to go. It did not look as though Spaulding was going to get his extra material in a timely manner.[41]

Despite such frustrating delays, Meade did not let his command waste its last hours north of the Potomac. Even as the engineers built their first bridge at Harpers Ferry and Meade's troops moved toward the river, Brigadier General Rufus Ingalls, the chief quartermaster of the army, was ordering supplies that had been stockpiled in Frederick, Maryland, shifted to Berlin. The resultant logistical build up on the Potomac would allow the replenishment of nearly empty supply trains and address at least the worst needs of some Union soldiers.[42]

Meade ordered his subordinates to make the most of Ingalls' efficiency by having their troops fill haversacks with three days' cooked rations. The same interval's worth of hardtack and "small rations" were to be loaded into regimental wagons and the various brigade, divisional, and corps supply trains. Any shoes or clothing needed were to be requisitioned from the depots. Once these instructions were fulfilled, each corps commander was to inform army headquarters and prepare to "continue the march at the earliest moment practicable."

40 Ibid., 690.

41 Ibid., 701.

42 Ibid., 703.

The veterans of the Army of the Potomac new what that meant: a crossing of the Potomac in search of a showdown fight with Lee's Rebels that might yet end the war.[43]

43 Ibid., pt. 3, 94.

CHAPTER 3

"One of the Hardest Fights the Cavalry Has Ever Been In"

Gregg's Division Crosses the Potomac River—Reconnaissance Toward Charles Town—Gregg Moves to Shepherdstown—Stuart Orders a Counterstrike—Fitz Lee Attacks—The Battle of Shepherdstown—Company D Makes an Impact—Gregg Withdrawals

UNTIL the bridge at Berlin was built, General Meade had little choice but to mark time north of the Potomac River. At Harpers Ferry, however, the effort to discover the exact whereabouts of General Lee's Army of Northern Virginia and hinder its supply line grew bolder.

On July 15, Brigadier General David Gregg, a native Pennsylvanian and first cousin of that state's powerful Republican governor, Andrew G. Curtin, took his 1st and 3rd brigades, commanded respectively by Colonels John B. McIntosh and John Irvin Gregg (who preferred to use his middle name) southwest to Halltown. Halting his command there, the general sent Lieutenant Colonel Charles H. Smith's 1st Maine Cavalry to scout the Harpers Ferry Pike toward Charles Town and find out what was waiting in that direction.

A half-mile after leaving Halltown, the Maine regiment ran into Rebel pickets. Over the next two hours the Southerners gradually fell back, surrendering several miles of territory without offering Smith much trouble. Near Charles Town, however, resistance stiffened and the troopers from Maine found themselves embroiled in a "smart little skirmish" with Rebel cavalry from Brigadier General William E. "Grumble" Jones' brigade holding a patch of woods about a mile from the village. While Smith deployed dismounted skirmishers to test the enemy's strength, the Confederates reinforced their position with Captain Roger Preston Chew's three-gun battery of horse artillery.[1]

Chew's pieces remained silent even though Smith's dismounted troopers focused their fire on the newly arrived cannon. For ten minutes the artillerists abided this annoyance, all the while waiting for a mark worthy of their powder. Then, at a distance of about a mile, the Rebels spotted two companies Smith had kept mounted in case he needed to order a charge. Lieutenant George M. Neese, commander of a 12-pounder Blakely rifle— the longest ranged fieldpiece in Chew's battery—knew this was the target he had been waiting for and gave the order to commence firing.[2]

With great satisfaction, Neese watched his first shell burst inside the Union formation. The exploding projectile produced what one observer called a "regular scatteration" amongst its victims and had an even more profound effect on the fighting. Well aware that his lone regiment could not cope with a battery supported by ample cavalry, Lieutenant Colonel Smith concluded he had learned what he had been sent to learn and ordered his regiment to slowly pull back toward Halltown. The Confederate cavalry gingerly followed, but avoided coming close enough to reignite any action.[3]

With Smith's return to his starting point, General Gregg determined to try his luck in another direction. Leaving the 13th Pennsylvania Cavalry and a three-company detachment of the 11th New York Cavalry to hold Halltown, Gregg moved McIntosh's and Irvin Gregg's brigades north toward Shepherdstown. In the face of only slight opposition, the Federals swept into the village a little after noon, capturing six prisoners, a few wagons, 81 enemy hospital patients, 50 barrels of flour, and 4,000 pounds of

---

1   *OR* 27, pt. 1, 978; Edward Tobie, *History of the First Maine Cavalry, 1861-1865* (Boston, MA, 1887), 181; William Brooke Rawle, *History of the Third Pennsylvania Cavalry 1861-1865* (Philadelphia, PA, 1905), 287; George M. Neese, *Three Years in the Confederate Horse Artillery* (New York, NY, 1911), 199-200.

2   Neese, *Three Years*, 199-200; For the armament of Chew's battery see Jennings Wise, *The Long Arm of Lee* (New York, NY, 1959), 163; Tobie, *First Maine Cavalry*, 181.

3   Tobie, *First Maine Cavalry*, 181; Robert Trout, *Galloping Thunder: The Stuart Horse Artillery Battalion* (Mechanicsburg, PA, 2002), 321; Neese, *Three Years*, 199-200. Despite the accuracy of Neese's fire, the Federals did not suffer any casualties.

Shepherdstown, Virginia
Library of Congress

bacon. The cost of this triumph was one man killed and two wounded, both in the 16th Pennsylvania Cavalry.[4]

Nestled along the south bank of the Potomac, Shepherdstown had been a thriving antebellum community, its 1,000 inhabitants prospering in no small part because of their proximity to a nearby ford, the C&O Canal, and a covered bridge spanning the Potomac. Unfortunately these attributes had also made the settlement useful to rival armies. The place had changed hands several times and showed the abuse that went along with such treatment. The bridge had been burned in June 1861. Its destruction, along with damage to the canal and nearby railroads, had cost the town most of its commerce.[5]

In September 1862, Shepherdstown became one vast hospital after the battle of Sharpsburg and subsequent fight at nearby Boteler's Ford. Although most of its young men had enlisted to fight for the Confederacy, the town had a fair number of pro-Union inhabitants against whom the majority held considerable ill-will. Those bitter feelings were hardly mitigated when Gregg's quartermasters gave Union sympathizers provisions from captured Rebel supplies.[6]

Now, Shepherdstown found itself once more near the epicenter of a coming fight. Probing northwest beyond the town toward Martinsburg and southwest toward Winchester, Yankee troopers found the roads "strongly picketed" by Southern infantry and cavalry. In the face of this discovery,

4   Thomas West Smith, *The Story of a Cavalry Regiment: Scott's 900, Eleventh New York Cavalry* (Chicago, IL, 1897), 105, 110; *OR* 27, pt. 1, 982; Rawle, *Third Pennsylvania Cavalry*, 287; *New York Times*, July 26, 1863.

5   Thomas McGrath, *Shepherdstown: Last Clash of the Antietam Campaign* (Lynchburg, VA, 2013), 39; Nicholas Redding, *A history and Guide to Civil War Shepherdstown* (Lynchburg: VA, 2012), 36.

6   Pyne, *First New Jersey Cavalry*, 169.

Gregg felt he could not advance until reinforced by his 2nd Brigade under Colonel Pennock Huey. Although General Pleasonton had issued orders that morning for Huey to move from Falling Waters to Harpers Ferry, those instructions did not direct the colonel to support Gregg. Indeed, Huey wasn't even aware his superior was over the river with the rest of the division. As a result, he rode without any particular urgency. Hampered by crowded roads, his brigade would not cross the Potomac River until the afternoon of the 16th. Ignorant of these facts, but certain little else could be done until Huey arrived, Gregg called a halt and settled his troopers in and around Shepherdstown for the night.[7]

Come dawn, additional reconnaissance confirmed David Gregg's impression of the previous afternoon that a significant body of Confederate infantry lay beyond Shepherdstown in the direction of Martinsburg. In light of that certainty, there was little else to do but wait for Huey's arrival. As the clock ticked toward noon, however, General Gregg—an aggressive 1855 graduate of West Point, veteran of the Indian Frontier, and participant of all of the Army of the Potomac's campaigns—wearied of the inactivity and finally concluded that his wisest course was to withdraw to Harpers Ferry and from there, seek an alternate route along which to strike Lee's communications.[8]

Unfortunately for David Gregg, Jeb Stuart had no intention of letting the Federals choose their field of maneuver. Late on the 15th, when he learned Yankees were menacing Martinsburg, Stuart issued orders for a counter-strike the next day. The general directed Fitz Lee to move his cavalry brigade from Leetown directly against Shepherdstown, with Brigadier General John R. Chambliss (commanding W. H. F. Lee's brigade) following in support. While they held Gregg's attention, Albert Jenkins' brigade, under Colonel Ferguson, would ride from Martinsburg with the purpose of hitting the Union right flank. Orders were sent to Jones to bring his brigade over from Charles Town and join the action. Because Jones' exact location was unknown to Stuart, however, no specific instructions as to the route he was to take or the timing of the ride were provided. If all went well, the

---

7   *OR* 27, pt. 1, 978; 959; 971; Richard Staats, *History of the Sixty Ohio Volunteer Cavalry*, 2 vols (Westminster, MD, 2012), Vol. 1, 329.

8   *OR* 27, pt. 1, 959.

Brigadier General Fitzhugh Lee
Library of Congress

Confederates would envelop Gregg, cut him off from Harpers Ferry, and destroy his two brigades against the south bank of a flooded Potomac River.[9]

As the Confederates rode northeast on the morning of July 16, the Federals—completely unaware of approaching danger—leisurely prepared to shift position and went about their daily chores. The 10th New York Cavalry was spread out to picket the several roads running out of Shepherdstown, its outposts on average about five miles from the community. Companies C, G, H, and L guarded the Winchester Pike, while companies K and M kept watch on the road leading northwest to Dam Number 4 (one of a series of such barriers built on the Potomac to funnel water into the C&O canal). The remaining companies were posted on the road to Martinsburg.[10]

The Union cavalry had not received an issue of rations or forage since crossing the Potomac almost three days ago. The men at least had gotten something to eat courtesy of the supplies captured in Shepherdstown. The horses, however, had consumed little but grass. Quite understandably, Colonel Gregg was grateful to receive a message from the 10th New York Cavalry that there was ample feed in the fields behind its picket line. Taking advantage of this unexpected windfall, Gregg instructed the 1st Maine Cavalry to send detachments down the Winchester Pike to obtain the proffered fodder. Wishing to gather as much forage as quickly as possible,

9 *OR* 27, pt. 2, 706.

10 Ron Matteson, *Civil War Campaigns of the 10th New York Cavalry, With One Soldier's Personal Correspondence* (Raleigh, NC, 2007), 134.

Lieutenant Colonel Smith decided to take his entire regiment on the mission rather than send out special details.[11]

That casual decision would prove most fortuitous, for the Maine troopers were unknowingly trotting right for Fitz Lee's brigade, which was on the verge of launching Stuart's plan to smash Gregg's division. The Southern cavalry chieftain would not oversee that effort, however. Just as his troopers were deploying for the attack, a courier arrived summoning Stuart back to Bunker Hill for a meeting with General Lee at army headquarters. Stuart, who departed immediately, left control of the pending engagement in the hands of Fitz Lee, a proven combat leader and the 27-year-old nephew of Robert E. Lee. Fitz attended West Point while his famous uncle was commandant of the academy, and was almost expelled for misbehavior. He avoided that potential humiliation and graduated in 1856 one year behind David Gregg, who he was now trying to bring to battle.[12]

Much to Fitz's irritation, it was taking longer for the fight to begin than was intended. The distance from Leetown to Shepherdstown was a mere nine miles, meaning the Confederate cavalry had to ride four miles or so before it encountered Union pickets. Despite an early start, the Southerners, delayed by the "very bad condition" of the roads around Leetown, had taken the entire morning to cover that handful of miles. It was midday before they passed through Walpers Crossroads, just beyond which lay the Federal picket line, and a little past noon before they were in a position to attack.[13]

When the Rebels did strike, however, they struck hard. Colonel James H. Drake, a 41-year-old officer known as an outstanding curser and "much beloved" by his men, led a furious attack by two squadrons of his 1st Virginia Cavalry. The charge drove in the 10th New York Cavalry's outposts and sent startled vedettes galloping for the rear. Hearing the clamor of this sudden onset, the Federal picket reserve, resting nearby, hurriedly mounted its horses and rushed to meet the assault. The New Yorkers formed unseen in a piece of woods and waited patiently for the Confederates to draw

11 Matteson, *10th New York Cavalry*, 133; *OR* 27, pt. 1, 980; Tobie, *First Maine Cavalry*, 181.

12 *OR* 27, pt. 2, 706; Faust, *Historical Encyclopedia of the Civil War*, 429; Warner, *Generals in Gray*, 178.

13 Robert J. Trout, *Memoirs of the Stuart Horse Artillery Battalion: Moorman's and Hart's Batteries* (Knoxville, TN, 1998), 59; Walbrook Swank, ed., *Sabres, Saddles and Spurs* (Shippensburg, PA, 1998), 83. Carter misspells Walpers as Walpin's.

near before unleashing a surprise volley that forced the Southern horsemen to retire.[14]

The stunned Confederates, now painfully aware of their enemy's position, quickly regrouped and came on again with twice as many men as before. While some attackers pressed down against the Yankee front, others slipped around the exposed Federal left and quickly had the New Yorkers caught in a deadly crossfire. At almost the same instant, Confederate artillery opened on the Union position. As far as the Federals were concerned, that decided the issue. Private Manning Austin admitted that when "shells began to burst over our heads . . . it got too hot." He and his comrades began to retreat, darting from tree to tree as they attempted to get to their horses and ride to safety.[15]

Thrown into complete confusion, outflanked, and outnumbered, the New Yorkers—some on horseback, some scrambling about on foot—fell back toward a wooded ridge about one mile to their rear and some four miles southwest of Shepherdstown. Luckily for the hard-pressed pickets, the 1st Maine's troopers lay directly in their path and a few of the mounted vedettes raced past Smith's column shouting that the Confederates were right behind them. Rather than halt or turn back, the regimental commander decided to move forward and confront whatever enemy was coming his way. The colonel ordered the column out at a gallop and headed toward a height just three-fourths of a mile ahead, from which thin wisps of gun smoke could be seen rising into the summer air.[16]

As the Federals closed on their objective, Smith watched the situation into which he was hastening deteriorate with disconcerting speed. Blue uniforms tumbled over the wooded crest to his front. Seconds later, several squadrons of enemy cavalry appeared on the same ridge. Between the triumphant Rebels and Smith's own command, the 10th New York's picket reserve was staging a fighting withdrawal to protect its wounded men and

14 Robert K. Krick, *Lee's Colonel's: A Biographical Register of the Field Officers of the Army of Northern Virginia* (Dayton, OH, 1992), 123; Swank, *Sabres, Saddles and Spurs*, 83; Manning, Austin, letter of July 23, 1863, www.10thnycavalry.org/morrishistory.html Manning Austin letter 7/23/63.

15 Austin Manning, letter of July 23, 1863.

16 Matteson, *10th New York Cavalry*, 134; Tobie, *First Maine Cavalry*, 181; *OR* 27, pt. 1, 980-1.

Brigadier General David M. Gregg
Library of Congress

horses, both of which were frantically attempting to get out of reach of the oncoming Confederates.[17]

Realizing the ridge offered a key defensive position, Smith ordered the two companies at the head of his column to retake the crest. Rapidly moving from column into line, Companies A and B dashed forward with "such impetuosity" that their attack completely surprised the Rebels who had believed, and not incorrectly, they were chasing a beaten foe. In the face of this sudden resistance the Virginians yielded the position with a loss of one dead and three wounded.[18]

Once Lieutenant Colonel Smith gained the high ground, the prewar teacher and law student from Eastport, Maine, deployed his men to hold onto it. He quickly established a heavy skirmish line under the command of Major Stephen Boothby into the woods along the crest. The rest of the regiment remained mounted and took position in line of battle on the reverse slope, its formation split by the pike in which Smith kept a single company mounted in fours.[19]

When he heard the sound of the initial clash between Fitz Lee's Rebel vanguard and the New York pickets, General Gregg hurried to the scene of the action. Gregg reached the ridge just retaken by the 1st Maine Cavalry, from which point he could see large numbers of Southern horsemen coming up the road from Leetown, and dismounted Rebels taking down rail fences in

17 Ibid.

18 Tobie, *First Maine Cavalry*, 181; *OR* 27, pt. 1, 981.

19 Ibid. Charles Henry Smith page, Arlington National Cemetery, http://www.arlington cemetery.net/chsmith.htm

front of the Federal position. Both were clearly harbingers of an impending attack.[20]

Despite the looming threat, division commander Gregg, whose stout frame and impressive beard suggested steadfastness more than anything else, exhibited an air of virtual nonchalance to those around him. He ordered McIntosh to take his brigade due south of Shepherdstown and form a line eastward, parallel to the Potomac, in order to protect the division's line of retreat back to Harpers Ferry. Gregg's brigade was ordered forward to meet the attack already underway. It would take time for those movements to bear fruit, however, and until they did, the troopers of the 1st Maine were on their own.[21]

In front of this single regiment the number of visible Confederates was increasing rapidly. Fortunately for the Maine troopers, the nature of the battlefield worked in their favor. The "very rocky and broken" terrain was divided into small fields by patches of timber and numerous high stone and rail fences. This made the area utterly unsuitable for mounted cavalry operations and compelled most of the attackers (and defenders) to fight on foot. The time consuming process of deploying for that kind of action meant Fitz Lee couldn't hurl his superior numbers against Smith in one quick and irresistible blow. Consequently, the pressure exerted by the Virginian grew slowly.[22]

For an hour, aided by these factors and having the advantage of an elevated and wooded position, Smith thwarted every effort to fling him backward. To achieve that success, however, he had to send more and more men onto the skirmish line. Before long virtually all his troops were committed, leaving only a modest three-company reserve. Moreover, the regiment was rapidly shooting up its ammunition and taking an increasing number of casualties, including Major Boothby, who was struck in the arm and forced to retire from the field.[23]

---

20 *OR* 27, pt. 1, 959.

21 Ibid; William Lloyd, *History of the First Regiment Pennsylvania Reserve Cavalry* (Philadelphia, PA, 1864), 65-66; Henry C. Meyer, *Civil War Experiences under Bayard, Gregg, Kilpatrick, Custer, Raulston, and Newberry: 1862, 1863, 1864* (New York, NY, 1911), 65.

22 Tobie, *First Maine Cavalry*, 184; *OR* Vol. 27, pt. 2, 706.

23 *OR* 27, pt. 1, 981; Tobie, *First Maine Cavalry*, 183-186.

Order of Battle: Shepherdstown, July 16, 1863

Confederate	**Union**

Stuart's Division
Army of Northern Virginia
Major General J.E.B. Stuart

Second Division, Cavalry Corps
Army of the Potomac
Major General David M. Gregg

Fitz Lee's Brigade
Brig. Gen. Fitzhugh Lee

First Brigade
Col. John McIntosh

1st Maryland Battalion, 1st Virginia Cavalry, 2nd Virginia Cavalry, 3rd Virginia Cavalry, 4th Virginia Cavalry, 5th Virginia Cavalry

1st Maryland, Purnell (Maryland) Legion, Co. A, 1st Massachusetts Cavalry, 1st New Jersey Cavalry, 1st Pennsylvania Cavalry, 3rd Pennsylvania Cavalry

Jenkin's Brigade
Col. Milton Ferguson

Second Brigade
Col. Pennock Huey

14th Virginia Cavalry, 16th Virginia Cavalry, 17th Virginia Cavalry, 34th Virginia Cavalry Battalion, 36th Virginia Cavalry Battalion

2nd New York Cavalry, 4th New York Cavalry, 6th Ohio Cavalry, 8th Pennsylvania Cavalry

W.H.F. Lee's Brigade
Col. John Chambliss

Third Brigade
Col. J. Irvin Gregg

2nd North Carolina Cavalry, 9th Virginia Cavalry, 10th Virginia Cavalry, 13th Virginia Cavalry

1st Maine Cavalry, 10th New York Cavalry, 4th Pennsylvania Cavalry, 16th Pennsylvania Cavalry

Jones' Brigade

Second Brigade Horse Artillery

Company D, 12th Virginia Cavalry
Captain Henry W. Kearney

1st United States, Batteries E & G
Captain Alanson Randal

Stuart's Horse Artillery

Breathed's Battery, one section, McGregor's Battery, one section, Moorman's Battery, one section

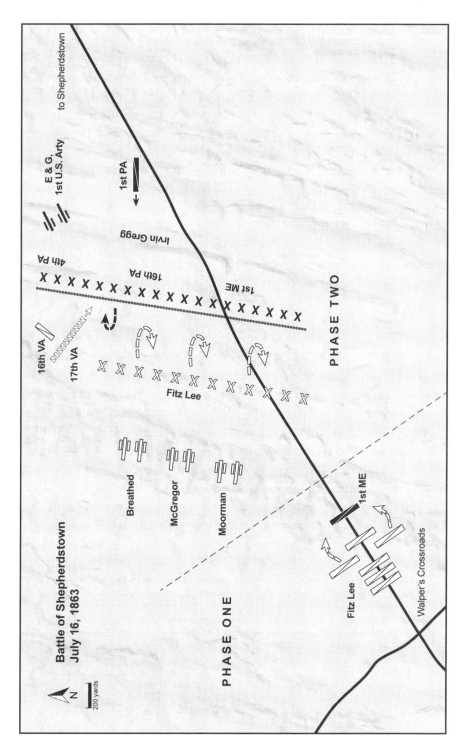

to Shepherdstown

E & G,
1st U.S. Arty

1st PA

Irvin Gregg

4th PA

16th PA

1st ME

X X X X X X X X X X X X X X X X X X

16th VA

17th VA

X X X X X X X X X X X X X
Fitz Lee

PHASE TWO

Breathed

McGregor

Moorman

1st ME

Fitz Lee

Walper's Crossroads

Battle of Shepherdstown
July 16, 1863

PHASE ONE

N
200 yards

While the Union regiment was growing weaker, Fitz Lee was gaining strength. Chambliss' brigade and elements of three batteries of horse artillery—a section each from Moorman's, Breathed's and McGregor's—reached the field, which allowed Lee to take the Federals under shellfire and extend his line of battle beyond the flanks of Smith's stubborn Yankees. Chambliss sidled to the southeast to confront McIntosh, with the apparent mission of merely holding him in place, while Lee struck at Gregg in anticipation of Ferguson ultimately storming down onto the Federal right flank.[24]

Now heavily outnumbered, with no reinforcements yet at hand and in danger of being outflanked, Smith knew his time was running out. When the Confederates surged forward across the entire front, further successful resistance simply became impossible and the Federals began falling back. Exultant Southerners rushed the ridge, and were soon firing at the blue troopers sullenly withdrawing on foot toward Shepherdstown.[25]

To buy time for these men to get away, Smith threw his last reserve into the fight and ordered a mounted attack against the ridge. Companies B, K, and M drew the mission and in line from left to right, respectively, "charged gallantly" toward the timber, which they quickly reached. Once there, however, the Federals could stay for but an instant. There were too many Rebels and too few Northerners on the height for the blue troopers to do anything other than fire a quick pistol shot or slash with a saber before turning around and racing back as fast as they had come. But the assault served its purpose—the strike broke the momentum of the Confederate advance and gained precious time for the skirmishers to escape.[26]

The 1st Maine Cavalry might be retreating, but the men in blue did not intend to go far. A half mile or so from the ridge, Smith's soldiers reined in

---

24 Trout, *Galloping Thunder*, 321. Southern accounts of the battle of Shepherdstown are sparse and there is no definitive count of how many Rebel guns took part. The number given by participants ranges from three to six to eight. It is likely that six is the correct number, which would mean one two-gun section from each of the three batteries that participated on the field. Chambliss' role in the battle is a surmise. McIntosh's regiments did not report any significant combat or casualties, nor did those of Chambliss. However, McIntosh clearly faced enough Rebels to require him to request artillery support from his division commander.

25 *OR* 27, pt. 1, 981.

26 Tobie, *First Maine Cavalry*, 182.

their mounts on a second elevation known locally as Butler's Woods. Though slightly lower, this alternative position was far superior to the one just yielded to the Rebels, benefiting not only from timber, but also from the presence of a stout stone wall stretching to the left and right of the pike for a considerable distance. Happily taking advantage of this accidental breastwork, the Maine troopers turned to make a stand.[27]

* * *

Not only were Smith's men no longer retreating, they were also no longer alone. Colonel Gregg had finally managed to get the rest of his brigade to the front along with four 12-pounder Napoleons from Batteries E & G of the 1st US Artillery under the command of Captain Alanson M. Randal. Gregg sent the 4th Pennsylvania Cavalry to support Randal and bolster Smith's flank. For the moment, he held the 16th Pennsylvania Cavalry in reserve. The 10th New York Cavalry, at last fully assembled after drawing in its scattered picket posts, was dispatched to the far right to guard against any Rebel attempt to sweep in from the northwest. Meanwhile, McIntosh's brigade was forming on Gregg's left to blunt any Confederate attack from the south.[28]

On the opposite ridge, the Confederate horse artillery had dropped trail and was now hammering away at the new Federal line. One howitzer, its crew a bit overzealous, moved too far forward and found itself within range of Union carbine fire, which forced the gunners to pull back to a safer distance. The rest of the Rebel artillerists made no such error and Southern cannons began to blanket Gregg's position with solid shot, canister, and shell.

By all accounts, the Rebel guns made quite an impression. General Gregg noted that Confederate artillery fire was "incessant," while one of his troopers simply labeled it "terrific." Lieutenant George W. Beale of the 9th Virginia Cavalry was taken by the precision with which the Southern guns were employed, observing that they fired in sequence singly, then by section, and finally by battery—a type of shooting more often associated

27 *OR* 27, pt. 1, 981; Tobie, *First Maine Cavalry*, 186.

28 *OR* 27, pt. 1, 959; 984-5; 982; 981; Tobie, *First Maine Cavalry*, 182; Matteson, *10th New York Cavalry*, 134.

with the drill field than the battleground. That sort of command and control made for great accuracy, a fact to which the Federals could unhappily testify.[29]

A soldier in the 16th Pennsylvania believed he had never witnessed Rebel batteries "better served," and considered their performance superior to what he had experienced in any previous fight. Confederate shells flew "all around and among" the Union cavalrymen, knocking down tree branches and throwing "huge fragments" of stone into the air when they struck one of the innumerable rock outcroppings in the area. Only the uneven nature of the ground prevented the Rebel fire from inflicting more casualties than it did.[30]

Captain Randal's Federal battery, posted on a higher ridge to the right rear of Gregg's line, replied in kind, but this initially caused more consternation than relief. Either through poor marksmanship or the result of defective ammunition, the first two rounds from the Federal guns fell short and struck the ground between the 1st Maine's front and its reserve. Word of this was quickly (and doubtless, pointedly) hurried back to the gunners. Adjusting their aim or procuring better cartridges, the Union artillery was soon sending its rounds over the Federal skirmishers, who had the uncomfortable experience of having shells flying above their heads in opposite directions at the same time.[31]

As the artillery dueled, more regiments entered the fight and the battle grew in intensity and size. Before long, the rival lines stretched for a mile and a half on either side of the Winchester Pike. As usual, how many friends or foes were on the field was a mystery to those doing the fighting. Indeed, it is probable that the officers directing the battle had only a vague idea of the strength of the opposing forces. The best guess is that David Gregg's division had between 1,600 and 1,800 troopers in the fight, split more or less evenly between its two brigades. Jeb Stuart probably fielded 2,000 to 2,500 men with Fitz Lee and Chambliss. If and when Ferguson and Jones arrived on the field, the Confederates might gain up to an additional 2,000 men. To Irvin Gregg's troopers, however, the most important fact was that there were

29 *OR* 27, pt. 1, 960; 981; Tobie, *First Maine Cavalry*, 185; George W. Beale, *A Lieutenant of Cavalry in Lee's Army* (Boston, MA, 1918), 122.

30 Tobie, *First Maine Cavalry*, 185.

31 Tobie, *First Maine Cavalry*, 182, 184.

more than enough Rebels concentrated on their front to make the odds most unpleasant.[32]

Whatever the number of soldiers in blue or gray, after two hours on the line the 1st Maine was nearing the end of its endurance and ammunition. As a result, Colonel Gregg sent the 16th Pennsylvania Cavalry forward to take its place. This movement was quickly spotted by the Confederates and their artillery shifted fire toward the maneuvering Yankee horsemen. The recipients of that attention did not relish the shells coming in "very disagreeable proximity" to their moving column, and counted themselves fortunate they incurred no casualties before the relief was affected.

The 1st Maine troopers retired to a reserve position as the 16th Pennsylvania Cavalry went into line on the left of the 4th Pennsylvania. Like its brethren Keystone state regiment, the 16th put three of its four squadrons on line and held one in reserve, the only difference being that the 4th's reserve squadron was detached to support Randal's battery rather than placed to assist the firing line. Very shortly after the 16th went into position, a pair of Randal's guns was shifted south in support of McIntosh, leaving only two Union cannon to contest six enemy pieces.[33]

The battle now settled into a contest of brute strength. Gregg's men were determined to hold their ground, with Stuart's men equally determined to drive them from it. The Confederates launched several attacks, "yelling like so many demons" and driving far enough forward to deliver their fire "with telling effect." The strain engendered by these assaults was enough to imperil the line of the 16th Pennsylvania, requiring Lieutenant Colonel Smith to send first one squadron, then two and finally his entire regiment back into the battle. With that extra help and the benefit of the stone fence, the Federals were able to fend off multiple attacks.[34]

---

32 *OR* Vol. 29, pt. 2, 636; On August 10, 1863 Stuart reported 10,200 men in his division. If we deduct 450 for the horse artillery, and 300 for Robertson's understrength brigade, then divide the remaining 9,450 by five brigades the theoretical average strength is 1,890. Certainly that number is too high for mid-July, a full three weeks before this report, and naturally the brigades were not all of equal strength. The figures in the text are an educated guess.

33 *OR* 27, pt. 1, 981; Tobie, *First Maine Cavalry*, 184.

34 *New York Times*, July 18, 1863; Tobie, *First Maine Cavalry*, 186; *OR* 27, pt. 1, 981. A cavalry troop is equivalent to an infantry company. A squadron consisted of two troops in July 1863.

Beaten back at each attempt, the Rebels caught their breath, redoubled their artillery fire, and tried again. On occasion, mounted Yankee reserves responded to the renewed pressure by rushing up to the stone wall, where they would "file to the right and left, rapidly deliver their fire, and gallop" off into protecting woods. Against a defense such as this, continued frontal attacks were sure to accomplish little more than enlarging the casualty lists.

In between assaults, Southern cavalrymen took advantage of the rocks, fences, and woods dotting the battlefield. From these vantage points they traded shots with the enemy, making for what one Rebel participant called "a great fight between sharp shooters." Anyone daring to rise up to fire took a serious risk. Among the numerous casualties from this bold behavior was a sergeant in the 1st Maine Cavalry who took it upon himself to ride back to fill canteens for thirsty comrades suffering under the 82-degree heat. Returning to the line, the good samaritan was riding along handing out canteens when a Southern bullet tore through his posterior and groin. The wounded sergeant had the presence of mind to throw the remaining canteens to the ground where others might recover them before galloping off, all the while cursing the luck he had so injudiciously tested.[35]

Such ill fortune did not reside solely on the Union side of the field. As the fight dragged on "as wickedly as ever," wrote one participant, color bearers became, as they almost always did, a preferred target for many marksmen. In front of the 16th Pennsylvania Cavalry, one Rebel flag was shot down three times in a few minutes. The next man to take up the banner made sure he avoided the same fate by holding the flag aloft while crouching behind a stone wall—as prudent a way to do one's duty as possible given the circumstances.[36]

Colonel Irvin Gregg, who was just three days shy of his 37th birthday, had better luck. Accompanied by an aide and a mounted escort, he "very leisurely" rode around the field tending to his duties. Nicknamed "Long John" by his men, the 6-foot 4-inch brigade commander and his entourage were readily spotted by Confederate artillerymen and subsequently,

---

35 Morrissett Diary, Museum of the Civil War; *New York Times*, July 18, 1863; *Richmond Dispatch* July 18, 1863 found in Frank Moore, *The Rebellion Record* (New York, NY, 1864) Vol. 7, 470. Robert Krick, *Civil War Weather in Virginia* (Tuscaloosa, AL, 2007), 104.

36 Tobie, *First Maine Cavalry*, 185.

wherever he and his staff went, Rebel cannon fire followed. Although shell fragments scattered all around the little cavalcade, Gregg "appeared to bear a charmed life and escaped unhurt." His men admired the colonel's courage and aplomb, no doubt, but probably didn't appreciate the bursting shells that arrived with him.[37]

On the other side of the field, Fitz Lee wasn't drawing enemy fire, but he was having a difficult afternoon nonetheless. Since driving the Yankees from their first position, Lee had seen each of his attacks repulsed by rapid-firing Union troopers safe behind stone walls. The only real hope the Virginian had of forcing the Federals from their position was to outflank them—which had been Jeb Stuart's original plan. But that was impossible without Jones or Ferguson—a tactical frustration Lee shared with Stuart when the cavalry leader returned to the battlefield later that afternoon.[38]

Purely by coincidence, Colonel Ferguson's longed-for brigade reached the scene shortly after Stuart's appearance. Unfortunately, this welcome reinforcement did not enter the field from the direction expected or needed. That morning, for some reason never fully explained, the colonel had led his command miles out of the way toward Leetown rather than riding from Martinsburg to Shepherdstown as Stuart had ordered. After hearing the firing about noon and realizing that a hot fight was in progress, Ferguson, perhaps sensing his error, pushed his men south as fast as possible. Nonetheless, his detour consumed several critical hours and completely deranged Stuart's battle plan.

When he reached Leetown, Ferguson turned his column left onto the Winchester Pike and moved toward the battlefield. As his troopers waded through the backwash of the fluid action, the arriving troopers passed large numbers of wounded going to the rear, some on foot and others in ambulances. Here and there, small knots of men were spotted burying dead comrades, while up ahead the noise of battle swelled and receded with each Confederate assault.[39]

---

37 Tobie, *First Maine Cavalry*, 184. Eric Wittenberg, "Bvt. Maj. Gen. John Irvin Gregg," *Rantings of a Civil War Historian*, January 2008, http://civilwarcavalry.com/?p=653.

38 *OR* Vol. 27, pt. 2, 706.

39 James H, Hodam, *Sketches and Personal Reminiscences of the Civil War as Experienced by a Confederate Soldier Together with Incidents of Boyhood Life of Fifty Years Ago* (Eugene, OR, 1996), 87-88.

It was late afternoon by the time Ferguson's four regiments reached the field. The colonel sent the 34th and 36th Virginia Cavalry battalions to support Chambliss (probably on Stuart's order) and brought the remainder of his brigade up behind Lee. Dismounting the 14th, 16th and 17th Virginia regiments, Ferguson deployed them into line from left to right, in that order, and began extending Lee's front to threaten the Union right flank.[40]

Late though they were, the arrival of Confederate reinforcements could not have been timelier. Just as these Southerners came onto the field, some of the troopers of the 16th Pennsylvania Cavalry became overly excited at the repulse of a Rebel assault, jumped over the stone wall, and launched a spontaneous (and wholly unplanned) counterattack. This was decidedly against the orders of David Gregg and Irvin Gregg. But once the impromptu attack was initiated, there was nothing anyone could do but await its inevitable result, which came quickly enough. In a mirror image of what the Confederates had suffered throughout the day, the Federals pushed their foe back into the woods where Rebel artillery lay in wait. Once their own men cleared the front, every Rebel gun on the field opened a vicious fire that sent the bluecoats reeling backwards.[41]

Quick to seize the opportunity offered by this repulse, the Southerners eagerly counterattacked with Ferguson's three fresh regiments leading the effort. Major Frederick Smith, commanding the 17th Virginia Cavalry, was ordered to advance up a "steep ravine" whose terminus was a mere 50 yards from the stone wall that marked the Union line of departure. "Stripped . . . of everything but revolvers and rifles," the regiment moved forward in an infantry-like column of fours. The gully provided excellent protection from enemy fire until the last few dozen yards, at which point the Virginians had to scramble out of their sheltered approach and dash up a steep grassy slope toward the wall.[42]

Maneuvering "by company into line," the attacking Confederate formation morphed into a column of companies, its men screaming the Rebel yell, as they hurtled toward the Federals. According to one attacker, the short time it took to cover those final yards seemed to last hours rather

---

40 Ibid.

41 Ibid. The Gregg officers were cousins.

42 Ibid.

than seconds. A savage crossfire struck the Confederates, hitting a lieutenant and then the regimental adjutant. Several privates went down as well, some dropped by bullets and others slipping and falling on the steep slope. Though wounded, Captain Edward Smith, commander of the 17th Virginia's Company B, waved his sword in the air and shouted for his men to keep going. No one stopped to fire. Success or failure depended solely on old-fashioned shock tactics and the question of whose nerves would break first.[43]

The 16th Virginia Cavalry hit the Union line on the left of the 17th Virginia, diverting some of the enemy's fire as Smith's troopers surged out of the ravine. Although the Rebels had no bayonets, their relentless advance and heart-stopping yells proved too much for the defenders. By the time the Virginians reached the wall, many blue troopers had abandoned its protection and were falling back. The Confederates drove the Federals rearward a quarter mile and managed to enfilade the right flank of the 1st Maine Cavalry before their assault lost its momentum and came to a fitful end.[44]

Peeved that his orders against counterattacking had been ignored, and in response to this crisis, an "anxious [and] irritated" Irvin Gregg was compelled to seek help from the rest of the division. General Gregg ordered McIntosh to send reinforcements, and the latter promptly dispatched the 1st Pennsylvania Cavalry commanded by Colonel John P. Taylor. Moving in a column of fours, the Pennsylvanians galloped over a mile of open ground to the Winchester Pike, then turned onto the road and dashed the last half-mile to the front, all the while under artillery fire.

When he reached the battle line, Taylor dismounted four companies. He sent two of the companies to protect the far right and the other pair to reinforce the 16th Pennsylvania Cavalry, whose reserve squadron had also entered the fight. The remaining four companies of the 1st regiment took position behind the line, waiting with drawn sabers to strike any Rebels who might break through. As it turned out, the precaution proved unnecessary. With the assistance of their reinforcements, the troopers of the 16th

---

43 Ibid.

44 Ibid; Brian Stuart Kesterson, *Campaigning With the 17th Virginia Cavalry Nighthawks at Monocacy* (Washington, WV, 2005), 48.

Pennsylvania established a new line against which the enemy's advance ground to a halt.[45]

Elsewhere along the front, attacks by Ferguson's other regiments produced one last flurry of fighting on the Union right. The 14th Virginia Cavalry hit the 4th Pennsylvania Cavalry around 5:00 p.m., though with no better luck than that enjoyed elsewhere along the line for most of the afternoon. As the Confederates drew back from this last effort, some blue troopers mounted the stone wall. Waving their hats and cheering, they taunted the Rebels with demands they try another charge. Such bravado was hardly wise, for the regiment was nearly out of ammunition. Its boastful members were fortunate the Southerners didn't take up the challenge.[46]

*   *   *

While Fitz Lee and Stuart hammered away at the Federals with only modest success, elsewhere a handful of men in Company D of the 12th Virginia Cavalry were making an outsized impact on the course of events. The members of this unit were mostly natives of Jefferson County—which encompassed Harpers Ferry, Halltown, Leetown, Charles Town and Shepherdstown—and they knew the area intimately. When Gregg's division began its advance on July 15, the company was on picket between Shepherdstown and a place called Engle's Hill. The Federal movement to Halltown had skirted the right flank of the company's line, and when Gregg led the bulk of his command northward to Shepherdstown, he unknowingly cut these Confederates off from the rest of Lee's army.[47]

Rather than react with alarm and seek a way back to their regiment, the company took advantage of its position to operate behind enemy lines. On the afternoon of the 15th, some Rebel troopers had captured a courier on his way to Harpers Ferry with dispatches from General Gregg. The unlucky messenger was 18 year-old Private Cicero C. Phelps of the 10th New York,

45 Tobie, *First Maine Cavalry*, 182, 185; Charles Miller, *History of the 16th Regiment Pennsylvania Cavalry, for the Year Ending October 31st, 1863* (Philadelphia, PA, 1864; Meyer, *Civil War Experiences*, 66-67.

46 Tobie, *First Maine Cavalry*, 185; *OR* 27, pt. 2, 984-5.

47 James C. Holland, ed., *Military Operations in Jefferson Count, Virginia (Now West Virginia) 1861-1865* (Hagerstown, MD, 2004), 10-11.

and the Virginians extracted "sufficient information" from him to suspect Union reinforcements would move from Harpers Ferry toward Shepherdstown the next day.[48]

On the morning of the 16th, armed with this knowledge, Captain Henry W. Kearney commanding Company D, assembled his roughly 100-man unit near a hamlet called Uvilla and hid it in a patch of woods. Picketing the road to the east and west, the Virginians waited in ambush for anyone wearing blue to come within reach. The hunting proved good, and by mid-afternoon Company D had captured almost 30 prisoners.[49]

While Kearney was scooping up captives, Colonel Huey's brigade of Gregg's division had plodded down congested roads toward Harpers Ferry. Crossing the Potomac into the town sometime after noon, the colonel found an opportunity to rest his troopers for a short time before receiving orders to reinforce Gregg at Shepherdstown. Sending his headquarters wagon with a small escort down an easier and supposedly safer route, Huey took his four regiments on a diverging course along a road paralleling the river.[50]

Unfortunately for the colonel, his wagon and its guards blundered into Captain Kearney's trap, and the Virginians gleefully pounced on the rich prize. About the same time Huey's vehicle and escort fell prey to Kearny's men, Major John L. Knott of the 12th Virginia Cavalry arrived at Uvilla. Knott, who assumed command, concluded that a captured headquarters wagon must mean there were a lot of Yankee horsemen nearby. Curious as to just where the enemy might be and what he was up to, the major sent the prisoners and captured wagon to the rear and ordered Company D north two miles to Moler's Cross Roads, a point on the river road between Harpers Ferry and Shepherdstown four miles equidistant from both.[51]

About 3:00 p.m., as the Rebels drew near Moler's, they spotted the advance guard of Huey's brigade topping a hill as it trotted down the road. The Confederates charged, capturing one of the Yankees and giving chase to

---

48 Matteson, *10th New York Cavalry*, 137; Holland, *Military Operations*, 11.

49 Holland, *Military Operations*, 12; *OR* 27, pt. 2, 767; The strength of Company D is based on a requisition for forage for 100 horses signed by Captain Kearny on July 31, 1863 at Charles Town, Va. In all likelihood there were fewer troopers with the command on July 16, but perhaps not significantly so.

50 *OR* 27, pt. 1, 972.

51 Holland, *Military Operations*, 12.

the rest, who managed to turn and run from their pursuers. Cresting the hill over which the Federals had fled, Knott and his men were shocked to discover an entire brigade of Northern cavalry, accompanied by artillery, materialize in their path. The stunned Virginians engaged in a brief exchange of fire before rapidly reversing course and falling back out of reach.[52]

Despite its brevity, this encounter paid unexpected dividends for the Rebels. Well aware of the fight at Shepherdstown, Huey was fearful his brush with Knott and Kearney might presage an enemy effort to cut Gregg off from Harper's Ferry. Taking no chances, the colonel halted his command, ordered his artillery to unlimber, threw his regiments into line of battle and deployed a heavy force of skirmishers to guard against further surprise. Huey stayed at Moler's Crossroads for three hours before concluding it was safe to resume his march to Shepherdstown. As a result of this delay, Huey did not report to General Gregg until 7:00 p.m.[53]

Sunset was a mere 30 minutes away and the Rebel attacks were petering out, though in places shooting would go on for some time after nightfall. Nonetheless, the addition of the 2nd Brigade's four regiments was most welcome. What was not welcome, however, was Huey's report of the clash at Moler's Crossroad. If the Rebels were that far north, it was safe to assume they were also astride every road leading back to Harpers Ferry.

In fact, the only thing between Gregg and the ferry was a very aggressive company of Virginia cavalrymen, but there was no way for the general to know that. Already facing three enemy brigades, he was keenly aware they could easily call on reinforcements from Southern infantry encamped near Martinsburg. Given the strength of Fitz Lee's assaults that afternoon, and Huey's encounter at Moler's Crossroads, it was not illogical to conclude the Union 2nd Division was surrounded on three sides, and that its only escape route led to a flooded and unfordable river. Low on rations and ammunition, there was no question of successfully continuing the fight on the morrow. The only option left to Gregg was to retreat before the enemy drew his noose closed.

If the mood at Union headquarters was foreboding, the Confederates were in a much more positive frame of mind. Though the Federals had obstinately maintained their position throughout the day, the Southerners

52 Ibid.

53 Holland, *Military Operations*, 12; *OR* 27, pt. 1, 972.

were positive they outnumbered their foes and could cut the Yankee line of retreat to Harpers Ferry. "We went to sleep, confidently anticipating that Gregg was caught in a trap from which he could not extricate himself," Lieutenant George Beale later recalled, adding that Southern troopers were probably never "more certain" that the next day would bring them a "great success and disaster to their enemies."[54]

Regardless of Rebel confidence, David Gregg was not despondent. After night finally put an end to the firing, the rival troopers prepared for the possible renewal of the contest in the morning. Each side built a barricade of stones across the pike to thwart any mounted charge while others went about the grim business of caring for those wounded who could be reached. Federal sergeants distributed what little ammunition and provisions were available to weary troopers resting in the positions they had held throughout the afternoon. The Confederates, similarly exhausted but not as destitute of provisions or ammunition, drew back from their forward positions about 9:00 p.m. to reorganize for a dawn attack.[55]

The move likely surprised and certainly pleased General Gregg, who could not have asked for a greater stroke of fortune. The farther the enemy line was from his front, the easier it would be for him to sneak away in the night down a narrow trail hugging the lapping waters of the swollen Potomac. The route, although at places barely wide enough for a single rider, was thought to be unobstructed by Rebels and hence the only perceived escape route open to the Federals.

A nighttime withdrawal in face of the enemy was perilous in the extreme. If the Confederates realized what was happening and launched an attack, the Federals would be in no condition to resist. The resulting chaos and confusion would likely rout, and possibly destroy, the division. Unless the move was made secretly, it could not succeed. Orders were issued prohibiting talking and directing everyone to take precautions to mute rattling equipment. The men needed little urging to obey, for everyone realized that "unless something could be done very soon," they would be "swallowed up."[56]

---

54 *OR* 27, pt. 2, 706; Beale, *A Lieutenant of Cavalry*, 122-123.

55 Tobie, *First Maine Cavalry*, 182; Pyne, *1st New Jersey Cavalry*, 169.

56 Matteson, 10th New York Cavalry, 135.

The exception to this silence came at 11:00 p.m., when General Gregg ordered drummers to beat the long roll in hopes of convincing Rebel ears that he was being reinforced by infantry. Whether that ruse worked or not (no Southern record mentions hearing drums), Federal regiments gradually began to pull out of the battle line. Due to the narrow road and the need for stealth, it would take considerable time to put the entire division on the march. The troopers in those commands slated to be at the tail of the retreat passed the intervening hours in exhausted tension. More than a few rested on the ground beside their saddled horses, reins in hand, and fell fast asleep despite the circumstances.[57]

Slowly, unit after unit quietly slipped toward the river to join the ever-lengthening column on the single lane leading to safety. The dead had to be left behind, so too the enemy hospital patients captured the day before and those Federals too badly wounded to be moved. These unfortunates were collected in a Shepherdstown church or private homes, where they were consigned to the care of the town's ladies and a Union surgeon who agreed to stay behind to help them.[58]

As the various regiments began retreating, a few men snuck away to say last goodbyes to friends being abandoned to the clemency of the enemy. Not all of these visitors were willing to forsake the injured, however. William Maloon, Jr., a bugler in the 1st Maine Cavalry, refused to leave the side of his brother Horton, a private in the same regiment who had been mortally wounded. William remained by his sibling's side until he expired, after which he fell into Rebel hands.[59]

The story of another suffering soldier had a happier ending. Shot through both lungs, Lieutenant John McKevitt of the 10th New York Cavalry was too severely hurt to be evacuated. Left at the home of the Chapline family, he was nursed back to health by the Chapline's young daughter, Maggie. She helped save the lieutenant's life and won his heart in the process. The two were later married.[60]

---

57 Ibid.

58 Meyer, Civil War Experiences, 59-60.

59 Tobie, First Maine Cavalry, 188.

60 Matteson, *10th New York Cavalry*, 136.

The rest of Gregg's troopers funneled onto the road and snaked their way back toward Harpers Ferry. The general and his staff joined the column a little after midnight. The rearguard did not leave Shepherdstown until just before dawn. As the Federals wound their way down the narrow trail they often had to ride single file and never had enough space for any formation other than a column of twos. This made for slow going, and it wasn't until sometime around 8:00 a.m. that the front of the division reached Harpers Ferry. A few exhausted soldiers who had fallen so soundly asleep they did not hear whispered orders to retreat showed up many hours later, sometimes pursued by Rebel patrols.[61]

If the breaking dawn brought relief to the Yankees, it brought consternation to the Confederates, who discovered too late that Gregg had escaped their trap. Southern horsemen swept up some stragglers and captured the wounded left in Shepherdstown, but otherwise were unable to do any further damage. The Yankees had squirmed out of the trap. Nonetheless, the Rebels held the field where the Federals had left their dead and could claim a victory, even if it was less of a victory than they had hoped.

For both sides the battle had been a hotly contested brawl, and an unusually severe one for cavalry. Writing home a few weeks later, Private John Sheahan of the 1st Maine Cavalry called Shepherdstown "one of the hardest fights that the cavalry has ever been in." A trooper in the 16th Pennsylvania Cavalry agreed, labeling the contest "one of the most desperate cavalry fights of the war." The casualty lists seemed to verify those descriptions. An official tally of the 2nd Division's losses listed 16 killed, 64 wounded, and 24 missing, for an aggregate of 104. Another 33 unlucky Federals were gobbled up by Company D of the 12th Virginia Cavalry, for a grand total of 137.[62]

John Gregg's brigade suffered the vast majority of those casualties. The 1st Maine Cavalry lost 4 killed, 18 wounded, four mortally wounded, and another nine captured. The 16th Pennsylvania listed 6 killed, 18 wounded, and 11 missing, and the 10th New York Cavalry reported a total of eight casualties. No record of the 4th Pennsylvania's Cavalry losses exists, but its

---

61 Meyer, *Civil War Experiences*, 60; Matteson, *10th New York Cavalry*, 135-136; Pyne, *1st New Jersey*, 169.

62 *OR* 27, pt. 1, 193.

regimental history noted that it "suffered more heavily" at Shepherdstown than "in any previous action."[63]

Southern casualties are harder to calculate. Jeb Stuart only reported that his command suffered "several killed and wounded," while claiming enemy losses were "heavy." A description of the battle written for the Richmond *Dispatch* on July 18 stated that casualties were "unofficially reported at from seventy-five to one hundred from all causes." Virtually all of those losses came from Fitz Lee's and Ferguson's brigades. Lieutenant Colonel William Carter of the 3rd Virginia Cavalry recorded the day's events in his diary. According to the lieutenant, Lee's brigade lost four killed and 35 wounded. One fatality that was certain was Colonel James H. Drake, the commander of the 1st Virginia Cavalry. Hit in the thigh, right breast, and through the right shoulder during the fighting around Butler's Woods, Drake died later that evening in a local home.[64]

Regardless of the exact losses, each side suffered more than 100 and maybe as many as 150 in killed, wounded, and missing or captured. The Confederates probably suffered more killed and wounded than the Federals, who lost a great many more men captured than the Rebels. The price of victory notwithstanding, Stuart and Fitz Lee had shoved Gregg's Union division back into Harpers Ferry. For the time being, it would pose no hazard to Lee's supply line or his army.

Unfortunately for the Confederates, a much graver threat was massing along the banks of the Potomac River just out of sight.

---

63 John Sheahan, *Cavalry Battles in Virginia* (Maine Memory Network www.mainememory.net/artifact/97584); Tobie, *First Maine Cavalry*, 183, 185, 673; William Hyndman, *History of a Cavalry Company: A Complete Record of Company A, 4th Penn'a Cavalry* (Philadelphia, PA,1870), 117; Frederick Phisterer, *New York in the War of the Rebellion, 3rd edition* (Albany, NY, 1912); Unknown, *History of the 16th Regiment Pennsylvania Cavalry, For the Year Ending October 31, 1863* (Ithaca, NY, 1864), 8, 15, 17-19.

64 *Richmond Dispatch*, July 18, 1863; *OR* 27, pt. 2, report 706; Holland, *Military Operations*, 12; Swank, *Sabres, Saddles and Spurs*, 84. Carter notes Fitz Lee's losses as 1st VA: 2 killed, 8 wounded; 2nd VA 8 wounded; 3rd VA 2 killed 7 wounded; 4th VA 12 wounded, 5th VA no casualties. Col. James Henry Blake memorial page can be found at http://www.findagrave.com/cgi-bin/fg.cgi?page=gr&GRid=1390105

CHAPTER 4

"You Need Have No Fear"

Bridging the Potomac—Reconnaissance into the Loudoun Valley—The Union Army
Crosses the River—the Confederates disappear—Meade's Doubts and Fears—
Halleck Scolds—Meade's Shrinking Army

THE real danger to the Army of Northern Virginia was not Gregg's division of Union cavalry, but George Meade's army waiting to cross the flooded Potomac River.

Under orders to construct a second bridge over the river, and undaunted by the unavailability of additional supplies, the bulk of the 50th New York Engineers had marched from Harpers Ferry to Berlin on July 15. The next day, after ferrying a squadron of the 3rd Indiana Cavalry to the south bank for protection, the New Yorkers went to work with the pontoons and planking at hand.

Their task was hampered not only by a shortage of material, but also the width of the river, which had expanded to a daunting 1,500 feet. Additionally, the swift current swept downstream a menagerie of debris that threatened to wreck the bridge before it could be finished. Entire companies of engineers had to be assigned the job of removing this flotsam from the river and keeping it away from the pontoons.[1]

1 F. J. Bellamy diary, Indiana State Library; Chapman diary, Indiana Historical Society; Malles, *Bridge building in Wartime*, 168-169.

This pair of pontoon bridges was laid across the Potomac at Berlin in October 1862, following the Battle of Antietam. Part of Meade's army used the same spot to cross back into Virginia after Gettysburg. *Library of Congress*

Ironically, this imminent menace proved a godsend to Lieutenant Colonel Spaulding, for among the drifting rubbish were the remains of General Lee's discarded Williamsport bridge and other floating spans that had come to grief earlier in the campaign. Spaulding's men opportunistically fished this refuse out of the Potomac, gathering an extra 700 feet of material—more than enough to complete their bridge by the early morning of July 17.[2]

In true army fashion, the additional pontoons ordered from Washington three days prior arrived on the afternoon the bridge was finished. It had taken these longer than expected to reach Berlin because it had taken longer than expected to bring the water level of the repaired C&O back to operational depth. Spaulding was philosophical about the delay. Reasoning that late was

2 *OR* 27, pt. 3, 715.

better than never, he put his engineers to work building a second span with the tardy material.[3]

With bridges now over the river at both Berlin and Harpers Ferry, Meade finally felt ready to send infantry into Virginia. At 2:00 p.m., he instructed Major General William H. French to cross his III Corps at Harpers Ferry and move three or four miles south before going into camp. The rest of the army would begin crossing the Potomac the next day (July 18). Major General George Sykes' V Corps and the II Corps under Brigadier General William Hays would follow the men of the III over the river. Major General Henry Slocum's XII Corps, meanwhile, was ordered to move as close to the bridge as possible before nightfall and cross if daylight remained; if not, it was to cross early on the 19th.

To the east, Major General John Newton's I Corps, the Reserve Artillery, Army Headquarters, and Brigadier General John Buford's 1st Cavalry Division (in that order) would use the newly laid bridges at Berlin. If these units got over the river before dark, Major General Oliver Howard's XI Corps would also cross. Major General John Sedgwick's VI Corps was instructed to follow suit if enough hours remained before nightfall. Otherwise, one or both of those commands would enter Virginia on July 19. Once these final formations passed into the Old Dominion the next phase of the Gettysburg campaign could begin.[4]

Meade's choice of setting for the resumption of his pursuit was a wise one. Berlin was situated on the north bank of the Potomac at the top of the Loudoun Valley, an 8- to 12-mile-wide and 34-mile-long geographic highway running southwest to northeast, parallel to the Shenandoah Valley. Framed on its eastern flank by the Bull Run Mountains and on the west by the Blue Ridge Mountains, Loudoun had long been a cockpit of the war and had featured prominently in several of the conflict's early campaigns.

By entering the valley at Berlin, while simultaneously crossing at Harpers Ferry, Meade greatly reduced the possibility he would meet Confederate resistance while his army straddled the Potomac. More importantly, once most of his army was inside the Loudoun Valley, it was largely invulnerable to attack and in an excellent jump-off position for offensive operations. The incredibly lush and agriculturally productive

3 Ibid., 715-716.

4 Ibid., 714; 718.

region was accessible only by a handful of passes in either of its bordering mountain ranges. These rugged gaps were easily defended by relatively small bodies of troops. Whoever possessed them was able to deny his enemy access to the valley for attack or reconnaissance.

Perhaps most important of all, custody of the gaps might allow an undetected Union army to suddenly pour out of Loudoun into the Shenandoah Valley or steal a march down the eastern slope of either mountain range toward the Rappahannock and Rapidan rivers. Such a move, if executed with speed and vigor, might trap the Army of Northern Virginia in the Shenandoah and cut it off from Richmond.

These geographic realities were as well known to Robert E. Lee as they were to George Meade, and there was a possibility the Rebel general would preempt the Union commander's scheme by occupying Loudoun first. This was a real fear, for once the Confederates crossed the Potomac they had, for all intents and purposes, disappeared from view, their exact whereabouts and movements unknown. In light of that fact, moving into Loudon, despite all its attractions, entailed considerable risk precisely because of its geographic utility. If Lee had managed to insert significant forces into the area he could attack and destroy the first Union units over the river before help could arrive.

Fortunately for Meade, in the days after Gettysburg Henry Halleck had done more than goad the Army of the Potomac to a vigorous pursuit. He had also sent forces south of the river to detect any enemy troops in Loudoun capable of coming to Lee's aid. As things turned out, this movement would also answer the question of whether it was safe to deploy Union forces into the region once the Rebels escaped back to Virginia.

On July 9, Colonel Charles R. Lowell III, commanding the 2nd Massachusetts Cavalry, had received orders to move his regiment from Poolesville, Maryland, to Washington, D.C. as quickly as possible. Reaching the city next day, Lowell reported to Colonel Percy Wyndham of the 1st New Jersey Cavalry, who had been given the job of collecting all "straggling cavalry" in the vicinity of the capital and organizing them for its defense during Lee's invasion. Wyndham handed Lowell instructions written by Halleck but issued through the headquarters of Major General Samuel P. Heintzelman, commander of the Washington defenses.

With his own regiment and whatever troopers Wyndham could spare, Lowell was to conduct an immediate reconnaissance into the Loudoun Valley as far south as Chester Gap. Specifically, he was to discover what

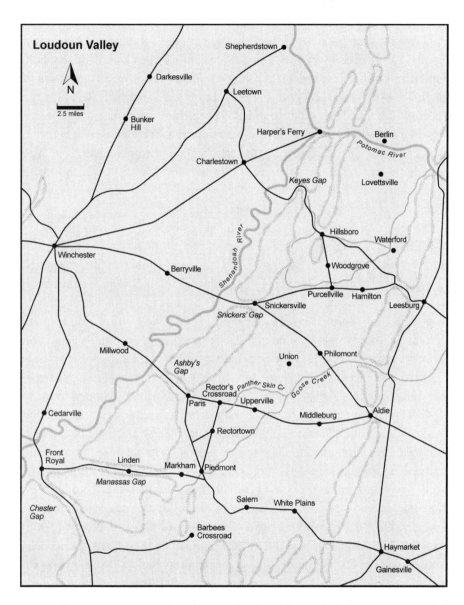

enemy forces were operating there and what, if any, Rebel troops occupied the passes of the Blue Ridge. If he could obtain a vantage point in the mountains, the colonel was also to make a visual survey of the Shenandoah Valley and report any Confederate movements he might discern.[5]

5   *OR* 27, pt. 3, 623; 717; *OR* 27, pt. 1, 1039.

Lowell began his mission on July 11, with the 340 troopers in his own regiment reinforced by 60 men from Wyndham's ad hoc command. By 6:00 p.m. he was at Aldie, the scene of a vicious cavalry action at the beginning of the Gettysburg campaign and just outside the valley proper. Thus far the Federals had found no evidence of any Rebel troops other than the expected presence of Colonel John S. Mosby's partisan rangers, who were a constant menace in this district. Learning that elements of Grumble Jones' cavalry brigade were near Middleburg, Lowell decided against following instructions to send 100 men to scout Thoroughfare Gap, electing instead to keep his force concentrated for the next day's push.[6]

On the morning of the 12th, the Yankees rode deeper into the valley expecting to encounter trouble. Despite rumors that two companies of enemy cavalry occupied Ashby's Gap and some force of undetermined strength held Snickers' Gap, Lowell's troopers had no difficulties until noon when they reached the little village of Paris outside the entrance to Ashby's Gap. Here, the Northerners encountered Rebel pickets who fired at them from inside the town, but did no damage before fleeing toward the pass, with Lowell's advance guard of three companies in hot pursuit.[7]

This, however, was exactly what the Rebels wanted and expected. Reaching the top of Ashby's Gap, the Federals found three platoons from the 5th North Carolina cavalry, about 75 men, drawn up in line of battle awaiting an attack. As it turned out, these defenders were merely bait meant to lure the Yankees into an ambush. When the Northerners neared the summit, dismounted graybacks opened fire from the cover of underbrush and stone walls. Two rapid volleys toppled nine Federals from their saddles and killed three horses, whose riders were captured. Stung by this sudden reversal of fortunes, the surviving blue troopers beat a hasty retreat. Colonel Lowell responded to this check by sending two companies to outflank the Rebels, who, in danger of being surrounded, were compelled to flee. Once again

---

6   *OR* 27, pt. 1, 1039.

7   Ibid; *Fayetteville Observer*, Sept. 14, 1863; Larry Rogers and Keith Rogers, *Their Horses Climbed Trees: A Chronicle of the California 100 and Battalion in the Civil War from San Francisco to Appomattox*, (Atglen, PA, 2001), 162.

Lowell's advance guard followed closely, but this time a bit more cautiously than before.[8]

The Union troopers trailed the Rebels down the western slope of the mountain and chased them for three miles along the east bank of the Shenandoah River, engaging in a brisk firefight with their opponents all the while. Satisfying though this was from a tactical point of view, the intelligence rewards were meager. The atmosphere was "so hazy," Lowell reported, that he could see nothing in the Shenandoah Valley, and all his vanguard could learn was that the river was in full-throated flood and impassable at Berry's Ferry, where they were shot at by 25 Confederates guarding a small supply dump on the western shore. The most pertinent piece of information appeared to be the prediction of locals that it would take 10 days for the flooding to subside.[9]

Finding the weather no more conducive to observation on the 13th than it had been the day before, Lowell decided his reconnaissance had accomplished all that was reasonably possible. Leading his men northeast to Leesburg via Mount Gilead, he camped at Dranesville (a few miles east of Leesburg) before heading back to Washington. On the 14th, Lowell sent a report of his efforts to General Heintzelman, in which he detailed his losses and the course of the expedition. Union casualties, he explained, were two dead, eight wounded, and another six captured. One man had taken the opportunity to desert. The Federals took 13 enemy prisoners, most of them from Jones' and Robertson's brigades, and claimed to have killed nine enemy troopers.[10]

Losses were incidental to the project, however, as was the reoccupation of Ashby's Gap by the evicted Rebel outpost. What mattered most to Halleck, and hence Meade, was Lowell's conclusion that "there is no force of Rebels on this side of the Blue Ridge north and west of Thoroughfare Gap." Given that Lowell's report was delivered in the immediate aftermath of Lee's successful withdrawal across the Potomac, the colonel's observations were freighted with an importance beyond their original

---

8 Ibid; James McLean, *California Sabers: the Second Massachusetts Cavalry in the Civil War* (Bloomington, IN, 2000), 44.

9 Ibid.

10 Ibid, Appendix A, 275-6; Rogers, *Their Horses Climbed Trees*, 162.

purpose, for they meant the Loudon Valley was open to the Army of the Potomac, and Meade could execute his river crossing as planned.[11]

*   *   *

Robert E. Lee's intentions at this stage of the campaign were unclear. Certainly he hoped to keep the Federals close to the Potomac for as long as possible, and to that end his current position in the lower Valley served a useful purpose. If Meade crossed the river into Loudon County, however, this would no longer be the case and the enemy could either move to strike Lee on unfavorable terrain around Winchester, or trap him in the Valley while the Union army made an unimpeded lunge toward Richmond.

Forestalling either eventually meant Lee had to know what was happening in Loudon. If the Federals were already south of the river, the Army of Northern Virginia would be compelled to shift east of the Blue Ridge Mountains, and quickly. But if the enemy was still north of the Potomac, it might be possible for the Confederates to claim Loudoun's geographic advantages for themselves. No matter which scenario he faced, Lee knew it was vital for him to hold the mountain passes, which is why he had called Jeb Stuart to army headquarters on the eve of the Shepherdstown fight to instruct him to reinforce whatever detachments currently occupied the gaps. Consequently, on the morning of July 17, Stuart ordered Grumble Jones to carry out Lee's directive and maintain control of that critical ground.[12]

Unfortunately, Jones quickly discovered that getting any additional troops into the passes would be extremely difficult, and perhaps impossible, because of the flooded state of the Shenandoah River. Indeed, during the entire week after Lee crossed the Potomac, only the 35th Virginia Cavalry Battalion, commanded by Lieutenant Colonel Elijah V. White, managed to move into Loudoun from the Shenandoah Valley. Both the unit and its leader were something of a special case. Lean and lanky, with a face that suggested he was a man not to be trifled with, 31-year-old White was a native of Poolesville, Maryland. He had gone west in his early 20s to fight against

11 Ibid.

12 *OR* 27, pt. 2, 324, 796.

Free Soil settlers in the Missouri-Kansas border dispute, but returned home about a year later to buy a piece of land and settle down. When the war broke out in 1861, White enlisted as a private in the 7th Virginia Cavalry. He worked his way up to his current rank, earning in the process significant praise from A. P. Hill, who considered White "one of the best cavalry officers" in the Confederate army. White's six companies had been raised in the area and, when not attached to Stuart, usually operated in Loudoun County, where their raids proved a constant irritation to Federal forces. During the invasion of Pennsylvania, the 35th had been assigned the job of screening General Ewell's corps and had performed commendably throughout the Gettysburg campaign. Upon returning to Virginia, however, White asked for permission to move his unit back into Loudoun, and Stuart had consented.[13]

On July 15, when the battalion reached the Shenandoah River at Castleman's Ferry, close to Snickers' Gap, it found the water "so high" it was "impassable." After waiting more than 24 hours for the river to subside, White and his men—all impatient to return to their homes and old haunts—decided to run the considerable risk of crossing the flooded river even as gloomy skies threatened more rain. While some troopers relied on a small skiff to get over the turbulent waters, others boldly swam their horses across. By the time twilight began to darken the overcast sky, 50 or so of White's troopers had managed to find somewhat dry ground on the river's east bank. While comrades on the opposite shore prepared to emulate their crossing, the men on the distant bank stripped off sodden clothing and kindled fires to warm themselves and dry their uniforms. Those plans were rudely upended, however, when a courier dashed into White's impromptu camp with an urgent plea for assistance.[14]

The messenger bore a dispatch from Lieutenant Thomas Moon, commander of a detachment of dismounted men from the 6th and 12th Virginia cavalry regiments, left to picket Snickers' Gap when Lee invaded Pennsylvania. According to Moon, Federal troops were advancing on the pass in strength, and it was highly unlikely he could halt them without help.

---

13 Krick, *Lee's Colonels*, 392; Frank M. Meyers, *The Comanches: A History of White's Battalion, Virginia Cavalry, Laurel Brig., Hampton Div., A.N.V., C.S.A.* (Marietta, GA, 1956), 206.

14 Ibid, 207. White crossed the river on the afternoon of July 17, 1863.

Quickly putting on wet uniforms and mounting their horses, White's troopers hurried north to render what aid they could, which turned out to be none at all.[15]

Well before Moon called for reinforcements, the 5th Michigan Cavalry, part of Brigadier General George A. Custer's brigade from Judson Kilpatrick's 3rd Cavalry Division, had captured a dozen dismounted Confederates searching for horses near the gap. When the Yankees rode deeper into the pass, they encountered Lieutenant Moon's troopers and a sharp skirmish broke out. The overmatched Rebels were unable to stand up to an entire regiment and Moon ordered a retreat. The fight cost the Federals two casualties, both wounded, but all things considered, that was a cheap price to pay for such an important objective.[16]

White met up with Moon's retreating contingent shortly after setting out to offer it some assistance. With the Federals in possession of Snickers' Gap, there was nothing more White could do but get the balance of his command safely over the Shenandoah River and then fall back to the next probable Yankee target—recently reoccupied Ashby's Gap. There, the colonel "resolved to make a fight" if the enemy came at him with anything close to equal force.[17]

Although White's resolve was commendable, the possibility that the Yankees would approach in anything less than overwhelming strength was remote. By nightfall on July 18, more than one-half of the Army of the Potomac was in the Loudoun Valley. That evening, Meade's headquarters camped at Loyettsville, the I corps at Waterford, and the II and III corps at Hillsboro—the latter having crossed the Shenandoah River from Harpers Ferry via a pontoon bridge and then marched on through Keyes Gap in the Blue Ridge Mountains to join the main army in the valley. The V Corps, along with the 1st Cavalry Division, bivouacked at Purcellville and the artillery reserve around Wheatland. Gregg's cavalry division remained at Harpers Ferry, while Judson Kilpatrick posted one brigade of cavalry at Harpers Ferry, another at Berlin, and third at Purcellville. The VI and XI corps were gathered at Berlin, and the XII corps opposite Harpers Ferry. All

15 Ibid; Consolidated Service Records, 5th North Carolina Cavalry, www.fold3.com; *OR* 27, pt. 1, 1039.

16 Meyers, *The Comanches*, 207; *OR* 27, pt. 1, 1001.

17 Meyers, *The Comanches*, 208.

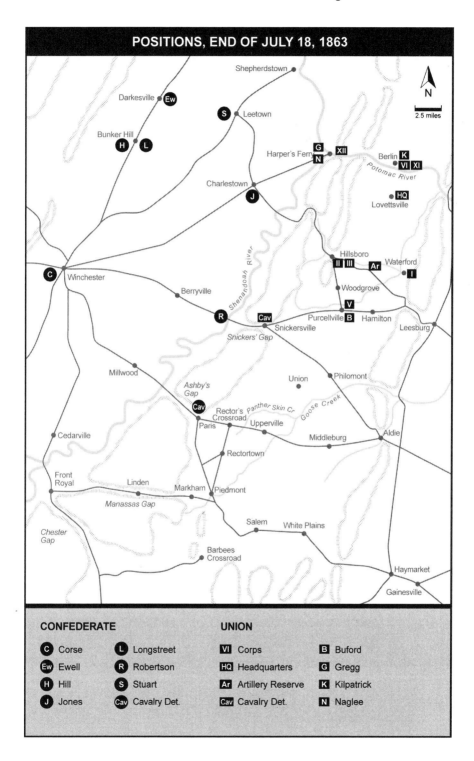

POSITIONS, END OF JULY 18, 1863

three of the infantry corps just mentioned prepared to cross the river the next day.[18]

*   *   *

However much this thrust over the Potomac River might satisfy the newspapers and the high command, starting the next phase of the campaign was not altogether conducive to high morale. In fact, many of Meade's soldiers were in something of a foul mood. One Union infantryman confessed that the crossing of the Potomac was made "amid the curses and groans of the men, who detest the soil of Virginia" and were anything but enamored of the commander ordering them back into the Old Dominion. Some complained that "Old Meade, the four eyed loafer" was again "leading them to the graveyard of the Army of the Potomac."[19]

The demeanor of Southern civilians did nothing to brighten the disposition of advancing Federals. Riding through Leesburg, a Union cavalryman observed that the "folks look awfully surly at us as we pass. We can see our unwelcomness." While Virginia's black citizens and Unionists clearly rejoiced in the return of blue uniforms, contempt for Northern soldiers was equally evident among the state's pro-Confederate female inhabitants. William White, marching with a Vermont regiment, noted the women wore "very long faces" and "pretty much all dressed in black."[20] Corporal Charles Engle of the 137th New York thought the female Virginians living near Kemper's Ford the "worst secessh" he had ever encountered. "They talk it right out," he wrote home, adding "they hate us the worst way." Major Winkler didn't need words to discern the opinion of the inhabitants of Middleburg. "Ladies curled their lips in proud distain as we passed," he observed, while some Virginians locked up their wells to prevent Northern troops from getting water."[21]

---

18 *OR* 27, pt. 1, 148.

19 James Mohr, *The Cormany Diaries*, 345; White letters, www.vermonthistory.org/educate/cwletter/whitelet.htm

20 Ibid.

21 Engle letter August 23, 1863, www.members.aol.com/jocy13/; Winkler letter July 21, 1863, www.russscott.com/~rscott/25thwis/26pgwk63.htm

Although his soldiers had no way of knowing it, entering Virginia made George Meade as ill at ease as it made them. On July 16, in a letter to his wife, he bemoaned the pressure coming from Washington to overtake and destroy Lee's army—something he confessed was "impossible" once the Rebels were over the Potomac and free to avoid battle. Painfully aware of the losses suffered at Gettysburg and the rigors of the last six weeks, he grumbled that his exhausted army was "greatly reduced and weakened by recent operations." Rather than renew its advance, the general felt it ought to pause for a much-needed period of "rest and reorganization."[22]

Two days later, as his men crossed the Potomac, Meade's outlook remained despondent. During the afternoon of July 18, the Union commander vented his strategic concerns to Halleck. While noting that his cavalry had seized Snickers' Gap and was moving along the eastern slope of the Blue Ridge with orders to occupy all similar terrain as far south as Chester Gap, Meade lamented that he had "no intelligence of any kind" as to Lee's whereabouts. Other than vague reports of the Rebels "moving on Winchester," the position of the Confederate army was a mystery. Scouts "sent in all directions" had done nothing to pierce the cloak of invisibility that seemed to have descended on the enemy.[23]

This lack of knowledge allowed Meade to conjure nightmares. He telegraphed Halleck, for example, that Southern newspapers were claiming that part of the Confederate Army of Tennessee had been dispatched to Lee's assistance. Although he feigned skepticism of these rumors for Halleck, telegraphing, "I presume if any reliable intelligence of this fact reaches you, I shall be fully advised," he wrote his wife on the same day that he considered the report "by no means improbable."[24]

Hearing that Meade feared Lee was being reinforced irritated an already irritable Halleck, who saw in such talk hints of the same equivocation that preceded Meade's failure to attack at Williamsport. Talking about bold action was one thing. Carrying through on it was something else, and thus far Meade had shown no disposition to make good on such promises. Fretting

---

22 George Meade, *Life and Letters of George Gordon Meade*, 2 vols (New York, NY, 1913), vol. 2, 135.

23 *OR* 27, pt. 1, 96.

24 Ibid; Meade, *Life and Letters*, vol. 2, 136.

about Lee being substantially reinforced today, after all, could become a handy excuse for failing to act aggressively tomorrow.

Halleck was determined to deny Meade any such safe harbor. That the commander of the Army of the Potomac considered it possible for his foe to be significantly reinforced was preposterous as far as the general-in-chief was concerned. Snapping off a reply, he lectured his commander: "You need have no fear . . . not a man will join Lee." Should that prove incorrect, Halleck reasoned, the only possible source of Rebel reinforcements was North Carolina, and even if troops were sent from there to Virginia, the Rebels, Halleck pointedly told Meade, would still be "far inferior in numbers" to his own force.[25]

So it might appear from Washington. But Meade's perspective was very different. The War Department might imagine that the more than 36,000 emergency volunteers hastily called to arms during the Rebel invasion provided the overwhelming strength necessary to destroy Lee, but Meade knew better. Not only were these semi-trained men of no "practical value," except for a handful of six-months' recruits, their enlistments were due to expire within a very short time.[26] In fact, the majority of these volunteers were slated for demobilization in early August and none later than September 1. On July 16, Major General Darius N. Couch, commander of the Department of the Susquehanna, reported that most of Pennsylvania's 15,000 emergency volunteers stationed at Harrisburg were refusing to leave the state and enter Maryland. The general informed Meade that he could only be certain of sending 800 cavalry to guard the north bank of the Potomac, although he hoped to convince "a few thousand infantry" to follow suit.[27]

The meaning of this was clear. Once the immediate threat to their state disappeared, these men had no intention of doing anything but going home as soon as possible. This was hardly a surprise and Meade knew it. In his mind it was little short of ridiculous to take these temporary soldiers into

---

25 *OR* 27, pt. 1, 96.

26 Meade, *Life and Letters*, vol. 2, 135.

27 Pennsylvania had sent 31,000 militia and ninety-day enlistees as well as 5,459 six-month Volunteers into the field between the middle of June and mid-July. New York had forwarded 19 regiments of infantry and a battery of artillery, while New Jersey contributed an infantry battalion. Meade, *Life and Letters*, vol. 2, 135; *OR* 27, pt. 2, 215-16; *OR* Vol. 27, pt. 3, 712.

account when calculating the balance of power between the Army of the Potomac and the Army of Northern Virginia.

Not only was Meade unimpressed by his supposed reinforcements, he was also less than enthused by his chief subordinates. The loss at Gettysburg of his two best corps commanders—Major General John F. Reynolds, shot dead on July 1, and Major General Winfield Scott Hancock, who was grievously wounded on July 3—was especially injurious, and Meade admitted that men of equal capacity could not be readily found to replace them. Worse, he considered many of his remaining generals neither "active" nor "energetic," and felt they could not be depended upon to take "care of themselves" or their commands.[28]

In addition to these woes, Meade's army was shrinking. The nine-month enlistment of the entire 2nd Vermont brigade, an over-sized outfit, whose 4,800 volunteers had performed magnificently at Gettysburg, expired just days after the battle and it was discharged. In good measure this subtraction was counterbalanced by the addition of a 5,000-man division under William French, which had joined the army on July 7. Meade had assigned the unit to the badly shot up III Corps, whose commander, Major General Daniel E. Sickles, had lost a leg on July 2. By virtue of seniority, French assumed command of the corps. The addition of this division, however, did little to make up for the 23,000 casualties suffered at Gettysburg.[29]

At any rate, if French had helped offset the loss of the tough Vermonters, no similar reinforcement was available for the army's mounted arm, which was dwindling due to hard service and worn-out horses. On July 16, Alfred Pleasonton reported that his strength had slipped below 10,000 men. Worse, there were fewer than 7,000 serviceable horses in the cavalry corps, meaning that 3,000 troopers present for duty could not be put into the field. This was an especially painful deficit since Pleasonton's horsemen were Meade's best hope of uncovering Lee's position and intentions.[30]

Under such circumstances, Meade believed President Lincoln ought to be "contented with driving Lee out of Maryland" and refrain from ordering a continuation of the campaign until the army was "largely reinforced and

28 Meade, *Life and Letters*, vol. 2, 136.

29 Meade, *Life and Letters*, vol. 2, 135; *OR* 27, pt. 1, 488.

30 *OR* 27, pt. 1, 95.

reorganized." As the general saw it, further pursuit of Lee was pointless until the Army of the Potomac was "put on such a footing that its advance was sure to be successful." What Meade thought should be done was completely at odds with the administration's wishes, not to mention the public's expectations, and he recognized that fact. Therefore, he would continue to follow a course he considered dangerous and one that might end in his defeat and dismissal. "This has been the history of all my predecessors," Meade wrote his wife.[31]

He was sure it would be his own in due course.

31 Meade, *Life and Letters*, vol. 2, 135-136.

Chapter 5

"I Desire to be Cautious"

General Kelley Pursues Lee—Fight Near Martinsburg—Lee Lacks Information—
Longstreet Ordered to the Rappahannock—Meade Deepens His Invasion of Loudoun
Valley

W HILE George Meade lamented the state of his affairs, Federal troops led by Brigadier General Benjamin F. Kelley were on the move in the Shenandoah Valley. Born in New Hampshire in 1807, Kelley had moved to Wheeling, Virginia at the age of 19, where he made a living first as a merchant and later as a freight agent for the B&O Railroad. When Virginia seceded, Kelley remained loyal to the Union and at the relatively old age (for a soldier) of 54, raised a regiment of 90-day volunteers organized as the 1st West Virginia Infantry. Commissioned colonel of the regiment, Kelley led it into a small battle at Philippi, Virginia, on June 3, 1861, where he was shot in the right breast—earning him the unhappy distinction of being the first Federal officer wounded during the war. With his lung damaged and his ribs fractured, many thought him mortally injured. Remarkably, after just a few weeks he returned to duty and was promoted to brigadier general. The bump in rank was bestowed mostly in recognition of his wound and efforts to promote the Union cause in the western reaches of the Old Dominion, rather than any pronounced military capability.[1]

---

1   Faust, *Encyclopedia of the Civil War*, 410; Ezra J. Warner, *General in Blue: Lives of the Union Commanders* (Baton Rouge, LA, 1977), 260-261; *Reports of Committees of the*

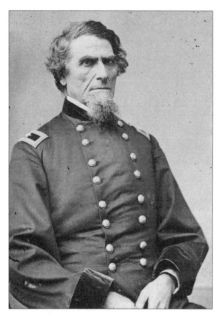

Brigadier General Benjamin F. Kelley
Library of Congress

Appointed commander of the freshly minted Department of West Virginia on June 2, 1863 Kelley had immediately received orders to harass General Lee's flank during the invasion of Pennsylvania. The primary mission of Kelley's department, however, was to guard the Baltimore & Ohio railroad, which necessitated that his units be widely scattered. Such dispersal was hardly conducive to offensive movement and consequently it took some time for Kelley to assemble a mobile force. Once he had his troops in hand, the New Hampshire-born general marched promptly. By mid-afternoon of July 14 he had reached Williamsport with 6,000 men, only to find the Rebels gone and the river "rising rapidly."[2]

Anxious to maintain pressure on the Confederates, Halleck ordered Kelley to cross the Potomac and do "some harm" to the enemy. Naturally, this was easier said than done, especially with the river spilling out of its banks. Nonetheless, orders were orders, and the general wasted no time in complying. On July 15 at a ford on the Potomac near Cherry Run Creek, Virginia, Kelley ferried six companies of cavalry—the Ringgold Battalion (5 companies) and the Washington (Pennsylvania) Cavalry—over the Potomac using three small skiffs.[3]

Each boat would take saddles and men over the river, while the horses of the passengers swam behind. It was a slow and tedious process that required "great labor" in the face of a current that swept boats a half-mile downstream

---

House of Representatives for the First Session of the Forty-Ninth Congress, 1885-1886, 12 Volumes (Washington, D.C., 1886), vol. 9, Report 2715.

2   OR 27, pt. 3, 699, 748. Kelley had 3,200 infantry in two brigades, 2,500 cavalry, and three batteries of artillery.

3   Ibid., pt. 1, 94.

from their starting point on every trip. Despite the difficulties it worked, and that was all that mattered. By afternoon this small mounted force was patrolling North Mountain, which jutted northeastward into a bend of the Potomac six miles east of Cherry Run and just below Williamsport.[4]

With the added contribution of three additional flat boats, Kelley continued his ferrying operation over the next two days. Although the technique remained "difficult and dangerous," the Federals kept at it until Kelley had all his troops safely in Virginia. Telegraphing this news to Washington on the evening of July 17, the general promised to advance with his entire force as soon as his wagons could be gotten across the Potomac.[5]

The same day that Kelley finished crossing the river, a patrol from the Ringgold Battalion captured a party of 17 Confederates near North Mountain Station (also known as North Mountain Depot), a stop on the B&O located at a gap through which ran a road to Martinsburg. The prisoners were from Wade Hampton's cavalry brigade, which the captives claimed was stationed close by. This information, combined with the sound of cannon fire heard the day before from the direction of Shepherdstown, indicated that Rebels indeed were not far away, and in strength.[6]

The next day Kelley continued to reconnoiter, sending cavalry patrols southwest to Shanghai in Back Creek Valley, which lay just west of North Mountain and extended from Winchester all the way to Williamsport on the Potomac. These patrols captured a few more prisoners and confirmed that Rebel cavalry was hovering in the area. The most important intelligence came from a Confederate deserter who entered Kelley's lines on the evening of July 18. According to the defector, Hampton's brigade was at Martinsburg, Ewell's Second Corps only four miles south of that point, while the rest of the Rebel army, including Robert E. Lee himself, was encamped at Bunker Hill.[7]

This knowledge made Benjamin Kelley uncomfortable. Although he was dutifully undertaking the logistical steps necessary to stay south of the Potomac—restringing telegraph lines, repairing the C&O canal, and

4 Samuel C. Farrar, *The Twenty-second Pennsylvania Cavalry and The Ringgold Battalion, 1861-1865* (Pittsburg, PA, 1911), 126.

5 *OR* 27, pt. 2, 281; Farrar, *The Twenty-second Pennsylvania*, 126.

6 *OR* 27, pt. 2, 281; Farrar, *The Twenty-second Pennsylvania*, 126.

7 Farrar, *The Twenty-second Pennsylvania*, 126; *OR* 27, pt. 3, 727.

The Ford at Cherry run in 1898. Almost everything in this photo would have been
under water when Kelley crossed here on July 15-16, 1863.

Maryland Geological Survey, Volume two by William B. Clark

facilitating repairs to the B&O—he wasn't sure his sojourn would be a long
one. The worried general kept a constant stream of telegrams flowing to
Halleck, asking what information Meade had on the enemy and if it
corresponded with his own intelligence.

Despite a lack of meaningful answers from the general-in-chief, Kelley
promised to push his cavalry to Martinsburg and drive the Rebels out of
town—unless of course, they were "found too strong" to dislodge. Although
willing to be aggressive, the general was concerned he might kick over a
hornet's nest and bring a large part of Lee's army down on his head. To
Halleck he emphasized a "desire to be cautious" with his "small force" lest it
bite off more than it could chew.[8]

Kelley assigned the job of testing enemy strength at Martinsburg to
Brigadier General William W. Averell's 4th Separate Brigade. This
command had only come into existence at the end of May and was still
something of a work in progress. The backbone of Averell's force was the
14th Pennsylvania Cavalry and three regiments (the 2nd, 3rd and 8th West

8   *OR* 27, pt. 2, 281.

Virginia) that had been converted into mounted infantry within the last month. In addition to these commands, Averell had the Ringgold Battalion and four independent cavalry companies: C of the 3rd West Virginia; A of the 1st West Virginia; and the Lafayette and Washington companies (both from Pennsylvania). The four guns of Battery G, 1st West Virginia Light Artillery, under the command of Captain Chatham Ewing, rounded out Averell's brigade, which altogether fielded about 2,500 men.[9]

Not all of these units would be marching against Martinsburg. On the morning of July 19, Kelley ordered the Ringgold Battalion out on another scout of North Mountain and Back Creek. The 3rd West Virginia Mounted Infantry was assigned to guard the road to Winchester. This left Averell with only the 14th Pennsylvania, 2nd and 8th West Virginia, Ewing's battery, and four cavalry companies to complete his mission.[10]

Despite the modest size of his force, Averell, an 1855 graduate of West Point, acted rather boldly. It didn't take his troopers long to encounter the vedettes of Hampton's brigade, with whom they had sparred for the past several days. This pestering vexed Rebel cavalrymen and annoyed Major General Edward ("Allegheny") Johnson's division of Ewell's corps, which had been busy destroying the B&O north of Martinsburg since July 17. Exasperating though these pinpricks were, the Southerners had become accustomed to them and considered the presence of Union cavalry in the area rather mundane.[11]

This morning, however, it quickly became apparent the Federals were up to something more than routine harassment. Confronted by three full Union regiments, Confederate pickets pulled back toward Martinsburg. By noon, the gray troopers were within a mile of the municipality and it looked very much as if Averell would soon capture the place.

When he learned of the Yankee advance, North Carolina native Colonel Lawrence Baker, a West Point graduate (Class of 1851) and veteran Indian fighter, acted swiftly to concentrate a force for the town's defense. The colonel, who was just days away from being promoted to brigadier, deployed the 1st North Carolina Cavalry and Cobb's Legion behind his

---

9 Ibid., 209.

10 Ibid. Confederate reports confirmed the composition of this relatively modest force as only three regiments and four fieldpieces. Ibid., 534.

11 Ibid., 534; Faust, *Encyclopedia of the Civil War*, 31.

retreating vedettes and ordered forward a section of guns from Hart's battery of horse artillery. An appeal for infantry support brought Colonel Alexander S. Vandeventer's 50th Virginia to Baker's aid as well.[12]

Whether this would be sufficient to halt the Federal advance and throw it into reverse depended upon how many Federals were nearby. Local citizens reported that the Yankees had as many as six regiments of veteran cavalry, a pair of mounted infantry regiments, and a six-gun battery approaching Martinsburg. If that was true, the Confederates would have to bring up a lot more troops and guns to engage in a protracted fight to save the town from capture.[13]

As it turned out, neither reinforcements nor a battle was necessary. Baker's concentration stopped the Yankees without firing a shot, largely because the Federals had less than half as many units on the field as Southern civilians claimed. Furthermore, Averell knew his small contingent couldn't take Martinsburg unless the Rebels had left nothing but a token force for its defense, which the appearance of Vandeventer's infantry made clear was not the case. Although Averell could push his advance and provoke a fight, Kelley had warned him not to bring on a general engagement "lest Ewell come to Hampton's support." With those instructions in hand and enough Rebels in his front to make him nervous, Averell decided to do the prudent thing and withdraw.[14]

The Federal retreat was anything but hurried. The Yankees pulled back "slowly and cautiously" while engaging in what one lieutenant in the 50th Virginia Infantry called a "right heavy skirmish." The fitful fighting lasted the rest of the day, waged with such deliberation that in late afternoon the Rebels had the leisure to replace the 50th Virginia with the 48th Virginia under the command of Lieutenant Colonel Robert H. Dungan. The action reached what passed for a climax about a mile and a half from Hedgesville, when Averell was reinforced by Kelley's infantry. Bolstered by this infusion of strength, the Union horsemen turned to make a stand, supported by Ewing's battery, which unlimbered and opened fire for the first time that

---

12 Warner, *Generals in Gray*, 14-15.

13 Ibid.

14 *OR* 27, pt. 2, 281.

day. The Confederates briefly probed the Federal line, but when they found it solid, withdrew out of reach.[15]

Although lengthy, the action had not been expensive. Johnson reported no casualties among his infantry, but claimed the enemy left six dead and one wounded on the field. Averell admitted having two officers and six men wounded, and reported five Rebels killed and a few taken prisoner. Neither Hampton's brigade nor Hart's battery made a report of casualties, but at least three men—two from the 1st North Carolina and one from Cobb's Legion, were killed or mortally wounded.[16]

Beyond that, the engagement revealed some very important information to both sides. Kelley found out that there was a lot of Rebel cavalry and infantry around Martinsburg, while the Confederates discovered the approximate size of Kelley's force and its location. What either side did with that knowledge remained to be seen, but from this point forward both would undoubtedly be on their guard.

In the larger scheme of things, what took place between Martinsburg and Hedgesville seemed of minor importance. Indeed, Robert E. Lee was infinitely more concerned about the possibility Meade had beaten him into the Loudoun Valley. Impatient for reliable intelligence, he directed Stuart to discover "as soon as possible" the truth to reports that Union troops had occupied Snickers' Gap and were threatening Ashby's. Lee stressed that he needed to know the "exact condition of things," and whether it was enemy infantry or merely cavalry operating against the passes.[17]

Just now, however, the flooding Shenandoah River and operations around Martinsburg and Harpers Ferry prevented Stuart from shifting troopers toward the Blue Ridge. The cavalry general was not without recourse, however, and the swollen river did not prevent at least some

15 Ibid., 210; 534-5; William Adolphus Smith papers, letter of July 20, 1863, Dolph Briscoe American History Center, University of Texas at Austin.

16 The Confederate dead were Privates William T. Boyd and Jesse A. Shipman, both from the 1st North Carolina Cavalry, and Private Thomas Salter of Cobb's Legion. OR 27, pt. 2, 210; 534-5; Harriet Bey Mesic, Cobb's Legion: A History and Roster of the 9th Georgia Volunteers in the Civil War (Jefferson, NC., 2011), 333; Consolidated Service Records, 1st North Carolina Cavalry; A. P. Corn to Andrew Shipman, July 20, 1863, and J. K. P. Shipman to Andrew Shipman, August 27, 1863, www.rarebooks.nd.edu/digital/civil_war/letters/shipman/5043-17.shtml

17 OR 27, pt. 3, 1020.

information from reaching his headquarters. By July 19, most likely courtesy of messages sent by Moon or White, Stuart was able to confirm that Snickers' Gap had been lost and Union cavalry was active in Loudon.

Although precisely what was happening east of the mountains remained a mystery, the lack of detailed information didn't render Lee indecisive or inert. Whether the enemy had entered Loudoun in strength or not, it was Meade's most logical move and Lee would operate on the assumption he had or would make it. That meant the moment had arrived to put the Army of Northern Virginia into motion for the first time since crossing the Potomac.

On the afternoon of July 19, Lee ordered Longstreet to shift his First Corps the following day from Bunker Hill to Millwood, just across the Shenandoah River from Ashby's Gap. Jones' and Robertson's cavalry brigades would provide whatever information they could about the enemy, but Longstreet's movements from Millwood were left to his discretion. If, in his judgment, it would be wise to cross the Shenandoah at Berry's Ferry and occupy Ashby's Gap (whose fate remained uncertain), the general was free to do so.[18]

If such action was unnecessary or impracticable, Lee wanted Longstreet to continue up the Valley to Front Royal, cross the Shenandoah on a pontoon bridge he had ordered constructed at that point, pass through Chester Gap, and assume a position along the headwaters of the Rappahannock River. Whether Longstreet remained in that location would be contingent on his ability to obtain enough flour in the region to feed his troops and whether Meade was trying to slip southeast toward Richmond. In the latter case, the First Corps was to move "by the most direct route" to a position south of the Rapidan River and block the Federal advance. If any forthcoming intelligence rendered it necessary, A. P. Hill's Third Corps would be dispatched to Longstreet's aid.[19]

Beyond these instructions, the bulk of Lee's order concentrated on logistics, and included details on how Longstreet should provision his corps. The specificity of these directives illustrated how heavily the problem of supply weighed on Lee's mind. Perhaps it also demonstrated the extent to which he had been disappointed by his subordinates at Gettysburg, where many officers had failed to act with initiative, speed, or sufficient care in

18 Ibid., 1024.

19 Ibid.

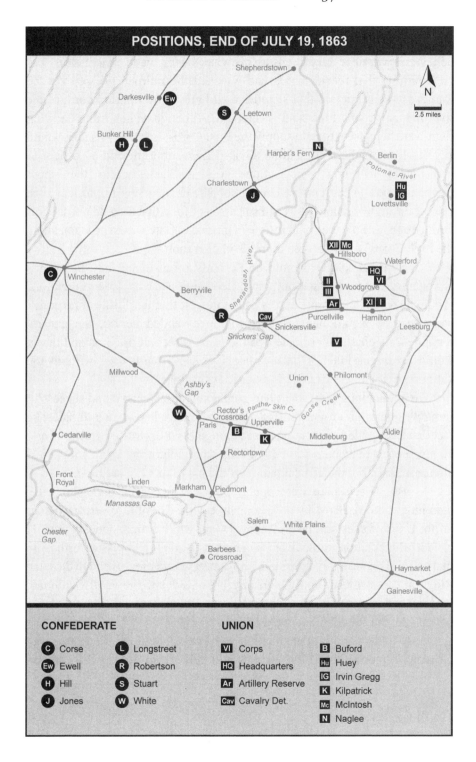

POSITIONS, END OF JULY 19, 1863

N

2.5 miles

Shepherdstown

Darkesville Ew

S Leetown

Bunker Hill
H L

Harper's Ferry N

Berlin

Potomac River

Charlestown
J

Lovettsville
Hu
IG

Shenandoah River

XII Mc
Hillsboro

Waterford

C Winchester

Berryville

II
III Woodgrove

HQ
VI

R

Cav

Ar

Snickers' Gap

Snickersville

Purcellville

XI I

Hamilton

Leesburg

V

Millwood

Ashby's
Gap

Union

Philomont

Goose Creek

Rector's
Crossroad

Panther Skin Cr

W

Paris

B

Upperville

K

Middleburg

Aldie

Cedarville

Rectortown

Front
Royal

Linden

Markham Piedmont

Manassas Gap

Salem

White Plains

Chester
Gap

Barbees
Crossroad

Haymarket

Gainesville

CONFEDERATE

C Corse
Ew Ewell
H Hill
J Jones

L Longstreet
R Robertson
S Stuart
W White

UNION

VI Corps
HQ Headquarters
Ar Artillery Reserve
Cav Cavalry Det.

B Buford
Hu Huey
IG Irvin Gregg
K Kilpatrick
Mc McIntosh
N Naglee

executing Lee's often discretionary orders. The army commander now believed it was necessary to ensure his wishes were made crystal clear.

Warning that recent floods had wrecked the railroad bridge over the Rapidan, Lee cautioned that supplies could not be transported north of the river in quantity until the span was rebuilt. Although wagon trains carrying flour were being sent to help supply the First Corps, Lee knew its men would have to live off the land, and he advised Longstreet to send an officer to investigate just how much flour was available along the upper Rappahannock. Additionally, Lee admonished Longstreet not to leave the district through which he marched so barren of food that it could not support Hill's troops, who were apt to follow in his wake. Care was to be taken along the First Corps' route to keep all mills in operation.[20]

Longstreet's soldiers would be decently provisioned, but the army's animals were a very different matter. Lee cautioned that "every attention" should be paid to the corps' horses and mules. Noting that "little or no grain" had been, or would be, available for an extended period, the general reminded his chief subordinate and the army's second in command that it would be impossible for draft animals to stand hard work without the "utmost care and relief from all superfluous weight."[21]

The meticulous Longstreet had conducted an extensive and successful foraging operation around Suffolk, and so already knew such things. The fact that Lee spelled everything out as though his most trusted general was a young second lieutenant served not only to highlight the army's logistical circumstances, but the critical nature of the move that lay before it.

As usual Lee's plan was vaguely phrased, but easily understood. By marching southeast to Millwood, Longstreet would be able to verify whether or not Union forces had taken Ashby's Gap, while simultaneously placing his corps in position to block any Federal thrust that might issue forth from that point. If no such threat existed, Longstreet would move through the Blue Ridge at Chester Gap and thwart any Union advance toward Richmond. Preferably this would happen along the upper Rappahannock, but if that was unfeasible, the Rapidan line would do.

Fully understanding the situation and Lee's intentions, Longstreet put his plans in motion. The First Corps would move from Bunker Hill early on

20 Ibid.

21 Ibid.

July 20. Pickett's division would lead the column, followed in turn by the divisions of Hood and McLaws. As a precaution, Corse's brigade, still camped at Winchester, would march directly to Front Royal and from there to Manassas and Chester gaps. Two batteries from Dearing's artillery battalion, both under the command of Major Jacob P. W. Read, would accompany the brigade. If necessary, Corse could keep the enemy out of the gaps until the rest of the First Corps arrived.[22]

On the other side of the Blue Ridge, Meade, like Lee, was making strategic decisions mostly in the dark. Knowing next to nothing of the Rebels' exact positions and determined to be careful, Meade pushed General Buford's 1st Cavalry Division well ahead of his infantry, which advanced only a handful of miles on July 19. By nightfall, Buford had a brigade at Upperville and another at Rector's Crossroads south of Philomont. The rest of the army ended the day with its lead elements—the III and I corps—on a line stretching from Purcellville to Hamilton.[23]

Happily, Buford had run into nothing more than Rebel guerrillas during the day, leading Meade to remain fairly certain Lee was moving up the Shenandoah Valley, probably with the intention of crossing the Blue Ridge on his way to the general area of Culpeper County. Still, the possibility that the Rebels were being reinforced and might resume the offensive remained a factor the general was unwilling to ignore. Uncertain whether he was about to be forced onto the defensive or presented an opportunity to launch an offensive, Meade decided to prepare for either eventuality.

That evening, he instructed his subordinates to continue their southward advance the next day at a brisker pace. Buford would probe toward Manassas and Chester gaps, while Custer's brigade of Kilpatrick's division seized Ashby's Gap in order to protect the army's western flank. Gregg's horsemen would keep watch on the army's rear and scout eastward toward Warrenton. Beyond that Meade was unwilling to make future plans. Until he learned something more definitive of Lee's position, he would take things one day at a time.[24]

22 Ibid., pt. 2, 362; 390; Walter Harrison, *Pickett's Men: A Fragment of War History* (New York, NY, 1870), 108.

23 *OR* 27, pt. 1, 97; 148.

24 Ibid., pt. 1, 97. The 1st Brigade of Judson Kilpatrick's division, led by Colonel Nathaniel P. Richmond, would move to Purcellville.

Chapter 6

"What Is Going On We Cannot Tell"

The Federals Seize Ashby's Gap—Longstreet Moves on Manassas and Chester Gaps—
A. P. Hill Ordered to Follow—Ewell Plans Kelley's Destruction—A Spy Saves
Kelley—Ewell Frightens Meade—The Army of the Potomac Comes to a Halt

OBEDIENT to Meade's orders, the Army of the Potomac began deepening its penetration into Loudoun County at dawn on July 20. As the blue infantry trudged south, a brigade of Federal cavalry from Kilpatrick's division rode toward Ashby's Gap. Waiting for them there was Colonel White's 35th Virginia Cavalry Battalion and a detachment from the 4th and 5th North Carolina Cavalry regiments of Robertson's brigade led by Lieutenant John Hines. From their mountain vantage point, the Confederates watched the "long lines of the Yankee army" spread out below them like so many blue snakes slithering through the grass.[1]

The sun had been up only a short time when the Rebels noted the appearance of Union scouts near Paris, at the eastern entrance to Ashby's Gap. The handful of enemy vedettes came no closer than the village outskirts and seemed happy to observe the mountains from a safe distance. For a long while, White waited for the blue cavalrymen to move forward, but nothing

---

1 *Fayetteville Observer* September 13, 1863; Clark, *NC Regts*, vol. 3, 464. Captain L. A. Johnson commanded the troops from the 4th North Carolina Cavalry. It is possible Lieutenant Moon's dismounted troopers, who lost Snickers' Gap a few days before, were also on hand, but it is more likely they had moved to Chester Gap.

happened. Finally tiring of delay, the colonel ordered Captain Franklin Myers to "stir up those fellows" and end the standoff. The captain dutifully sent six men to drive away the enemy horsemen. The gray troopers chased the Union men over a small knoll and out of sight.[2]

A few seconds later, however, the Southerners came thundering back in hurried retreat, their rapid withdrawal occasioned by the discovery of an entire Yankee brigade on the other side of the hill. As the Rebels galloped rearward, dismounted troopers from the 5th Michigan Cavalry, hidden in the underbrush, "sprang up as if by magic" and began advancing toward the pass. Witnessing this sudden manifestation of danger, Captain Myers matter-of-factly inquired if the colonel would like the enemy "stirred up any more." Appreciating the joke, if not the circumstances, White dryly responded, "That would do just now."[3]

What would not do, of course, was to allow the Federal advance to sweep up and into Ashby's Gap before the Confederates could get away. The "stirred up" Yankees moving on the mountain were five regiments of cavalry—the 1st, 5th, and 6th Michigan, the 1st Vermont, and 5th New York—accompanied by Battery M, 2nd U.S. Artillery, the whole under the command of Colonel Charles H. Town. Although White had earlier boasted he would defend the gap against anything like equal numbers, these odds were anything but equal. Given the magnitude of what was coming at him, his only reasonable course was retreat, and that is what he proceeded to do.[4]

To cover his withdrawal, the colonel sent two of the 35th's companies—A and C, led by Captain Myers and Captain Richard Grubb, respectively—into Paris with orders to delay the oncoming Yankees as long as possible. Reaching the village ahead of the enemy, the officers dismounted their troopers and ordered them to take shelter amid its buildings. When a column of Union cavalry neared, the Rebels opened fire and drove the Northerners back. This check kept the enemy at bay long

---

2 Meyers, *The Comanches*, 208.

3 Ibid.

4 *OR* 27, pt. 1, 1017; Louis Boudrye, *Historic Records of the Fifth New York Cavalry: First Ira Harris Guard* (Albany, NY, 1865), 74; *OR Supplement*, vol. v, pt. 1, 287. Town led the brigade because Custer had taken temporary command of the 3rd Cavalry Division after Kilpatrick took sick leave on July 16, 1863.

enough to allow Myers and Grubb to successfully disengage and give White an ample head start.[5]

With their opposition in flight, the Federals easily took control of the gap. Satisfied with that accomplishment, they declined to pursue the retreating Confederates. Hines' makeshift command headed south to Front Royal. The 35th Virginia, on the other hand, lingered near the western exit of Ashby's Gap, hoping to pounce on any unsuspecting Federals who blundered into their path. That wait proved in vain, however. Meade had seized the position for purely defensive purposes, and no Union troops other than a handful of pickets ventured westward beyond the pass. A few days later, White led his men toward Snickers' Gap and Harpers Ferry in search of better luck, and by doing so rode his unit out of the balance of the campaign.[6]

Ironically, as Confederate cavalry was abandoning Ashby's Gap, Rebel infantry was marching hard to get there. True to plan, General Longstreet was on the road at sunrise of the 20th. A warm morning soon turned into a hot day, with the thermometer hitting 87 at 2:00 p.m., so the columns set a measured pace. Despite the heat George Pickett's men covered 14 miles before dusk and his lead elements reached Millwood that night. Montgomery Corse's brigade clocked nearly 16 miles and bivouacked at Cedarville, just five miles shy of Front Royal.[7]

At Millwood, the Confederates found the Shenandoah River still spilling over its banks and the Federals in occupation of Ashby's Gap, their cavalry pickets posted all the way to the riverbank. Careful observation discerned no evidence of Union infantry in the area, but there was no longer any doubt that Meade was in Loudon Valley and probably maneuvering to cut Lee off from Richmond. In light of the river's condition and the fact that Union troopers already held the gap, Longstreet saw no practical means of recapturing the pass, or merit in attempting to do so.[8]

---

5 Meyers, *The Comanches*, 208; John Divine, *The Thirty-fifth Battalion Virginia Cavalry* (Lynchburg, VA, 1985), 37-38.

6 Divine, *The Thirty-fifth Battalion*, 37-38.

7 *OR* 27, pt. 2, 362; 390; George Wise, *History of the Seventeenth Virginia Infantry, C.S.A.* (Baltimore, MD, 1870), 160; Krick, *Civil War Weather*, 104; Edgar Warfield, *A Confederate Soldier's Memoirs* (Richmond, VA, 1936), 151.

8 *OR* 27, pt. 2, 362.

The matter of Manassas and Chester gaps now dropped onto the table. If Meade's infantry was marching south behind the barrier of the Blue Ridge, it was most likely aiming for those two vital points. The loss of either might enable the Federals to strike into the Shenandoah Valley or block Longstreet's movement toward the Rappahannock. Corse's brigade and Read's guns were already less than a half a day's march from the gaps and should be able to occupy them before the Federals arrived. If Meade was aiming for the passes, however, Corse would need help sooner rather than later, so Longstreet issued orders for his corps to march on Front Royal first thing the next day.[9]

Having taken these steps, the general composed a dispatch to Lee informing him of the situation at Ashby's Gap and the First Corps' plan for the next day. Once Longstreet's message reached army headquarters, it would fill a hole in the strategic puzzle that had been yawning dangerously open for several days. Longstreet knew Lee could be counted on to fit the piece into place quickly and act accordingly.[10]

In fact, Lee had already anticipated Longstreet's findings. On the morning of July 20 he had written Ewell that unless information contrary to what he currently possessed came to hand, A. P. Hill's corps and army headquarters would follow Longstreet toward the Rappahannock next morning. Stuart would maintain his cavalry screen in the Lower Valley until enemy strength near Harpers Ferry was "sufficiently reduced" to render it safe for him to withdraw, at which point Stuart was to "interpose his forces" between the Federals and that "portion of the army east of the Blue Ridge."[11]

For the time being, Ewell's corps would continue in the lower Valley. Lee thought it probable that Ewell would have to follow the rest of the army in a few days, and that his Second Corps should be prepared to move on short notice. Brigadier General John D. Imboden's cavalry brigade, as well as a brigade of infantry detached from Major General Sam Jones' department in southwestern Virginia, were under orders to move to Winchester and should

9 Ibid.

10 Ibid.

11 Ibid., pt. 3, 1026.

arrive any day. Ewell was to assume command of these troops and use them as he saw fit until Lee called him east.[12]

As was his habit, Lee left dispositions and movements to his subordinate's discretion. However, he did suggest that it might be judicious to shift the Second Corps toward Berryville or Millwood so that it would be better prepared "to vacate the Valley if pressed by superior numbers" or ordered to join the main army. In any event, it was likely Union activity would prevent Ewell from taking the same route through Chester Gap that Longstreet and Hill intended to use. If that proved the case, Lee wanted Ewell to proceed west of Massanutten Mountain and then move on Culpeper County via Thornton's or Swift Run gaps. Lee closed his message by reminding Ewell to forward any information on the enemy which he might "deem important."[13]

As it turned out Ewell had something to share along those lines. Forwarding news of the previous day's fight around Martinsburg, the general added that a civilian just returned from Hedgesville reported enemy strength there to be about 10,000 men. Ewell told Lee that he and his division commanders thought they could destroy these interlopers with a quick strike and asked for permission to make the attempt.[14]

Lee did not think Kelley's force "as large as represented," but he did find the Union general's position odd. Either the Yankees were ignorant of Ewell's proximity, or they were planning a joint attack against him in coordination with Federal troops around Harpers Ferry. Either way, a bold strike toward Hedgesville was likely to disrupt Union plans and might scare the Federals enough to inspire a defensive overreaction. Certainly Lt. Gen. Thomas "Stonewall" Jackson, dead now just nine weeks, had proven last year just how sensitive the enemy was to Rebel troops doing unexpected things in the Shenandoah Valley.[15]

Therefore, Lee assented to Ewell's maneuver. Given the overall situation it was an opportunistic and somewhat audacious move, but the

---

12 Ibid.

13 Ibid.

14 Archie McDonald, ed., *Jedediah Hotchkiss: Make Me a Map of the Valley: The Civil War Journal of Stonewall Jackson's Topographer*, (Dallas, TX, 1973), 162; *OR* 27, pt. 3, 1027.

15 *OR* 27, pt. 3, 1027.

Boydville, where Ewell and his division commanders plotted
Kelley's destruction on the afternoon of July 20, 1863.
*©)2002 Jane Flulkner Wiltshire Snyder, great granddaughter to
Senator Charles James Faulkner II, used with permission.*

possible rewards justified the attempt. Certainly, an easy victory would provide a welcome boost to Southern morale, and it was reassuring to hear Ewell talking aggressively after his disappointing performance at Gettysburg. At any rate, swatting away the Federals at Hedgesville would give Lee one less thing to worry about as he began leaving the Valley. Kelley's force was marked for destruction.[16]

After receiving Lee's authorization to strike, Ewell convened a meeting of his generals at Allegheny Johnson's headquarters near Martinsburg at Boydville, the elegant home of Lieutenant Colonel Charles James Faulkner. The owner had been President James Buchanan's ambassador to France before the war, and was now an assistant adjutant general on Ewell's staff.[17]

16 Ibid., pt. 2, 449; 324; McDonald, *Make Me A Map*, 162; *OR* 27, pt. 3, 1027.

17 McDonald, *Make Me A Map*, 162; John Elwood, *Elwood's Stories of the Old Ringgold Cavalry: 1847-1865, The First Three Years of the Civil War* (Coal Center, PA, 1914), 166-167. Krick, *Staff Officers in Gray: A Biographical Register of the Staff Officers in the Army of Northern Virginia* (Chapel Hill, NC, 2003), 125.

In these comfortable surroundings and tended by a black house servant lent to the Faulkners by their nephew, Dr. Elisha Pendleton, the generals developed a plan to encircle and annihilate Kelley's Federals. While Johnson, reinforced by Major General Robert E. Rodes' division, held the Federals' attention with an advance from Martinsburg, Major General Jubal A. Early would take his division across North Mountain and march down Back Creek Valley to strike the Yankee rear at Hedgesville. Trapped between three Rebel divisions, hemmed in by impassable mountains and an unfordable river, Kelley would either have to surrender or fight under extremely unfavorable circumstances.[18]

That night, around 7:00 p.m., Early undertook the first step toward Kelley's demise by marching his troops five miles south to Mills Gap near Gerardstown at the foot of North Mountain. The Confederates went into camp there, ready for an early start the next morning. Cavalry from Hampton's brigade crossed the mountain and moved down Back Creek, bivouacking for the night at Tomahawk Springs. Unbeknownst to the Southerners, however, Unionist civilians were already undermining Rebel prospects of victory.[19]

As it turned out, Ewell had chosen the location for his strategy conference with an eye for comfort and convenience when he should have been more concerned about security. The Pendletons were Northern sympathizers who had instructed their servants to keep eyes and ears open while in the presence of the Confederate generals. No sooner did Ewell's conference at Boydville end than the Faulkners' borrowed slave hurried home to inform Lucinda Pendelton of what he had heard.[20]

Realizing the Rebel plan would succeed if Kelley was not alerted, Mrs. Pendleton attempted to send her servant through the lines to warn the Federal general of the impending danger. That effort failed when suspicious Southern pickets refused to let a black man pass their posts. Refusing to be foiled, Pendleton dispatched her 10-year-old son, Nathaniel, to carry the message. Armed with an empty basket and claiming he was going to pick blackberries, the boy managed to make his way past Confederate sentries to

18 Ibid.

19 Terry Jones, ed., *The Civil War Memoirs of Captain William J. Seymour: Reminiscences of a Louisiana Tiger* (Baton Rouge, LA, 1991), 81.

20 Elwood, *Elwood's Stories*, 166-168.

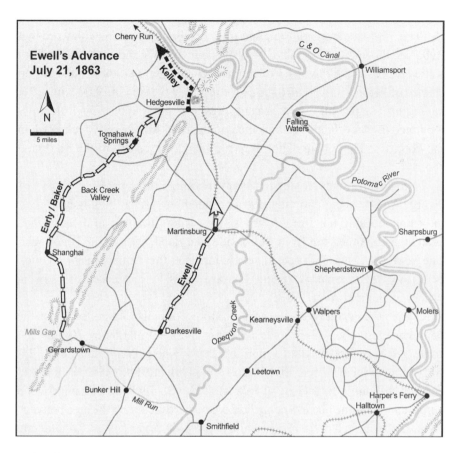

Union lines. Stopped by Federal troops, the youngster demanded to be taken to General Kelley and refused to divulge anything to anyone until his demand was met. Finally relenting, a Union officer put Nathaniel on his horse and carried him to headquarters, where Kelley agreed to see him.[21]

Initially the child's story came across as incoherent and sensationalistic, a prediction that "all the Yankees" with Kelley "were going to be killed." Gradually, the patient general coaxed enough information out of the boy to discern the import of his message. The outline of the Confederate plan was certainly plausible, and Kelley ordered a cavalry patrol into Back Creek Valley with orders to find evidence confirming or refuting Pendleton's tale.[22]

21 Ibid.

22 Ibid.

The troopers returned from their mission about 7:00 p.m. with word that Rebel cavalry was at Tomahawk Springs a mere four and a half miles from Kelley's bivouac. Convinced of the danger, the general knew he stood no chance of successfully confronting an entire Rebel corps. At 9:00 p.m., after having his troops build up their campfires to make it appear his little army remained in place, Kelley put his men on the road for Cherry Creek Ford on the Potomac. Three hours later they commenced crossing to the Maryland shore.[23]

While Kelley was stoking his campfires and pulling back out of danger, George Meade was pondering new and potentially vital intelligence. This information came not from Ashby's Gap, where the two armies brushed against one another, but from well inside Maryland, deep in the Union rear. The source of this unexpected revelation was the commander of Union troops in Hagerstown, who sent forward news he had obtained from an officer in General Averell's brigade.

The message, received at 9:15 p.m. from Colonel William Brisbane, the commander of the 4th Brigade of Pennsylvania Emergency Volunteers, contained the first detailed report of Lee's whereabouts since July 14. According to the dispatch, Ewell's corps was still at Darkesville, with Lee at Bunker Hill and Major General John Bell Hood's division of Longstreet's corps near the same place. Enemy horsemen were picketing the area between Hedgesville and Harpers Ferry, while at least six regiments of Confederate cavalry were at Martinsburg, in front of which skirmishing had taken place throughout the 19th.[24]

The intelligence report surprised Meade, whose confidence in his assessment of Lee's movements evaporated completely, leading him to take counsel of his fears and succumb to the same instinctive caution he had displayed at Williamsport six days earlier. Brigadier General Marsena R. Patrick, Meade's provost marshal, West Point classmate, and personal friend, recorded his commander's worries in his diary. Meade, he noted, believed Lee remained in the lower Shenandoah Valley to await

---

23 Ibid.

24 *OR* 27, pt. 1, 97; *OR* Vol. 27, pt. 3, 731. Colonel William Brisbane sent the message, and the source of his information was a "Major Bryson of Averell's Cavalry." I have been unable to locate rosters for Averell's units, and did not find anything matching a "Major Bryson."

reinforcements from Rebel armies in Tennessee or South Carolina. Convinced his foe would be massively reinforced, despite Halleck's stern assurance that no such thing would happen, Meade dreaded that a strengthened Lee was about to resume the offensive by moving north of the Potomac and threatening Washington, DC.[25]

If this was indeed the case, the roles of pursued and pursuer might soon be reversed. If Meade pushed his Union army deeper into Loudoun Valley, a void would open behind him into which Lee could plunge, inserting his force between Meade and the capital. Determined not to fall into whatever trap the Rebels had concocted, Meade decided to halt the movement of his infantry and keep his army in place throughout July 21, lest the continuance of its march enable Lee to get into his rear and "interrupt or interfere" with his communications.[26]

Just at the moment when a bold advance might pay huge dividends, Meade shrank from taking the chance. He was a good general, but he seems not to have seriously contemplated the possibilities offered by Brisbane's intelligence. If Lee's army was deployed as the news suggested, a quick breach of the Blue Ridge and the thrusting of his army into the Shenandoah Valley south of the Confederates offered substantial dividends. Without doubt such a move would have been daring and logistically difficult, but it would have also placed the Army of the Potomac between Lee and his sources of supply and reinforcement. Thus isolated, Lee would once again find his army backed up against the Potomac River, giving Meade the opportunity to do on the river's south bank what he had failed to do at Williamsport one week earlier.

Meade understood strategy, but in his risk-averse mind, looming peril trumped grand opportunity—especially since danger was easily imagined. Considering Lee's record of confounding and defeating each of Meade's predecessors, this was hardly an inexplicable attitude. Nonetheless, given the circumstances, it was an unjustifiably timid one.

Unable to think himself into Lee's shoes and envision the difficulties that beset his rival, Meade obsessed about the poor state of his own army, which Marsena Patrick, doubtlessly echoing the prevailing view at

---

25 David Sparks, *Inside Lincoln's Army: The Diary of Marsena Rudolph Patrick, Provost Marshal General, Army of the Potomac* (New York, NY, 1964), 273-4.

26 *OR* 27, pt. 1, 97-98.

headquarters, felt was in "no condition to fight." Not only was it worn out and in need of reinforcements and supplies, the army's discipline had become so "horrible" that the provost marshal worried that if something wasn't done to improve it, there would be "few troops to put into action" should a battle occur.[27]

Meade's misgivings were not without foundation. His men were in need of rest and Gettysburg had been a serious blow to the army's organization and efficiency. The record of the Army of Northern Virginia spoke for itself. The bulk of Lee's command was, as reported, still around Bunker Hill and Martinsburg, while Longstreet's Corps had only just begun to move. The strategic transfer of troops from one of the other Rebel armies to Lee was feasible. Still, all of this added up to danger only if one ignored context.[28]

The loss of the Mississippi River Valley by the fall of Vicksburg and Port Hudson, coupled with the abandonment of central Tennessee and dire threat to Chattanooga left Confederate forces throughout the Western Theater in disarray. Braxton Bragg's Army of Tennessee and other Rebel forces scattered across the Confederacy faced superior Union forces and were in no condition to ship troops off to help anyone. Meade could not have been unaware of these facts. Unless he believed the Confederacy's armies were much stronger than they really were, he should have realized Halleck's promise that Lee was not and could not be reinforced at that time was logical and accurate.

It was true that the Rebels were displaying their customary aggressiveness against Kelley, and it seemed equally certain that General Lee would attempt to seize the initiative at the first opportunity. But it was also true that the Army of Northern Virginia had been severely handled at Gettysburg, and certainly could not recover from that bloody ordeal any more quickly than could the Army of the Potomac. Therefore, any belief that the Rebels were on the verge of resuming the offensive was not grounded in a realistic appraisal of the situation. Yet, this is precisely what Meade concluded was possible.

---

27 Sparks, *Inside Lincoln's Army*, 273-4.

28 In fact, less than two months later the Rebels would undertake just such an effort, although the reinforcements (most of Longstreet's First Corps) would flow from Lee's army in Virginia to General Braxton Bragg's Army of Tennessee in Georgia. The arrival of Longstreet and his men would help win a decisive tactical victory at Chickamauga.

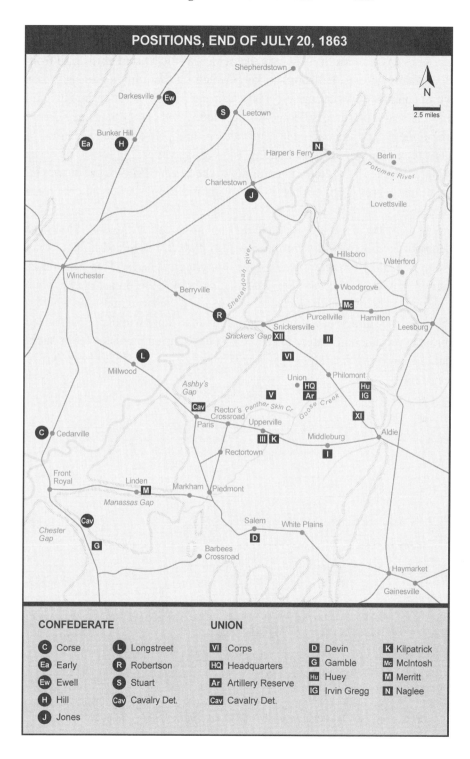

POSITIONS, END OF JULY 20, 1863

N

2.5 miles

Shepherdstown

Darkesville Ew

S Leetown

Bunker Hill

Ea H

Harper's Ferry N

Berlin

Potomac River

Charlestown

J

Lovettsville

Hillsboro

Waterford

Winchester

Berryville

Shenandoah River

Woodgrove

R

Purcellville   Hamilton

Mc

Snickersville

Snickers' Gap XII   II

VI

Leesburg

L

Millwood

Union

Philomont

Ashby's Gap

HQ

Hu

IG

V

Ar

Cav

Rector's Crossroad *Panther Skin Cr.*

Goose Creek

XI

Paris   Upperville

C Cedarville

III K

Aldie

Rectortown

Middleburg

I

Front Royal

Linden

M

Markham Piedmont

Manassas Gap

Salem   White Plains

Cav

Chester Gap

G

D

Barbees Crossroad

Haymarket

Gainesville

CONFEDERATE

C	Corse
Ea	Early
Ew	Ewell
H	Hill
J	Jones

L	Longstreet
R	Robertson
S	Stuart
Cav	Cavalry Det.

UNION

VI	Corps
HQ	Headquarters
Ar	Artillery Reserve
Cav	Cavalry Det.

D	Devin
G	Gamble
Hu	Huey
IG	Irvin Gregg

K	Kilpatrick
Mc	McIntosh
M	Merritt
N	Naglee

Except for Buford's cavalry, which had orders to occupy Manassas and Chester gaps, and McIntosh's brigade, which would be sent northward from Purcellville back to Hillsboro to keep watch on the army's rear, Meade's entire command was brought to a halt. Throughout the night of the 20th and into the next day, rumors floated through the Union camps that Lee's Army of Northern Virginia had been reinforced by troops from Bragg's Army of Tennessee and was "again making for Pennsylvania." Whether this was widely believed is unclear. Up and down the chain of command, however, uncertainty prevailed. "What is going on we cannot tell," one sergeant confessed.[29]

In fact, no one knew the actual strategic situation. Meade, almost as uncertain as his men, did not have a firm plan and believed he could not make one until he better understood his circumstances. This much was certain, however: A great deal depended on what Buford discovered when he struck at the mountain passes. What happened there might dictate whether the blue army turned back toward the Potomac to face an invasion, or lunged into the Shenandoah Valley in search of a battle its commander felt it ought not to fight.

---

29 Cassedy, *Dear Friends at Home*, 298-299; Sparks, *Inside Lincoln's Army*, 273-4.

CHAPTER 7

"The Sun . . . Seemed for Hours to Stand Still in the Sky"

Longstreet and Hill March for the Gaps—Ewell Moves Against Kelley—Early Discovers the Yankees Gone—Corse and Federal Cavalry Reach the Gaps—Gallant Fight of the 17th Virginia—Pickett Foils the Enemy—Merritt Fooled

EARLY on the morning of July 21, General Meade's troops awakened to learn the unexpected news that they would enjoy a day of rest. The opponents did not share the same fate, and the Shenandoah Valley that day quickly became a hive of Confederate activity.

Longstreet's First Corps troops marched for Front Royal, while Montgomery Corse's brigade headed toward Manassas and Chester gaps. A. P. Hill put his Third Corps in motion toward Winchester, where the sick and wounded who could bear the agony of wagon transportation were being prepared for evacuation to hospitals at Staunton and Harrisonburg. Hampered by the poor condition of its exhausted animals, which dictated a slow methodical pace, the Third Corps artillery rumbled ahead of Hill's footsore infantry. General Ewell's Second Corps supply train, meanwhile, trundled along behind Hill's column in order to give it a head start on the journey south even as Ewell was launching his offensive in the opposite direction against Kelley's Federals. Despite orders to prepare three days rations and what one Confederate called abundant rumors swirling through their Leetown camps, Stuart's cavalry brigades remained firmly in place. Even though they were marking time, the gray troopers knew their regiments would be joining the southward movement very soon.[1]

A few miles west of Gerardstown, Jubal Early's division of Ewell's corps crossed North Mountain via Mills Gap at daylight, and, together with Baker's cavalry, moved rapidly down Back Creek toward Hedgesville. Screened by the cavalry of Hampton's Legion, Ewell's two remaining divisions under Rodes and Johnson began their advance on the same point at 5:00 a.m. Ewell's plan to trap Kelley appeared to be working to perfection until Baker's forward troopers reached the Potomac just in time to see the last boatload of Yankee infantry disembark on the Maryland shore. Thanks to his advance warning from Mrs. Pendleton's son, Kelley had taken wing and escaped Ewell's grasp.[2]

Early's soldiers took the disappointment in stride. No doubt, some of them were happy to see their enemy flee without fighting a battle. As partial compensation for their difficult march of 23 miles to no useful purpose, the troops were delighted to discover their trek ended in what one described as an "immense field of blackberries." Before long everyone in the division seemed to be picking fruit, leading those wittily disposed to claim the entire expedition was nothing more than a foraging expedition. In contrast to Early, the divisions of Rodes and Johnson had marched a mere seven miles before the attack was called off. Although their troops found neither an enemy to destroy nor blackberries to feast upon, the generals salvaged something from the movement by ordering their men to wreck another six miles of B&O track before going back to camp.[3]

The abortive offensive accomplished little, but it did allow Richmond newspapers to ridicule Kelley for having "illustrated the science of skedaddling after the most approved Yankee style." Sadly, this did nothing

---

1 *OR* 27, pt. 3, 1031; pt. 2, 609, 615; Jubal Early, *Lieutenant General Jubal Anderson Early, C.S.A. Autobiographical Sketch and Narrative of the War Between the States* (New York, NY, 1994), 284; Michael Marshall, *Gallant Creoles: A History of the Donaldsonville Canonniers* (Lafayette, LA, 2013), 218.

2 Jones, *Reminiscences of a Louisiana Tiger*, 81; Louis Leon, *Diary of a Tar Heel Confederate Soldier*, electronic edition, University of North Carolina, Chapel Hill, 1998, http://docsouth.unc.edu/fpn/leon/leon.html; 31, *Morissett diary*, MOCW.

3 Jones, *Reminiscences of a Louisiana Tiger*, 80-81; Leon, *Diary of a Tar Heel*, UNC-CH, 31.

to mitigate the distasteful truth that he had escaped destruction with the help of Union sympathizers. At the end of the day, the most the Confederates could claim was that they had chased Kelley away and potentially given Meade something to worry about.[4]

Elsewhere in the Shenandoah Valley there were no such disappointments, and everything seemed to be going smoothly for the Army of Northern Virginia. The continuance of such good luck, however, was predicated on the Yankees remaining distant and doing nothing to interfere with Lee's program, Longstreet's progress, or his unfettered access to the passes of the Blue Ridge. Unfortunately for the Rebels, Union cavalry soon proved unwilling to play its assigned role.

In fact, John Buford had every intention to complicate Lee's plans by seizing the gaps before the Confederates had a chance to do so. Unfortunately, his desire to capture the passes on the morning of July 20 had been delayed by rumors of a potential Rebel threat from Ashby's Gap. Those accounts—most likely spawned by Longstreet's march toward Millwood—forced the Federal horsemen to detour in that direction. The reports proved false, but they cost the division several hours. Although the cavalry had ridden out of Philomont at 7:00 a.m., it wasn't until around 5:00 p.m. that its column reached Rectortown, a mere 14 miles south of its starting point.

At this juncture, Buford divided his command into three components. Brigadier General Wesley Merritt's Reserve Brigade, accompanied by Battery K, 1st US Artillery, turned west toward Manassas Gap 13 miles away. Colonel William Gamble's 1st Brigade, along with batteries B & L, 2nd US Artillery, continued south in the direction of Chester Gap another 24 miles distant. The division supply train and Buford's 2nd Brigade, under Colonel Thomas C. Devin, rode on to Salem, where both would await future developments.[5]

Later that evening, Merritt went into camp about a mile east of Manassas Gap. On his way to Chester Gap, Gamble encountered mild opposition from Mosby's partisan rangers. The Rebel guerrillas forced the Federals into one brief fight, but otherwise were easily brushed aside. Nevertheless, the day's

4 *Richmond Daily Dispatch*, July 28, 1863.

5 *OR* 27, pt. 3, 729, 734-35; Chapman diary, Indiana Historical Society; Bellemy Diary, Indiana State Library.

various delays meant that by nightfall Gamble had only reached Piedmont Station, well short of his objective.[6]

Dawn on July 21 found the various columns of Union cavalry and Confederate infantry arrayed for the last leg of a race to control the Blue Ridge passes. Merritt was within a mile of Manassas Gap and Gamble was 22 miles away from Chester Gap. Pickett's Rebel division, at the head of Longstreet's column, was at Millwood, some 24 miles distant from both passes. Corse's brigade and Read's batteries were at Cedarville, just nine miles from Manassas Gap and 11 miles from Chester Gap. Ownership of those vital points would go to whichever side acted with the greatest alacrity and brought the most force to bear before nightfall.

Corse had his command up before dawn. After allowing time for a hurried breakfast, the general put his brigade on the road about daylight, which broke at 4:54 a.m. If his troops needed explanation for their early departure and brisk march, they obtained it from Rebel cavalrymen (probably Hines' North Carolinians) who volunteered that Snickers' and Ashby's gaps had been captured by the Federals. Since several of the brigade's regiments had been raised in this part of Virginia, the men easily inferred that their haste was to prevent Manassas and Chester gaps from suffering the same fate.[7]

The distance from Cedarville to Front Royal was five miles, but the length of the march, which was made at a rapid pace, was not the principle obstacle to the hurrying column. That difficulty arrived when the formation reached the confluence of the north and south forks of the Shenandoah River, a mile and a half north of town. The pontoon bridges Lee had ordered laid at Front Royal were not yet in place, but circumstances would admit of no delay. Corse ordered his men across.

Traversing the North Fork of the Shenandoah required some effort, but was accomplished without particular trouble. The much larger South Fork was a different proposition. The water was especially formidable, for it was both deep and racing downstream at a hazardous pace. Some troops joined hands to help one another across; others held onto the tails of horses and

---

6 Ibid; James Williamson, *Mosby's Rangers* (New York, NY, 1896), 81.

7 Wise, *Seventeenth Virginia*, 160; Krick, *Civil War Weather*, 104; Jack Sullivan, "The Dark Clouds of War: the Civil War Diary of John Zimmerman of Alexandria," *The Alexandria Chronicle, Alexandria Historical Society*, Fall 2014, 2.

The strategic importance of Front Royal is readily apparent in this May 1862 drawing by Edwin Forbes. The view is looking eastward. The town (marked 2) is in the center distance. The number 1 indicates Manassas Gap. The number 3 indicates Chester Gap.

Library of Congress

allowed themselves to be pulled to the opposite shore. No matter how a man chose to make the crossing, holding a 9-pound musket and full cartridge box out of the water while negotiating the swift-flowing stream's rocky bed and keeping one's balance proved tricky. Inevitably, a number of soldiers lost their footing and were swept away. These unfortunates were spared from drowning only by the quick action of mounted officers, including General Corse, who naturally "spared no effort" to save them.[8]

Gamely overcoming the challenges involved, the brigade successfully crossed both forks of the river. It was around 9:15 a.m. when the Confederates marched into the little village of Front Royal, whose population of less than 600 souls had already seen plenty of the war. Among those watching the troops pass through town was Lucy Buck. Like many,

---

8 Wise, *Seventeenth Virginia*, 160; *OR* 27, pt. 2, 390; Warfield, *Confederate Soldier's Memoirs*, 151; Sullivan, *The Dark Clouds of War*, 2.

she was hoping to catch a glimpse of the Warren Rifles, now Company B of the 17th Virginia, which had been raised in the Front Royal area.[9]

Lucy managed a brief exchange of greetings with two "dusty and bronzed" friends, who fell out of ranks to see her before the brigade hurried out of town. After her companions ran back to rejoin their company, she watched their "receding figures gradually lose themselves in the throng of martial forms" and with tears in her eyes, "looked after the regiment as long as it could be seen." As the brigade faded from view, Corse took four regiments—the 30th, 29th, 32nd and 15th Virginia—south toward Chester Gap. His fifth regiment, the 17th Virginia under Major Robert H. Simpson, was detached and ordered north to Manassas Gap.[10]

Sending the 37-year old Simpson on this isolated duty was an inspired decision. The 5-foot 8-inch gray-eyed major graduated from the Virginia Military Institute in 1845, taught at the Front Royal Male and Female Academy before the war, and knew the Manassas Gap region well. A brave and experienced officer with prewar militia experience, Simpson enlisted in the Confederate Army and was made a captain in the 17th Virginia in April 1862. Just two months later on June 30, he was captured at Frayser's Farm during the Seven Days' Battles. After spending four weeks in a New York Harbor prison, Simpson was exchanged and returned to his command in time to fight at Second Manassas, where he was wounded. After he recovered, he was promoted to major on November 1, 1862. General Corse was confident Simpson could handle any trouble that might unfold in the pass—not that any was expected.

A good deal of what the Confederates did that morning was done under the prying eyes of the US Army Signal Corps, which had established lookout stations at Snickers' and Ashby's gaps. Using high-powered telescopes and benefiting from clear skies, the signalmen could see across all 25 miles to Winchester, where they noted the town's fortifications were still occupied by Rebel troops. The visibility was so good that the Federals clearly saw Pickett's division break camp at Millwood and take to the road shortly after

9 Elizabeth R. Baer, ed., *Shadows on My Heart, the Civil War Diary of Lucy Rebecca Buck of Virginia* (Athens, GA, 1997), 232. Front Royal was the scene of a battle on May 23, 1862, during Stonewall Jackson's Valley Campaign.

10 Ibid; Wise, *Seventeenth Virginia*, 160; Robert Krick, *30th Virginia Infantry*. Virginia Regimental Series (Lynchburg, VA, 1983), 40; Warfield, *Confederate Soldier's Memoirs*, 152.

Major Robert H. Simpson
Ben Ritter, Winchester, Va.

dawn. Afterwards, the Northern signal station observed the passage of what was described as a "large body of troops" through the village. At 9:00 a.m., Captain Davis E. Castle, who commanded the signal station at Snickers' Gap, sent a message to his superior, Captain Lemuel B. Norton, that Rebel infantry had been marching through Millwood since 7:00 a.m. and was still moving through the town alongside a wagon train at least two miles long.[11]

Norton promptly forwarded Castle's message to Meade's headquarters, where it created quite a stir. Clearly something was up, and Meade wanted as much information as he could get, as soon as he could get it. At 10:00 a.m., General Humphreys, Meade's chief of staff, thanked Norton for his valuable intelligence and told him it was "highly important" that the commanding general "know at the earliest moment everything that can be observed" in the Shenandoah Valley. Humphreys requested that the signalmen "report as frequently as practicable."[12]

The pace of events picked up considerably throughout the day. At times it seemed as if the movements leading to the first clash at Gettysburg were repeating themselves, with the rival armies following intersecting roads toward a seemingly inexorable collision. Buford's 1st Cavalry Division was at the tip of that impending crash, just as it had been in Pennsylvania twenty days earlier. And just like July 1, columns of gray foot soldiers [this time Longstreet's men instead of A. P. Hill's troops] were on an intercept course with blue horsemen.

11 *OR* 27, pt. 3, 733-4.

12 Ibid.

As Corse's 1,200 men hurried toward their struggle with the branches of the Shenandoah River, Merritt's cavalry brigade chased away a handful of Rebel guerrillas in its path and rode into the small village of Linden, which sat at the 945-foot-high apex of Manassas Gap astride the railroad bearing the same name. A historic little community, Linden was surrounded by more than two dozen apple orchards and graced with the steeple of a Methodist Church. A well-known stop for travelers, it was also the spot where John Lederer and John Catlett had officially discovered the gap in 1669.[13]

Mindful of his instructions to hold the pass "at any and every cost," Merritt deployed his four regiments (the 1st, 2nd, 5th US and 6th Pennsylvania cavalry) into defensive positions. The clean shaven New Yorker looked much younger than his 29 years. After graduating from West Point in June 1860, he spent the first two years of the war on various staff assignments. Once the Chancellorsville Campaign ended, he was given command of the 2nd United States Cavalry, part of the Reserve Brigade of the 1st Cavalry Division, even though he was still a captain. Merritt performed well at the Battle of Brandy Station on June 9, 1863, where he displayed personal courage by engaging in a saber duel with Confederate Brigadier General William H. F. "Rooney" Lee—the second son of General Robert E. Lee. During the encounter Rooney Lee's slashing sword just missed Merritt's head and knocked off his hat. The New Yorker's counterthrust proved more accurate and severely wounded Lee in the leg.[14]

The captain's subsequent outstanding performance during the initial cavalry clashes of the Gettysburg campaign burnished his reputation as a daring, competent, and aggressive leader. Hoping to insert that kind of spirit into the upper ranks of the Army of the Potomac's Cavalry Corps, General Pleasonton prevailed upon Meade to promote Merritt (along with Elon Farnsworth and George Custer) to brigadier general on June 29, 1863 and give him command of the Reserve Brigade.[15]

13 Theophilus Rodenbough, *From Everglade to Canyon with the Second United States Cavalry* (Norman, OK, 2000), 296.

14 Faust, *Historical Encyclopedia of the Civil War*, 488; Warner, *Generals in Blue*, 321; Eric Wittenberg, *Rantings of a Civil War Historian*, http://civilwarcavalry.com/?p=206. Rooney Lee was recuperating from this wound when he was captured by Union cavalry.

15 Ibid. See Wittenberg, et. al., *One Continuous Fight*, 96-97, 133-34, 208-209, for a fine account of the role Merritt played in the pursuit of Lee.

Brigadier General Wesley Merritt
Library of Congress

At Gettysburg and thereafter, Merritt had vindicated his superiors' estimation of his skills. Those talents were about to be put to an extreme test, with the general on his own and far from any chance of rapid support. Although Merritt had accomplished his initial assignment, Buford and Meade now required additional efforts and sent the cavalryman orders "to do all in his power to find out the enemy's position and movements." In response, Merritt dispatched the 1st US Cavalry toward the western exit of Manassas Gap with instructions to "penetrate as far as practicable toward Front Royal."[16]

While Union troopers organized their defenses around Linden, the 270 men in Major Simpson's 17th Virginia were toiling eastward from Front Royal, their column enveloped in a cloud of dust that rendered the hot temperatures even more taxing. About a mile and a half out of town the road to Manassas Gap split, with one route following a path more or less parallel to the railroad and another swinging off slightly to the north over the lower slopes of the gap's northern face to the hamlet of Wapping.

The tiny village, sometimes referred to as Wappen, consisted of little more than a mill and a few houses. The settlement derived its name from the nearby home of John and Sarah Hansbrough, which was known as Wapping House. The one and a half story dwelling had been a stagecoach relay station and was licensed in the early 1850s as an "ordinary"—an establishment that

---

16 Rodenbough, *Everglade to Canyon*, 296. The 6th US cavalry was detached from the brigade on July 11 and assigned as the escort for Cavalry Corps Headquarters. Donald C. Caughey and Jimmy J. Jones, *The 6th United States Cavalry in the Civil War* (Jefferson, NC, 2013), 122; *OR* 27, pt. 3, 734-735; *OR* 27, pt. 1, 945.

Wapping House gave its name to the surrounding country and a battle. In the aftermath of the fighting on July 23, 1863 it was used as a Union hospital. The dwelling, expanded in 1895 to include an impressive Greek style portico, still exists and is located on Dismal Hollow Road, just south of Interstate 66 and across the street from a Virginia Department of Highways Park & Ride location. *Warren Heritage Society*

provided food, liquor, and lodging for passengers traveling through Manassas Gap.[17]

The business reached its end in 1854 after Irish construction crews arrived to build the railroad. The workers, who named the high ground around the Hansbrough residence Wapping Heights, were rowdy fellows—hard drinkers and harder brawlers. Predictably, maintaining law and order soon became a challenge, leading Warren County to shut down all ordinaries and deny all liquor licenses between Linden and the western exit to the pass. Of course, this only accelerated the inevitable, since the railroad killed the stagecoach lines, and customers for ordinaries quickly disappeared. Subsequently, the Hansbroughs became farmers, and their fields, along with those of their neighbors, represented the only clearings to be found in a

17 Rebecca Poe, "Wapping or Dismal Hollow?" *Warren County Historical Society*, no date.

landscape otherwise dominated by steep densely wooded and rugged mountains.[18]

Determined to avoid any surprises, Major Simpson detailed Companies B and C (together numbering just some 63 men) to take the mountain road to Wapping and watch out for the regiment's left flank. The remaining eight companies of the 17th Virginia continued east along the main road, where, just south of Wapping the major led his regiment twenty yards into the woods, halted, fronted toward the road, and stacked arms.[19]

It wasn't quite 11:00 a.m., the Virginians had already forded two rivers and hiked nearly 10 miles, the last four and a half uphill into Manassas Gap, an elevation 400 feet higher than Front Royal. The men were sweaty, grimy, tired, and hungry. Nonetheless, Simpson exercised the standard precautions and detailed Companies A, E, and G (approximately 55 men) under the overall command of Captain James W. Stewart for picket duty. The regiment's adjutant, Lieutenant William Zimmerman, was given the job of selecting the location of Stewart's outpost line and promptly led the little band down the road toward Linden. The remaining five companies (about 150 men) were allowed to fall out and rest.[20]

There was no sense of impending danger. Southern troopers in Front Royal had assured their Virginia infantry comrades that Confederate cavalry still held the gap. Although the Yankees were expected eventually, no one supposed that a sizable Union force was nearby. When any enemy did appear, whatever Rebel horsemen were up ahead would encounter them first and provide ample warning. Secure in that knowledge, Simpson's men wandered into the woods to harvest the profusion of blackberries gracing the mountainside.[21]

Their complacency was misplaced. In fact, there was no Confederate cavalry in Manassas Gap other than the handful of partisans who had faded

18 Ibid; US Census records, 1860, www.fold3.com.

19 17Sullivan, *Dark Clouds of War*, 2; Consolidated Service Records, 17th Virginia Records of Events; Wise, *Seventeenth Virginia*, 161; Company strengths of the 17th Virginia are based on a March 1863 requisition for rations found in Consolidated Service Records on www.Fold3.com; Warfield, *Confederate Soldier's Memoirs*, 152-3.

20 Sullivan, *Dark Clouds of War*, 2; Warfield, *Confederate Soldier's Memoirs*, 152-3; Wise, *Seventeenth Virginia*, 161.

21 Warfield, *Confederate Soldier's Memoirs*, 153-154; Sullivan, *Dark Clouds of War*, 2.

away with "little or no resistance" before Merritt's veteran Union cavalry brigade. Why such a vital position was left without even a small scout for protection remains open to speculation, but in all probability the reason was simply command confusion.[22]

The small contingents from Jones' and Robertson's brigades under Lieutenants Moon and Hines had been out of touch with their parent units since late June. There is no evidence they had any contingency orders in the event Snickers' and Ashby's gaps fell into enemy hands. Although evidence concerning their subsequent movements is circumstantial at best, Hines appears to have fallen back toward Front Royal in the hope of linking up with his parent brigade, while Moon moved to Chester Gap, whether before or after the loss of Ashby's is hard to say. Both lieutenants may have assumed that White's 35th Battalion would cover Manassas Gap. White, however, had no orders to do so and had taken his command in the opposite direction. The stage was set for a fight that would arrive as a surprise to both sides.

*   *   *

After marching a mile or so, Captain Stewart's 55-man picket detail (Companies A, E, and G) came abreast of open ground to its right and was surprised to see a body of horsemen about three quarters of a mile away. Because everyone assumed Southern cavalry was guarding the pass, Stewart thought he was looking at friends. Some in the ranks concurred, while others were vocal in declaring the distant figures wore blue. Deciding to take counsel of prudence, Stewart ordered his men to form a battle line and load their muskets.[23]

It was too late. The suspect riders were the vanguard of the 1st US Cavalry and they had spotted the Rebels about the same time the Confederates had seen them. The Federals charged, simultaneously shouting and gesturing to their main column to come up on the double. The onrushing cavalrymen were almost on top of Stewart's three companies before they knew it. Realizing he was about to be swamped, the captain ordered his men

22 Rodenbough, *Everglade to Canyon*, 296.

23 Sullivan, *Dark Clouds of War*, 2-3.

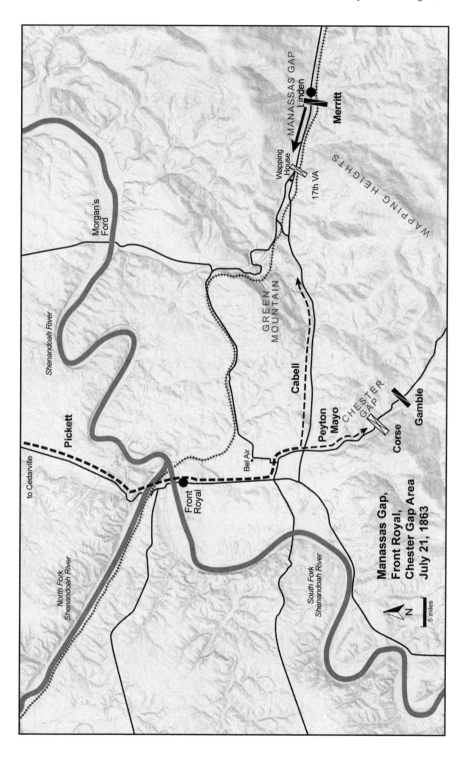

Manassas Gap,
Front Royal,
Chester Gap Area
July 21, 1863

to make a run for it, shouting at them to take to the woods and try to get back to the regiment.[24]

Chaos ensued as the Confederate infantry scattered, some racing down the road and others heading deep into the forest. A few men darted between the road and the trees, seeking the least obstructed and fastest route to safety. Regardless of their individual decisions, the Confederates were at a severe disadvantage. Not only were they on foot and being chased by men on horseback, but the Virginians were also exhausted after their long climb from the Shenandoah's lowlands to the heights of Manassas Gap. Captain Stewart and about one-half of the fugitives somehow managed to outpace their pursuers—either hiding in the woods or managing to find a way back to the regiment. The other half, however, were not as fortunate; the pursuing Yankees scooped up nearly 20 prisoners, including four officers, in the first few minutes of the encounter.[25]

One of those who escaped was Lieutenant Zimmermann. The mounted officer raced back toward the regiment shouting at the top of his lungs, "To arms! Fall in! The enemy is coming!" As he galloped to the rear, Zimmermann passed Privates Edgar Warfield and Mason Washington, who were chatting with Dr. John Leftwich, the 17th's surgeon. All three were standing in the middle of the road a few hundred yards east of the line of stacked muskets, Leftwich holding the bridle of his horse, when the adjutant sped by.[26]

Zimmerman's warning set off what one man described as "a helter-skelter race" as Virginians rushed from all directions toward their weapons, anxiously falling in and awaiting the arrival of comrades so that the stacks of muskets could be broken apart. Running back down the road toward the assembling Virginians, Private Warfield and his companions suddenly heard the thunder of hooves close behind them. Looking around, Private Washington cried, "Here they are!" Dr. Leftwich tossed his bridle into Warfield's hands and shouted for him to take the horse and hurry back to Front Royal for help. Even before he finished speaking, the surgeon was

---

24 Ibid, 3.

25 *OR* 27, pt. 1, 945-6, ibid, pt. 3, 735-6; Wise, *Seventeenth Virginia*, 160-161: Warfield, *Confederate Soldier's Memoirs*, 152; Sullivan, *Dark Clouds of War*, 3.

26 Warfield, *Confederate Soldier's Memoirs*, 153.

hopping a fence and hurrying into the woods to join the now prepared infantrymen.[27]

Warfield needed no further instructions. Leaping into the saddle, he turned the horse around and dashed down the road, some of his comrades shouting encouragingly as he hurried past. Immediately behind him came the advance guard of Yankee cavalry, about 10 in number, intent on catching Warfield. Alternately shooting at him and yelling for their prey to surrender, the Federals failed to see the 17th Virginia's line of battle in the woods running parallel to the road. As the blue horsemen galloped past, Major Simpson cautioned his men to aim for the Northern riders and not their mounts then ordered a surprise volley. The lead rounds toppled most of the Yankees from their saddles, while wounding only one horse. The lucky survivors circled about and beat a hasty withdrawal.[28]

Another contingent of the 1st US arrived on the scene shortly thereafter. Private John Zimmerman, who had hidden in the woods after Stewart's pickets had scattered, heard the Yankees gallop up, "shouting and swearing at a furious rate," and watched clandestinely as the column paused at a bend in the road, changed formation into line of battle, then charged ahead. Within seconds, the two forces collided, the Federals "popping away" with their carbines and the Virginians letting loose a yell and "returning their fire very lively."[29]

Although he had been surprised to encounter Rebel infantry, Captain Eugene M. Baker, commanding the 1st US Cavalry, was determined to knock the Confederates out of his way and proceed to Front Royal as ordered. To that end he progressively threw more squadrons into the fight until his entire regiment was committed. Baker also varied his tactics, attacking first in line and then in column as he attempted to dislodge the stubborn Southerners.

When none of his options worked, the Union officer deployed dismounted skirmishers into the woods in an effort to drive the enemy back. In many ways going forward through dense timber in search of an often invisible foe was more terrifying than launching a mounted charge. As he

---

27 Ibid.

28 Ibid, 153-154.

29 Sullivan, *Dark Clouds of War*, 3.

watched the Federals sweep through the forest a few feet from his hiding place, Zimmerman thought he had never seen "a more nervous, scared lot of men." Frightened or not, the Northern troopers plowed ahead, only to blunder into the Confederates and be repulsed once again.[30]

As the fighting escalated behind him, Warfield raced back to Front Royal. Reaching the town, he remembered hearing that some of the brigade's officers were being entertained at the home of a soldier in his regiment. When he arrived there, he discovered a number of officers from Pickett's staff as well as the commander of the 17th Virginia, Lieutenant Colonel Arthur Herbert, who was returning from sick leave. After relating what was happening at Manassas Gap, Warfield was ordered to ride on and find General Pickett and repeat his news.[31]

As Colonel Herbert galloped off toward the gap to join his men, Private Warfield took to the road in the other direction. Shortly after swimming his horse across both branches of the Shenandoah, Warfield met Pickett at the head of his column. While the soldiers closest to the general crowded in to hear, Warfield breathlessly explained what was transpiring at the gap. Incredulous, Pickett asked for further details about the 17th Virginia's position and enemy strength, and after learning all he could from Warfield, exclaimed, "Where in the devil is our cavalry?"[32]

Not expecting an answer to his inquiry, but fully grasping the extent of the crisis, Pickett ordered Major Joseph R. Cabell, commanding what was left of Lewis Armistead's brigade after it was shot to pieces in the July 3 attack at Gettysburg, to rush to Simpson's aid. Much to his astonishment, Warfield was told to accompany Cabell as a guide. Word that they were to rescue fellow members of their own division worked like a tonic on Cabell's troops, who "started off at a rapid gait" toward the river. Fording both branches of the Shenandoah, the brigade headed through Front Royal and then hurried toward Manassas Gap at a fast route step.[33]

The rest of Pickett's command reached the North Fork of the Shenandoah River between 3:00 and 4:00 p.m., only to find Confederate

---

30 Ibid. Private Zimmermann was eventually spotted by the dismounted Federals and taken prisoner.

31 Warfield, *Confederate Soldier's Memoirs*, 154-55.

32 Ibid., 155.

33 Ibid.

This photo, taken circa 1954, looks eastward from the southern portion of Green Hill toward Linden/Manassas Gap and shows the area where the 17th Virginia Infantry made its stand on July 21, 1863. *Western Heritage Society*

engineers had, in the words of one eyewitness, "hardly begun" to lay the pontoon bridges Lee had ordered constructed. After negotiating the smaller stream, the division crossed the South Fork by using flatboats to carry rifles and ammunition to the opposite shore, while the troops waded their way over. Once in Front Royal, Pickett sent the remnants of Richard Garnett's and James Kemper's brigades, also unfortunate participants in the misnamed "Pickett's Charge," to reinforce Corse's men at Chester Gap.[34]

Between Linden and Wapping the fighting had continued unabated. Frustrated by his inability to shove the Rebels out of his way, Captain Baker called upon Merritt for assistance. The general sent the 2nd US Cavalry to join the battle, which produced another round of combat during which the 17th Virginia had two colors bearers shot down in quick succession. At some point Colonel Herbert managed to reach his regiment and assume command from Major Simpson, who had done an extraordinary job with meager resources. His troops had repulsed each Union attack, and even made several advances of their own to keep the enemy off balance.

All of this had worked much better than the Southerners had a right to expect, but their successful defense could not be prolonged indefinitely. Merritt had some 1,000 troopers in his brigade and should he choose to throw all of them into the fight at once, he could easily overwhelm the roughly 250 soldiers Herbert could call upon. The pressure was bad enough as it was, and grew worse about 3:00 p.m. when Merritt sent Captain Julius W. Mason's 5th US Cavalry to outflank the Southern line.[35]

Moving off the main road, Mason followed the route leading over the mountain toward Wapping in hopes of skirting Herbert's line and falling on his rear. Fortunately for the Rebels, Major Simpson had posted two companies on this path earlier in the day. When the blue column drew near, concealed Virginians delivered an unexpected volley that struck down a corporal in the front ranks and threw the cavalrymen into rapid retreat.[36]

Small tactical triumphs, however, could not alter the fact that the 17th Virginia was vastly outnumbered, virtually surrounded, and expending its

34 Baer, *Shadows on My Heart*, 233; *OR* Vol. 27, pt. 2, 362.

35 Sullivan, *Dark Clouds of War*, 3; Warfield, *Confederate Soldier's Memoirs*, 154.

36 *OR* Vol. 27, pt. 1, 945; Corporal George T. Crawford, 5th US Cavalry letter lot, www.ebay.com/itm/5th-US-Cavalry-Co-C-8-Civil-War-Letter-Lot-by-KIA-Corporal&_tr ksid=p2047675.m4100.

ammunition at a steady rate. Lieutenant Lewis Slaughter, among others, wondered just how much longer the fighting could go on. Hoping desperately for night, he instead thought the sun crawled so slowly across the sky it "seemed for hours to stand still." While time seemed suspended, he continued, the enemy grew stronger and "charged again and again." Whatever the hour, there was little doubt the men of the 17th were reaching the end of their fortitude—hungry and thirsty they continued to hold, but with increasing frequency glanced over their shoulders, searching in vain for help that apparently was not going to come.[37]

At 4:00 p.m., however, the beleaguered Virginians heard the sound of drums beating behind them. This time, however, their hopeful glances were rewarded with what one man described as the "glorious sight" of a Confederate battle flag drifting over a "long gray line of veterans" rushing to their assistance. Under Warfield's guidance, Cabell had formed Armistead's brigade into line west of Wapping before beginning his final advance toward the gap. Within a few hundred yards, the brigade ran into Federal skirmishers who had infiltrated behind the 17th Virginia, and soon Cabell's "entire force was engaged." Although the brigade was a mere shadow of what it had been at Gettysburg, numbering this day just 600 men, Cabell easily shoved the Union troopers out of his way and linked up with the beleaguered men of the 17th.[38]

As ranking officer, Lieutenant Colonel Herbert took command of the brigade and ordered a general attack. The Confederate line surged forward and the Northern cavalry fell back rather than meet the onslaught, yielding at least a mile of ground before the tired Rebels decided to break contact. When the fighting stopped, the 17th Virginia took stock of its losses. Surprisingly, despite the length and brief periods of intense fighting, the regiment suffered but four wounded (one mortally) and 22 men taken prisoner (one of whom escaped a few days later). Yankee carbines had proven less effective in the rugged country than the Springfield rifles handled by the Virginians, who had the advantage of firing downhill from defensive positions. As a result, the Federals suffered a good deal more than their tenacious opponents.

37 Warfield, *Confederate Soldier's Memoirs*, 157.

38 Ibid., 156-57; Consolidated Service Records, 17th Virginia Record of Events, www.fold3.com.

Manassas & Chester Gap Forces Actually Engaged, July 21, 1863

Confederate	Union
Pickett's Division	*1st Cavalry Division*
Major General George Pickett	Brigadier General John Buford

Corse's Brigade	*First Brigade*
Brig. Gen. Montgomery Corse	Col. William Gamble
15th Virginia Infantry	8th Illinois Cavalry
17th Virginia Infantry	12th Illinois Cavalry
29th Virginia Infantry	3rd Indiana Cavalry
30th Virginia Infantry	8th New York Cavalry
32nd Virginia Infantry	2nd United States, Batteries B & L

Garnett's Brigade	*Reserve Brigade*
Maj. Charles Peyton	Brig. Gen. Wesley Merritt
8th Virginia Infantry	6th Pennsylvania Cavalry
18th Virginia Infantry	1st United States Cavalry
19th Virginia Infantry	2nd United States Cavalry
28th Virginia Infantry	5th United States Cavalry
56th Virginia Infantry	6th United States Cavalry
	1st United States, Battery K

Kemper's Brigade
Col. Joseph Mayo
1st Virginia Infantry
3rd Virginia Infantry
7th Virginia Infantry
11th Virginia Infantry
24Th Virginia Infantry

Armistead's Brigade
Maj. Joseph Cabell
9th Virginia Infantry
14th Virginia Infantry
38th Virginia Infantry
53rd Virginia Infantry
57th Virginia Infantry

Dearing's Artillery Battalion
(Detachment)
Maj. Jacob Read
Hampden Artillery (Caskie's Battery)
Virginia Artillery (Blount's Battery)

Merritt described his losses as "very severe," and reported nine killed, 12 wounded, and eight missing.[39]

The struggle at Manassas Gap sputtered to a close as the afternoon sun began to sink toward the horizon. Neither side had won all that it had hoped to win, but neither had anything been lost. From a defensive standpoint both Merritt and Herbert could claim victory, each having, at least for the moment, denied his enemy the ability to move through the pass. How long they would be content with the current stalemate depended on what their respective superiors chose to do the next day. Those decisions, in turn, relied upon what was happening a few miles to the south at Chester Gap.

And there, at Chester Gap, the Federals had even less luck than they did around Linden. After detaching the 17th Virginia, Montgomery Corse and the rest of his brigade, accompanied by Read's two batteries, had marched hard for Chester Gap and arrived at the crest of the pass about 3:30 p.m. This time the infantry found Confederate cavalry, most likely Lieutenant Moon's contingent from Snickers' Gap, guarding the eastern entrance to the pass.[40]

About the same time that Corse ended his trek, William Gamble's Union cavalry brigade arrived on the scene after a 20-mile ride from Piedmont Station. A mile short of the pass the Federals ran into Rebel pickets. Either the Southerners proved stubborn or Gamble was in no mood for half measures, because he immediately dismounted six full squadrons and sent them to deal with whatever resistance lay in his front. Having already raised the alarm, and thus accomplished their primary mission, the Confederate pickets fell back to the crest of the gap, where Corse's infantry waited along with Major Read's two batteries: the Virginia Artillery, armed with four 12-pounder Napoleons under Captain Joseph G. Blount, and the Hampden Artillery, commanded by Captain William H. Caskie, manning one 10-pounder parrot, one 3-inch rifle, and two 12-pounder Napoleons.[41]

39 Consolidated Service Records, 17th Virginia Record of Events; *OR* 27, pt. 1, 194, 945.

40 *OR* 27, pt. 1, 937. The identity of the Rebel cavalry is unknown. No Confederate report names them and Stuart's report of the campaign makes it clear that he was unable to get any mounted unit into the area until July 23. Federal accounts describe the cavalry as one regiment from Jones' brigade, information likely collected from prisoners. Moon's detachment was the only force from that brigade east of the Shenandoah and therefore the most plausible cavalry unit to be present at Chester Gap on July 21.

41 Piedmont Station is modern day Delaplane; *OR* 27, pt. 1, 937; Stewart Sifakis, *Compendium of the Confederate Armies: Virginia* (Berwyn Heights, MD, 2003). 12-13.

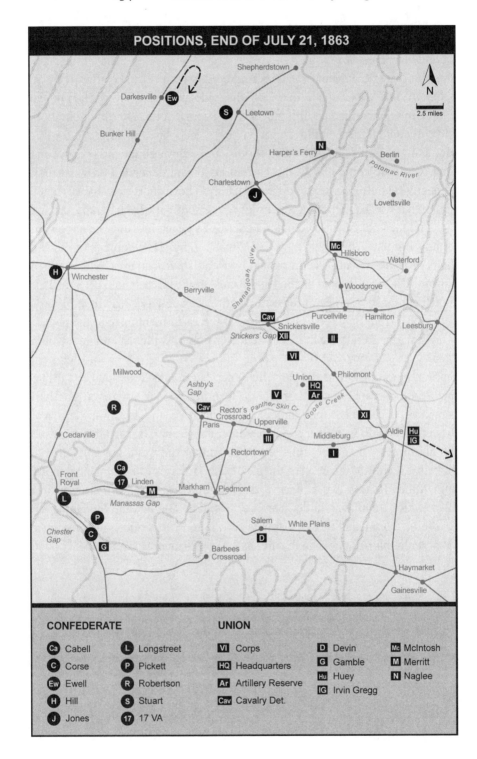

POSITIONS, END OF JULY 21, 1863

Infantry and artillery was more trouble than the Union colonel had bargained for, and he soon realized he lacked the strength to drive the Rebels away. Reflecting on the fact that the nearest possible support for his command was 20 miles distant, Gamble chose to seek safer ground. The Federal cavalry retreated a mile and a half to the point where the road leading from Chester Gap diverged, one fork running to Barbee's Crossroad and the other to Sperryville. There, Gamble ordered his men into bivouac, but only after unlimbering his guns and deploying a strong line of pickets to cover his front and flanks.[42]

Gamble's brigade, however, was still out on a limb and exposed. Colonel George H. Chapman, commanding the 3rd Indiana Cavalry, confessed to his diary that he did not like the position and was "somewhat uneasy" about remaining there. If the enemy decided to make a night march, they might surround the troopers in the dark and destroy the command come dawn. Gamble, however, thought the risk was worth the reward of blocking the intersection and hoped that the next day Meade would send infantry to help. Having captured during that day 654 cattle and 602 head of sheep destined for Longstreet's column, at least his men wouldn't go without supper.[43]

42 *OR* 27, pt. 1, 937.

43 Chapman Diary, IHS; *OR* 27, pt, 1, 937.

CHAPTER 8

"It Is Not Understood
What Meade's Plans Are"

Confederates Bridge the Shenandoah—Ewell Heads South—Longstreet Crosses the River—Lee Makes Plans—Meade Learns of Kelley's Retreat—The Federals Remain Uncertain

As William Gamble's Union cavalry troopers hunkered down for the night, the Army of Northern Virginia finished a day of hard marching.

A. P. Hill's corps had completed its 13-mile hike from Bunker Hill to Winchester by late afternoon on July 21. After parading through the town with bands playing, its regiments moved south another two miles before going into bivouac. Hill's artillery camped farther down the road on the grounds of Grand View, a mile beyond the small burg of Newton. Following their fruitless thrust toward Hedgesville, the divisions of Rodes and Johnson retraced their steps and returned to the Second Corps' camps around Darkesville for the night. Early's division along with Wade Hampton's brigade, now the northernmost elements of the army, stopped for the evening on the eastern side of North Mountain, a mile or so below Hedgesville.[1]

1 OR 27, pt. 2, 615; Austin Dobbins, ed., *Grandfather's Journal* (Dayton, OH, 1988), 152; Early, *Memoirs*, 284; McDonald, *Make Me a Map*, 162; Marshall, *Donaldsonville Canonniers*, 218-19.

Farther south, Richard Garnett's and James Kemper's brigades of Pickett's division reached Chester Gap just as Gamble began his withdrawal. The divisions of John Bell Hood and Lafayette McLaws (the former led by Brigadier General Evander M. Law since Hood's wounding at Gettysburg) reached the Shenandoah sometime around midnight. About the same time, Confederate engineers finished their pontoon bridges over both forks of the swollen river.[2]

Longstreet's First Corps wagon trains began crossing as soon as these pontoon spans were ready. Law's men, at the head of Longstreet's column, were forced to ford both branches of the Shenandoah. Under the modest glow of a one-quarter moon and bonfires, they found the swift-flowing, waist-deep, water no easier than had Corse and Pickett had earlier in the day. Several men who attempted to wade the river alone were "seized by the current," wrote one observer, and saved from drowning only with great difficulty. Benefiting from that poor example, the 5th Texas and other units settled upon a safer method, sending five or six men into the river at a time with their arms locked together for mutual support against the current. Although it is unclear from contemporary accounts, it is likely they ferried their arms and ammunition across the river in flat boats, as Pickett had previously done.[3]

By the time McLaws' troops were ready to follow Law, the pontoon bridge over the south branch was available for use, leaving them to ford only the smaller and less risky north fork. After managing to get across the river, both divisions went into camp alongside the Shenandoah near Front Royal. Rations were short and many men begged food from the locals, an effort that stretched late into the night. While the soldiers sought meals from sympathetic citizens, Longstreet's wagons and artillery continued to rumble across the pontoons. The laborious process continued at least until dawn.[4]

2 Letter of J. H. Reinhardt, 16th Georgia in *Southern Watchman*, August 5, 1863; *OR 27*, pt. 2, 362.

3 Joe Joskins diary, University of Texas, San Antonio, http://digital.utsa.edu/cdm/compoundobject/collection/p15125coll10/id/8440/rec/1.

4 James W. Silver, ed., *A Life For The Confederacy from the War Diary of Robert A. Moore, Pvt., CSA* (Wilmington, NC, 1987), 157; Baer, *Shadows on My Heart*, 234; *OR 27*, pt. 2, 390; Gary Gallagher, ed., *Fighting for the Confederacy, The Personal Recollections of General Edward Porter Alexander* (Chapel Hill, NC, 1989), 274.

General Lee pitched his headquarter tents amongst the mass of Hill's troops that night and began reviewing reports on the day's events. As usual, the intelligence was fragmentary and devoid of anything that provided absolute certainty regarding enemy plans and intentions. Still, there were enough puzzle pieces for the Virginian to get a handle on the strategic situation. Kelley's retreat across the Potomac made it clear that there was no danger of an attack on Ewell. The fighting at Manassas Gap and the presence of Union cavalry at Chester Gap, on the other hand, seemed to verify that the Federals were moving up the Loudoun Valley. As of yet, Lee did not know the location of Meade's infantry, but this now no longer mattered. The decision to shift the army from the Shenandoah Valley to the Rappahannock had been correct, and must be pushed to completion.

Having reached these conclusions, Lee acted with customary decisiveness. Orders went out for the movement south and east to continue in the morning. Longstreet would resume his advance through Chester Gap toward Culpeper Court House. A. P. Hill would move to Front Royal and trail Longstreet through the Blue Ridge. As previously anticipated, Ewell was ordered to follow the rest of the army. Rodes and Johnson would march their divisions for Winchester, while Early's goal for the day would be Bunker Hill.

Jeb Stuart's cavalry drew multiple missions. Beverly Robertson's small brigade was ordered to cross the Shenandoah River, overtake Longstreet and assume duty as his advance guard. Grumble Jones would maintain his position in front of Harpers Ferry as long as necessary to protect the army's flank as it headed south, then follow in its wake. Baker's regiments would remain with Ewell's corps and act as his rearguard. Stuart's remaining three brigades under Fitz Lee, Chambliss, and Ferguson, would make a forced march from Leetown to Manassas Gap with the goal of occupying the pass and denying its use to the enemy.[5]

Knowing he was leaving the lower Valley vulnerable to Union occupation, Lee did what he could to protect the region. In the aftermath of Gettysburg, Major General Sam Jones, commander of the Department of Southwestern Virginia, had been ordered to reinforce Lee with two brigades of infantry. Jones had responded enthusiastically and promised to send two batteries of artillery as well. However, those plans were quickly disrupted by

5 *OR* 27, pt. 2, 707.

a Union advance that threatened the vital salt works, lead mines, and rail lines his command protected. The situation precluded Jones from personally leaving his department or sending more than half of the promised infantry support. Colonel C. Gabriel Wharton's 1,100-man brigade and two batteries were all the troops Jones could offer, and he stressed that he needed them returned as soon as possible. It took almost ten days of considerable telegraph traffic to and fro between Jones and the War Department before even this much was decided upon. Then, to further complicate matters, Wharton's departure was delayed for several days by damage to the railroad caused by saboteurs.[6]

For the most part, General Lee was left out of this decision-making process. Not until July 18 did Jones write to inform him that Wharton's brigade and a battery were on their way from Staunton to Winchester, with another battery to follow on the 22nd. Whether any additional units would be joining them was open to doubt, dependent upon fluid circumstances and War Department orders.[7]

This message had not reached Lee by the afternoon of July 21. Therefore, as he plotted the next day's movements, the general remained uncertain whether Jones or any troops besides Wharton's were headed to the lower Valley. Regardless, that evening he sent dispatches to Jones, Wharton, and Brigadier General John Imboden, explaining to each that enemy movements "obliged [him to] withdraw the army east of the Blue Ridge." In face of this necessity, Imboden was ordered to move his cavalry from Staunton to Winchester as quickly as possible. Wharton was told to continue to that same point and take command there until either Jones or Imboden arrived. As soon as Ewell's Second Corps reached Winchester from Darkesville, Wharton was to confer with its commander and decide whether it was necessary or advantageous to keep his brigade in the city for a few extra days.[8]

In the event Jones did not appear with more troops—and Lee thought this a distinct possibility—he cautioned Wharton that it would be impossible for a small force to hold Winchester should the enemy decide to take it. Still,

---

6 Ibid., pt. 3, 978, 981-982, 985, 987, 991, 995, 999, 1020.

7 Ibid., 1022.

8 Ibid., 1031-1032.

he would leave it to Ewell and Wharton to decide if it would be wiser for the colonel to stay in the town or retire up the Valley to some other point. Imboden and his cavalry were another matter, and Lee wanted him in the lower Valley "as soon as practicable." Once on the scene the brigadier was to take charge of the region and deploy his troops to protect it from enemy "depredations."[9]

*   *   *

In sharp contrast to the activity of Army of Northern Virginia, Federal infantry spent July 21 in bivouac twenty or more miles from Manassas Gap. Road-weary Union soldiers used their unanticipated break to advantage, writing letters, washing clothes, repairing equipment, drilling, or simply resting. Their commanding general, on the other hand, spent the day in fretful uncertainty.

Worried that Lee had been significantly reinforced and was preparing another invasion, Meade was determined not to take another step southward until he had positive knowledge of the Rebel's position and movements. Unfortunately, the news that came into army headquarters throughout the 21st was alternately alarming, informative, contradictory, and misleading. None of it did much to ease the general's anxiety.

At 10:00 a.m., Halleck sent Meade a telegram informing him that "Hill's corps" had advanced on Martinsburg and compelled Kelley to retreat north of the Potomac. However, since Meade had warned Halleck on the night of the 19th that he would be out of telegraphic communication until his army reached Warrenton, it is not certain this message was received.[10]

News of the Confederate thrust managed to reach Meade independent of Halleck. Ironically, at exactly the same time the general-in-chief was warning Meade of the Rebel lunge, Meade was writing Halleck that he had reports that Hill had forced Kelly over the Potomac. By whatever means Meade learned of it, Ewell's offensive thrust lent credence to rumors that Lee was plotting a movement north of the Potomac River.[11]

9   Ibid., 1031-1032.

10 Ibid., pt. 1, 97.

11 Ibid., pt. 1, 97.

Information sent from Manassas Gap and lookout stations farther north, however, seemed to point to another conclusion. At 3:20 p.m. signal officers at V Corps headquarters passed along a message from observers at Ashby's Gap stating that the Rebels were "moving up the Valley in considerable force this a.m." The message also noted that "their train is immense." An hour and forty minutes later, an aide Pleasonton had sent to check up on affairs at Manassas Gap reported that blacks living nearby were claiming Longstreet's corps had entered Front Royal during the morning and was moving on both Manassas and Chester gaps. What they had seen and reported on was Corse's brigade, not Longstreet's entire corps. But the 4:00 p.m. appearance in the pass of what the aide described as a "superior force" of infantry seemed to give credence to the story.[12]

Amplifying this report were a pair of dispatches Merritt sent sometime after the struggle at Manassas Gap ended—one to Buford, the other to Cavalry Corps headquarters—telling his superiors that he had captured a number of pickets from the 17th Virginia and engaged in "two small fights" with the Rebels. The general confessed that at first he had thought he was facing only a single enemy regiment. Now, however, he believed he had run into "Hoover's brigade of Corse's division," which his prisoners claimed were 600 and 10,000 men strong respectively.[13]

That news added to Union confusion. There was no such thing as Corse's division, and "Hoover" was really Herbert, who led a 250-man regiment, not a 600-man brigade. Indeed, Cabell and Herbert together mustered just over 800 muskets. The fact that Wesley Merritt believed otherwise was a testament to the fight the 17th Virginia had put up and the quality of the lies told by Southern prisoners. But if Merritt got the details of his skirmish wrong, he was able to echo reports that Longstreet was at Front Royal and sending troops to Chester and Manassas gaps. Otherwise he passed along the testimony of his prisoners that the rest of Lee's army had not crossed the Shenandoah.[14]

Pondering these messages throughout the evening of the 21st, Meade found nothing to dispel his indecision. Dispatches from Manassas Gap

---

12 Ibid., pt. 3, 735-6.

13 Ibid., pt. 3, 735, ibid., pt. 1, 945.

14 Herbert started the day with 270 men, but lost about 20 as prisoners before the fighting began. *OR* 27, pt. 3, 735.

pointed toward a Rebel withdrawal through the mountains. But reports of Ewell's advance on Kelley lent credibility to the idea that Lee was about to launch an offensive. What Meade did not know, and could not discern, was which of these alternatives pointed toward the enemy's real intentions.

Doubt as to Confederate purposes meant irresolution as to the proper course of action for the Army of the Potomac. If the Rebels were abandoning the Valley, Meade should march south at once to block their path and hit them on the move. But if he did so, and the Confederates stormed through Snickers' or Ashby's gaps into his rear, the enemy would cut the Union army off from its base of supplies and Washington. In short, Meade was trapped in the same dilemma in which he had found himself on the night of July 20. In face of that unfortunate reality, there was little more he could do than maintain his present stance. The army's infantry would sit and wait until the situation clarified itself, hopefully sometime tomorrow morning.

For the men in the ranks, and even for general officers, this was all very confusing. Provost Marshal Marsena Patrick spoke for almost everyone when he confessed to his diary that "it is not understood what Meade's plans are." Was the army on the verge of breaking into the Shenandoah Valley in search of a fight? Was it about to leap eastward to Warrenton? Was it preparing for a defensive battle in Loudon or readying itself to re-cross the Potomac to face another Rebel invasion?

No one knew, because Meade did not know himself.

CHAPTER 9

"The Shenandoah Valley . . .
Is Alive With Wagons"

The Confederate March Continues—Gamble's Stand at Chester Gap—Wofford's Plan—Pickett's Attack—Longstreet's Corps Flows East—Skirmishing in Manassas Gap—Lee Visits Bel Air

ON July 22, Southern columns once again filled the Valley's roads. Cavalry commanders Fitz Lee, Ferguson, and Chambliss, accompanied by Major Robert Beckham's battalion of horse artillery, rode out of Leetown before dawn with orders to make a forced march for Manassas Gap. Traveling over what one Confederate described as "a terrible, bad and dusty road," the column passed through Rippon and Berryville on its way to Millwood. Before nightfall, the cavalry would make camp on the west bank of the Shenandoah just six miles from Front Royal. When the artillerists realized they would not be able to ford the swollen river, they turned their guns right at Millwood and later went into bivouac a mile and half south of Stone Bridge. Overall it was a "disagreeable" march that covered some 25 miles.[1]

Like their mounted brethren, Ewell's infantrymen were also on the move that morning, with Jubal Early pushing his men toward Bunker Hill as Rodes and Johnson guided theirs to Winchester. A. P. Hill's Third Corps

1   OR 27, pt. 2, 707; Morissett, diary, MOCW; Nunnelee Diary, MOCW; Swank, *Sabres, Saddles and Spurs*, 85.

troops left their bivouacs at 4:00 a.m. on the way to Front Royal. Meanwhile, Imboden's cavalry and Wharton's brigade moved north from Staunton toward Winchester.[2]

The critical locations that day were Manassas and Chester gaps. If these passes could not be secured, Lee's entire plan of campaign would be disrupted and he may well find his army cut off from its communication and supply lines. Fortunately for the Confederates, James Longstreet knew that Yankee cavalry in the passes the previous day might portend greater danger on the 22nd. Aware that Federal infantry could appear at any time, he acted accordingly. Although his troops hadn't finished crossing the twin forks of the Shenandoah River until well after midnight, Longstreet roused them after only a few hours' sleep and put everyone back into motion before daybreak.

Lafayette McLaws pushed his division for Chester Gap about sun up, moving ahead of the ponderous supply trains winding their way toward the mountains behind his column. At roughly the same time, John Hood's division under Evander Law marched for Manassas Gap, where it was to relieve infantry officers Herbert and Cabell, who would then move their small commands to rejoin Pickett's division. With Law at Manassas Gap to guard against Yankee interference, Longstreet's other two divisions would deal with any Union troops obstructing the eastern exit of Chester Gap.[3]

It took only a few hours for McLaws to get into position. Once at the western entrance to the gap, his troops were allowed time to cook rations before continuing their march. Brigadier General William T. Wofford's five Georgia regiments were assigned the task of leading the advance. Wofford was 39. The prewar lawyer, state legislator, and Mexican War veteran had opposed secession, but threw in with the Confederate cause once his home state of Georgia left the Union. Following standard procedure, Wofford deployed a skirmish line ahead of his brigade and sent it forward. Once it was far enough in front to provide ample warning of anything unexpected, Wofford ordered his column eastward. A few minutes later, the rest of

2   Jones, *Reminiscences of a Louisiana Tiger*, 82; Robert T. Douglass War Diary www.localhistory.morrisville.edu/sites/letters/owen10.html.

3   *Southern Watchman*, Aug 5, 1863.

Brigadier General William T. Wofford
Generals in Gray
(1959 LSU edition by Ezra J. Warner)

McLaws' division and the corps supply train moved as well, slowly filing into the road behind the Georgians.[4]

Reaching the crest of the gap about 8:00 a.m., Confederate skirmishers spied Union soldiers— some occupying a hill to their left and others blocking the exit to the pass. The enemy proved to be dismounted troopers of Gamble's brigade, supported by six 3-inch Ordnance Rifles from Lieutenant Edward Heaton's batteries B & L, 2nd US Artillery. As soon as the Rebels came within easy range the Federals opened fire. Wofford's skirmishers took up the challenge and the steep mountainsides forming Chester Gap reverberated with gunfire.[5]

The firing was noisy, but not particularly dangerous. Heaton's gunners were ramming their rifled cannon with what one man described as "the very worst kind of ammunition," and only one out of every dozen of his shells exploded. Those that detonated, however, did so prematurely over the heads of Yankee cavalrymen rather than the more distant Confederate infantry. The Rebels knew nothing of this, but they did appreciate that Union artillery was dangerous. Longstreet's wagon train, as well as most of McLaws' division, drew back out of range. Wofford's brigade, however, wasn't going anywhere and deployed to support its skirmishers, who took cover and kept up a continuous exchange of fire with the enemy.[6]

Although he knew he was vastly outnumbered by the Rebels clogging the pass, Gamble refused to budge. His troopers, eyeing the long wagon train

---

4 Ibid.; *OR* 27, pt. 1, 937; Warner, *Generals in Gray*, 343-344.

5 *Southern Watchman*, Aug. 5, 1863; *OR* 27, pt. 1, 937; Owen's letter, July 24, 1863, LV.

6 *Southern Watchman*, Aug. 5, 1863; *OR* 27, pt. 1, 937.

in the gap waiting to come down understood that by holding their ground, they were preventing the Confederates from exiting the gap. This was an accomplishment that might count for a great deal if Meade was pushing infantry to Gamble's support.[7]

Naturally, the Rebels were as alert to this possibility as the bluecoats and were anxious to knock the Northerners out of their way. This was easier said than done, however, for in terrain such as this, even a small body of determined men posed a considerable tactical challenge. Although Confederate skirmishers drove their Union counterparts back onto the main Federal line, the enemy clearly meant to yield no more ground. Just as clearly, any frontal attack designed to push the Yankees out of the way promised to be bloody.[8]

Rather than just bull ahead, Wofford proposed a less costly and potentially more decisive maneuver. He suggested that he hold his position and keep the enemy occupied, while another column made a clandestine march through the mountains to strike the Union flank. Once that flanking attack began, Wofford continued, he would send his men forward. Hit from two sides, and hopefully in the flank by surprise, the Federal line should crumple easily. Not only would this clear the road, it might destroy whatever hostile formation lay in the First Corps' path.[9]

Wofford had about as much experience as anyone, so his tactical advice carried real weight. As the commander of the 18th Georgia Infantry when it was part of Brigadier General John B. Hood's Texas Brigade, Wofford had helped break the strong Federal line at Gaines Mill in June 1862. After Hood was promoted, Wofford led the Texas Brigade as its senior colonel through the battles of Second Manassas and South Mountain. At Sharpsburg, his counterattack through the Miller Cornfield helped save the embattled left flank of the Army of Northern Virginia. When his regiment was transferred to Brigadier General Thomas R. R. Cobb's brigade, Wofford took charge of the brigade when Cobb fell at Fredericksburg. Given permanent command of Cobb's brigade and promoted to brigadier in January 1863, the Georgian missed Chancellorsville but launched a powerful assault against the Union

---

7   *OR* 27, pt. 1, 937.

8   Chapman Diary, IHS.

9   *Southern Watchman*, Aug. 5, 1863; *OR* 27, pt. 2, 362.

Confrontation at Chester Gap: Forces Engaged, July 22, 1863

Confederate	Union

Pickett's Division
Major General George Pickett

1st Cavalry Division
Brigadier General John Buford

Kemper's Brigade
Col. Joseph Mayo
1st Virginia Infantry
3rd Virginia Infantry
7th Virginia Infantry
11th Virginia Infantry
24th Virginia Infantry

First Brigade
Col. William Gamble
8th Illinois Cavalry
12th Illinois Cavalry
3rd Indiana Cavalry
8th New York Cavalry

2nd United States, Batteries B & L

Garnett's Brigade
Maj. Charles Peyton
8th Virginia Infantry
18th Virginia Infantry
19th Virginia Infantry
28th Virginia Infantry
56th Virginia Infantry

McLaws' Division
Maj. Gen. Lafayette McLaws

Wofford's Brigade
Brig. Gen. William Wofford
16th Georgia Infantry
18th Georgia Infantry
24th Georgia Infantry
Cobb's Legion Infantry
Phillips Legion Infantry

III Corps at Gettysburg late on the afternoon of July 2. He was an officer who knew what he was about.[10]

Longstreet approved Wofford's idea and gave George Pickett the job of outflanking the Union position. He, in turn, assigned the task to the brigades of Garnett and Kemper. Since both those officers had fallen at Gettysburg (the former killed and the latter severely wounded and captured), Garnett's

10 Warner, *Generals in Gray*, 343-344.

command was now in the hands of Major Charles S. Peyton, while Kemper's was being led by Colonel Joseph Mayo, Jr. The regiments under Peyton would lead the flanking move, with instructions to take a route designed to conceal their presence from enemy eyes until the last possible moment.

Whatever the tactical merit of Wofford's scheme, it would consume a considerable amount of time—perhaps a good part of the rest of the day. There was also the very real chance that the hours lost would allow additional Union troops to reach the field and find Longstreet's command divided. This seems not to have overly concerned Longstreet, or he calculated the stratagem more justified if the Yankees were in considerable force.[11]

*　　*　　*

Though the Southerners had no way of knowing it, any concerns about Federal infantry marching to reinforce Gamble were groundless. Meade's foot soldiers were encamped well to the north and no help was on its way to the embattled cavalryman. The Rebel plan was almost guaranteed to succeed, and it was merely a matter of time before the Yankees were driven away and the road opened. The only questions that remained were whether Gamble's force would be wrecked or merely displaced, and how long it would take to determine the result.

The answer to the second of those queries would be the interval it took Pickett's men to complete their part of the maneuver and get in place to attack. As it turned out, this was rather time-consuming. Meandering through the mountains over difficult side roads and pursuing a course that favored stealth over speed, the flanking column took nearly eight hours to get within striking distance of the Federal position.

Finally reaching a dense wood where he could deploy unseen, Peyton detailed the 18th Virginia as skirmishers and formed his line of battle to its rear. This was the first time since their disastrous assault on July 3 that Pickett's men were poised to go into combat. Both Peyton's and Mayo's brigades were woefully under strength, and a number of their regiments were led by mere captains. Moreover, the commands had been slaughtered at

11 *OR* 27, pt. 2, 362.

Captain Henry T. Owen
Library of Virginia

Gettysburg, so their discipline was unsteady and morale rather low. How well the Virginians would stand up to another fight remained to be seen.[12]

This question must have been on the mind of Captain Henry T. Owen, who was one of only three officers in the 18th Virginia to survive the Pennsylvania battle. By virtue of seniority, he now commanded the 68 men left in his regiment. The carnage of July 3, coupled with the loss of so many comrades, left Owen depressed and suffering from survivor's guilt. Why had he been spared when so many others had fallen? These thoughts and others tortured the man. A short time after the battle he suffered through a nightmare in which he relived the assault on Cemetery Ridge over and over again. Throughout his dream, as the Confederates advanced into the hellish vortex of Union fire, Owen saw a thin, dark shadow moving ahead of him constantly. No matter how he tried to veer away, the shadow stayed in front of him until somehow he emerged from the fighting unscathed. Once past the terror of enemy fire, the shadow spoke to him: "I am the Angel that protected you. I will never leave nor forsake you." Reassured by his dream, Captain Owen found the strength to carry on.[13]

During the retreat from Gettysburg and in the weeks that followed, Owen encountered difficulty enforcing discipline in the regiment, especially among men who were not part of his own company. Just six days shy of his 32nd birthday, the Virginian knew something about the problems of leading independent-minded volunteer soldiers, having himself been court-martialed twice and cashiered once in 1861 because of his head-strong

12 Henry T. Owen papers, letter of July 24, 1863, Library of Virginia.

13 Kimberly Ayn Owen, Graham C. Owen & Michael M. Owen, *The War of Confederate Captain Henry T. Owen* (Berwyn Heights, MD, 2004), 111-112.

attitude in his dealings with his regimental commander, Colonel Robert E. Withers. His ability to learn from and overcome these early setbacks had made him a solid company officer. Fearful that "some would not behave well" in action because they were "not accustomed" to his authority, Owen called his soldiers together before shaking them into a skirmish line. Assuming a humble tone that he hoped would inspire obedience when the engagement commenced, he told them they knew "as much about fighting and their duty in battle" as he did, and expressed regret that "a more experienced leader" was not available to take them into the coming action.[14]

Knowing that his men well understood "the importance of driving the Yankees from Chester Gap," the captain asked if they would fight as well today as they had fought heretofore. To his great relief, they promised they would. His confidence bolstered, Owen deployed his troops and commenced the advance.[15]

By this time it was almost 6:00 p.m. The 18th Virginia began moving through the woods, its skirmishers spread out at the standard interval of five paces and all expecting the outbreak of "a little fight" at any moment. Following behind in line of battle were the other four regiments under Major Peyton's command, who were followed in turn by Mayo's brigade. Crashing through the dense underbrush and moving relentlessly, as Owens later put it, "over hill and bottom," the Virginians eventually stepped within view of Gamble's cavalrymen. At that moment, Wofford's Georgians, as previously planned, began their own advance against Gamble's front, their general leading them on horseback with hat in hand urging them forward to capture Heaton's guns.[16]

Astonished to find at least five grey regiments bearing down on his left and the recently complacent Georgians now pressing his front, Gamble realized he was in serious trouble. Outflanked, his artillery all but useless, and confronting "overwhelming numbers" arrayed in a battle line "more than a mile in length," the only thing his command could do was get out of the way before it was crushed.[17]

14 Ibid, 41-50; Henry T. Owen papers, letter of July 24, 1863, Library of Virginia.

15 Henry T. Owen papers, letter of July 24, 1863, Library of Virginia.

16 Ibid; *Southern Watchman*, Aug. 5, 1863.

17 *OR* 27, pt. 1, 937; Chapman diary, IHS; Bellemy diary INSL; *OR* 27, pt. 2, 362.

This it did, and in hurried fashion. Robert Myers, surgeon of the 16th Georgia, boasted that upon hearing the yell of Wofford's skirmishers, the Federals fired one shot from their cannon and "ran off at a good speed." Captain Owen concurred, reporting that the Yankees "took out and would not let us come near them." The Southerners pursued the fleeing horsemen northward, knocking them back to Barbee's Crossroads before night put an end to the chase. Just as dusk fell, Hebert, who was leading Armistead's brigade, together with the 17th Virginia, arrived on the scene after trudging over the mountains from Manassas Gap. Although weary from their march, they provided a welcome reinforcement as Mayo and Peyton put their men into bivouac for the night.[18]

Wofford's plan had succeeded handily. Moreover, Pickett's brigades had performed competently and had helped score a vital victory at little cost—a fact of which they were keenly aware. In the wake of their Gettysburg experience, this inexpensive triumph along with their earlier stout defense of Manassas Gap went some distance toward restoring the division's self-confidence and élan.[19]

The view of events looked the same in the Federal camps, for there was no denying the Confederate success. Colonel Chapman forthrightly admitted the Rebels had driven his cavalry "back hastily" over a distance of several miles. For his part, Gamble was willing to acknowledge being pushed rearward, but by no means would he characterize the withdrawal as hasty. Instead, he reported retiring slowly without abandoning his mission of "watching the enemy." Whatever the speed of their retreat, the Yankees had been ejected from Chester Gap, losing by their own count one man killed, eight wounded, and 16 missing in the process. In contrast, Wofford had six men wounded, while Pickett reported only a few men "slightly hurt." Moreover, the Confederates captured several horses and reacquired many of the cattle Gamble had seized the day before.[20]

Longstreet was pleased by the result, but not surprised that more had not been accomplished, noting later that the "plan of catching cavalry with infantry was not successful, although General Wofford thought for a time his

---

18 Owen, letter of July 24, 1863, LV; Lt. Robert Pooler Myers Diary, MOCWW. Barbee's Crossroads is modern day Hume. Owen, letter of July 24, 1863; Myers diary, MOCW.

19 Owen, letter of July 24, 1863, LV; Silver, *A Life For The Confederacy*, 158.

20 Chapman diary, IHS; Bellemy diary, ISL; *OR* 27, pt. 1, 937-8.

trap was well laid." The enemy's escape, however, was inconsequential to the purpose of the day's maneuvers. What mattered was that the gap had been opened and the First Corps could continue its movement toward the Rappahannock River, which it proceeded to do as soon as the blue cavalry was shoved safely out of the way. Once the Confederate column lurched back into motion, it would travel all night to make up for lost time and not halt until 8:00 a.m. the next morning, July 23.[21]

* * *

The day's events at Manassas Gap were far less dramatic. At dawn, Law led Hood's division from Front Royal into the pass, where he relieved Cabell and Herbert. As the Virginians began marching via side roads toward Chester Gap, Law spread Brigadier General Henry L. Benning's command across the valley floor. He also sent elements of his other brigades out onto its flanks. This done, he began probing eastward to discover the whereabouts of Merritt's Union cavalry.[22]

As part of this movement, Captain John R. Woodward, acting major of the 1st Texas Infantry, was ordered to deploy a strong skirmish line and move to the top of one of the mountains embracing the pass. After dispersing onto the steep slopes of the defile, Woodward's troops began toiling upward. The men, recalled one of the Texans, kept their intervals "tolerably well" while negotiating the difficult terrain and managed to obtain the summit without encountering enemy resistance.[23]

Since his soldiers were "pretty well fagged out" after their long climb, Woodward ordered a halt to allow them to catch their breath. As best the Texans could tell, the Yankees were still some distance to the east, if they were nearby at all. Therefore, it was quite a shock to see the captain, standing in a clearing and fanning himself with his hat, suddenly drop to the ground. When several men rushed to his side and asked if he was alright, Woodward

21 James Longstreet, *From Manassas to Appomattox: Memoirs of the Civil War in America* (Secaucus, NJ, 1984), 431; Gallagher, *Fighting for the Confederacy*, 274.

22 *OR* 27, pt. 2, 415; Jeffrey D. Stocker, ed., *From Huntsville to Appomattox* (Knoxville, TN, 1996), 130.

23 Mary Lasswell, *Rags and Hope: Recollections of Val C. Giles: Four Years with Hood's Brigade, 4th Texas Infantry 1861-1865* (New York, NY, 1961), 208-209.

replied somewhat incredulously that he had been shot. Although no one had heard gunfire, the captain had, indeed, been struck by what one soldier described as "a small bullet" that broke his thigh bone near the hip.[24]

Where the round originated was impossible to tell. Some men said they had spotted a handful of cavalry on the "spur of a lofty mountain" 1,000 to 1,500 yards away, but that was the sole sighting of enemy troops reported. The Texans concluded that the only plausible explanation was a long-range shot by a sharpshooter who was either extraordinarily skilled or lucky. Good fortune was not Captain Woodward's lot, however. He was carried back to Front Royal, where he would linger for more than a month before dying on August 26.[25]

The loss of a good officer was always tragic, but Woodward's fate was all the more regrettable because the Confederates weren't trying to provoke a fight at Manassas Gap. Rather, Law's mission was to safeguard against any Yankee movement through the pass. He had no reason to push hard against Merritt's troopers, and he didn't. Desiring to keep the Federals on the defensive, however, he maneuvered aggressively enough to push the Yankee pickets and their reserves nearly back to Linden amid skirmishing that lasted more or less all day.[26]

Because the poor condition of the roads around Manassas Gap made the pass impracticable for use by artillery or wagons, Merritt did not believe the Rebels were attempting to force their way through or do anything more than essentially "feel" his lines. Nonetheless, the enemy exerted enough pressure to compel his retreat until the six 3-inch Ordnance Rifles in Captain William M. Graham's Battery K, 1st US Artillery went into action and helped stop the Rebel advance. Now aware there was an entire Confederate division in his front, Merritt sent a message to General Buford saying that he was "sorely pressed," and implied the pass could not be held much longer unless reinforcements were received soon.[27]

*   *   *

---

24 Ibid.

25 Ibid; Consolidated Service Records, 1st Texas Infantry, www.fold3.com

26 *OR* 27, pt. 1, 945; *OR* 27, pt. 2, 417; Stocker, *From Huntsville to Appomattox*, 130.

27 *OR* 27, pt. 1, 945; *OR* 27, pt. 3, 742; Stocker, *From Huntsville to Appomattox*, 130.

About 2:00 p.m., while Pickett, Law, and Wofford dealt with Union cavalry, A. P. Hill's corps reached the Shenandoah River. Traffic slowed to a crawl as the long line of troops funneled toward the pontoon bridges spanning the two branches. Assaulted by the hot July sun, the men endured the frustratingly familiar accordion-like motion of a column negotiating an obstacle. Forced to stand for long periods while awaiting the opportunity to move, they then had to rush ahead when the column suddenly pitched into motion, only to halt a few hundred yards down the road and repeat the process over again.[28]

Also threading its way toward the Shenandoah was the Virginia army's headquarters, which had marched south with Hill the previous day. About 4:00 p.m., Lee and his staff crossed the rivers via the bridges and were met on the far shore by William Buck, a prominent local citizen and father of the young lady who had tearfully watched the 17th Virginia march toward Manassas Gap the day before. Mr. Buck invited the general to stop for refreshments at his impressive two-story residence known as Bel Air, just a quarter mile east of town. Lee graciously accepted and a short while later he and his staff arrived at the Buck home.

As most of the junior officers took their ease under some Aspen trees, Lee, Colonel Robert H. Chilton (the army's chief of staff), and a few others retired to Bel Air's front porch, where the general was introduced to Buck's daughters Lucy and Nellie. Predictably, the girls were awed to be in the presence of the famous Virginian, and 20-year old Lucy was especially thrilled when Lee asked her to sit beside him. When she told Lee what an honor it was to see him, he teased her (as he was wont to do with young ladies), telling her he wished he was "more worthy of being seen" and suggested the "gallant young beaux" on his staff were more deserving of her gaze.[29]

When the guests moved inside, the officers rested for a brief time while enjoying fresh buttermilk and pleasant conversation with the Buck family. Lee asked the girls to sing some "Southern songs" and stood happily by the piano while they played. His fatherly banter and "courtly, dignified bearing," recalled an eyewitness, could not hide the war entirely from view. Lucy noted that the general's hair had "silvered" and his "brow [was]

---

28 Douglass diary, www.localhistory.morrisville.edu/sites/letters/owen10.html

29 Baer, *Shadows on My Heart*, 236.

Bel Air, the home of the Buck family, hosted Robert E. Lee and his staff on the afternoon of July 22, 1863. The residence and its occupants enjoyed a front row seat for the fighting in Manassas Gap the next day. *Warren Heritage Society*

marked with thought and care." Catching General Lee's "quick glance through a window toward the road where the columns of gray came marching on," she knew that "courteous interest" hid his true thoughts, which were with his "brave troops wading the Shenandoah and straining every nerve" to slip through the Blue Ridge before the Federals could interfere.[30]

After an interval that was all too brief, Lee rose to depart. He signed the girls' autograph books and expressed hope the family would remain unmolested by the enemy. Once more bantering with the ladies, he warned they shouldn't "let any of those fine young Yankee officers carry" them off. The girls responded that they were counting on him to see that didn't happen. With the pleasantries at an end, Lee led his staff to their horses, though he stopped along the way to kiss Lucy's infant brother who was sleeping in his

30 Baer, *Shadows on My Heart*, 236; *The Anderson Intelligencer*, January 3, 1906, 2.

buggy. With that, the general mounted his horse and, together with his staff, rode away.[31]

*   *   *

Thus far, the Confederate plan of operations was working almost perfectly and Lee had reason to be pleased. By the time the commander of the Army of Northern Virginia departed Bel Air, Pickett and Wofford had opened the exit of Chester Gap, and Longstreet's Corps with its accompanying trains were flowing eastward toward Gaines Crossroads in Culpeper County. A. P. Hill was almost completely across the swollen Shenandoah, Jeb Stuart's troopers were closing on Manassas Gap, and two-thirds of Ewell's corps was at Winchester. Only Early's division was more than a day's march from the Blue Ridge.

Inexplicably, Federal infantry had kept its distance. Another 24 hours would put the bulk of the Rebel army safely behind the Rappahannock River and again squarely between the Yankees and Richmond. Whether Meade would allow him to do so without a fight remained to be seen.

---

31 Baer, *Shadows on My Heart*, 236-237.

CHAPTER 10

"The Great Chess Board"

Northern Expectations—Meade Gets the Intelligence He Needs—The Army of the Potomac Resumes Its Advance—Buford's Dispatches—Three Missions—Meade Plans an Offensive—Misunderstanding the Situation

IF Robert E. Lee had reason to be pleased it was because he knew, and had known for several days, what he was trying to accomplish and how close he was to achieving his goal of slipping through the mountains and repositioning his army on the banks of the upper Rappahannock before the Federals could intervene.

George Meade could make no such claim. For him, the dawn of July 22 brought only continued uncertainty and more of the relentless pressure that had borne down on him since Gettysburg. From the moment that fight ended, extraordinary expectations had been heaped upon his shoulders by the public and the Lincoln administration. In the aftermath of Lee's escape across the Potomac River, Meade was certain those expectations were increasingly unrealistic, yet he still felt compelled to attempt their realization.

Already oppressed by the opinions of President Lincoln and General Halleck, Meade was also besieged by a gaggle of Northern newspaper editors who continued to imagine and editorialize that the Union army commander had a chance to annihilate General Lee. Indeed, even as the Confederates went about transferring the seat of war from the Shenandoah Valley to the Rappahannock River line, these newspapermen were telling their readers to "expect stirring news" from the Army of the Potomac at any moment.[1]

An editorial in the *New York Times* published that very morning offers a case in point. Commenting on the similarities between the current military situation and that following the September 1862 battle of Antietam, the paper noted that then, as now, Lee had been allowed to retreat across the Potomac after losing a battle. But the similarities ended there, the *Times* assured its readers, and there was "no reason to fear" the aftermath of Gettysburg would mimic that of Antietam.[2]

This confidence, continued the editorial, was predicated on the "new vigor and energy" animating the Union army. Meade had taken the lessons of 1862 to heart, the paper avowed, and would not repeat the blunders made by Major General George B. McClellan the previous fall. Although the *Times* confessed it lacked enough information to "forecast the nature of the coming campaign," it felt the "character of the great chess-board [was] so well understood" it would soon be easy to surmise the "general aspect of the grand game."[3]

With the Army of the Potomac on the strategic flank of the Rebels, only two moves were open to General Lee. He could either make a stand in the northern end of the Valley around Winchester, or he could shift his army east of the Blue Ridge Mountains toward Culpeper. If the Rebels chose the latter course, Meade could—or as the paper implied, *should*—seize the passes through which the enemy must march. Once this was done, Lee would have to stand and fight or retreat south up the Valley, allowing Meade to, in the first instance, engage Lee far from his base or, in the second circumstance, jump the Rappahannock River and cut him off from Richmond. Partaking of no speculation past these contingencies, the *Times* left little doubt that either eventuality would greatly hasten a victorious conclusion to the war. At least, this is how the "great chess-board" appeared to the newspapers and their readers above the Potomac.[4]

---

1   *The Washington Republican*, "The Pursuit of Lee," July 22, 1863 reprinted in *Troy Weekly Times*, July 26, 1863.

2   *New York Times*, July 22, 1863, "The New Campaign in Virginia."

3   Ibid.

4   Ibid.

George Meade would have liked little more than to have shared the certainty of success promised by Northern journals. But as day broke, he and his army remained frozen in place by contradictory intelligence. Until the fog of war dissipated, nothing could be done to meet the soaring hopes of the press or even the more modest desires of the army's commander.

The early morning ticked by with agonizing slowness as Meade waited for the information he so desperately needed. It was 7:00 a.m. before the first hints of Rebel intentions became available. They arrived courtesy of George Custer, who sent word that he had a prisoner from the 4th Texas who swore Hood's division had marched through Millwood 24 hours earlier on its way to Front Royal. Furthermore, the captive said pontoon bridges had been emplaced there and his impression was that Lee's army was "going back" to where it had "first started" its invasion of the North.[5]

Any claims by prisoners have to be considered carefully, for they are as apt to be lies and exaggerations as they are to be truth. Corroborating facts, relayed from observation posts on the mountains, however, soon verified this Texan's honesty. At 10:00 a.m., Custer sent a second dispatch stating that his lookouts at Ashby's Gap could see "large columns of troops . . . moving toward Front Royal." An "immense train" was headed in the same direction even as a large congregation of wagons went into park near the town. Two and a half hours later, Union signalmen at Snickers' Gap reported "a very large body of cavalry" passing through Berryville. A wagon train accompanied by "a strong escort" had already cleared the town and was "moving rapidly" ahead of the mounted column.[6]

It took time for these messages to filter into army headquarters, of course, and until they did, Federal soldiers enjoyed an extension of the rest they had been granted the day before. Their respite, however, would not survive the morning.

By 11:00 a.m., well before he received the info from the Snicker's Gap signalmen, Meade had seen enough dispatches to feel "satisfied" Lee was "in full movement" toward Culpeper or Orange Court House. Although he was still not willing to completely disregard the specter of a Confederate strike at Snickers' or Ashby's gaps, the general finally saw a chance to go over to the offensive and catch the Rebels at a disadvantage. If he could

5   *OR* 27, pt. 3, 740.

6   Ibid., 741.

shove three or more corps west through Manassas Gap and seize Front Royal, his army might cut off and overwhelm whatever part of Lee's force remained in the northern reaches of the Shenandoah Valley.[7]

Any meaningful hope of seizing this chance, however, meant Meade would have to act quickly. The morning had already worn away, and the clock was racing relentlessly toward midday by the time he issued a circular to his corps commanders, who were to move "immediately" upon its receipt. He knew it would be noon before any of them was likely to get on the road, but that couldn't be helped. During the half day that remained, the army would simply have to do its best to make up for some 35 hours of delay.

Meade began his move by directing William French's III Corps to advance 11 miles to Piedmont Station and "look to" Manassas Gap "with a view to supporting the cavalry" already there and maintaining possession of the pass. The V Corps, under Major General George Sykes, would simultaneously advance to Rectortown in support of French. Once Sykes was in place, but not before, the III Corps was to send a division to reinforce Merritt's cavalry in Manassas Gap. Meanwhile, the I Corps, now under Major General John Newton, would advance southeast to White Plains and act in support of French and Sykes, if needed.

To the north, the II Corps, temporarily led by Brigadier General William Hays, was to advance 10 miles to Paris and "be prepared to hold" Ashby's Gap "in the event of an attempt" by the Rebels to retake it. Major General Henry W. Slocum's XII Corps would remain at Snickersville with orders to likewise defend Snickers' Gap. The VI Corps, commanded by Major General John Sedgwick, was to accompany Brigadier General Henry J. Hunt's Artillery Reserve to Rector's Crossroads. Meade's last corps, the XI under Major General Oliver Otis Howard, would hold its position at Mountville southeast of Middleburg, but was to be ready to move on short notice. Army headquarters would be established at Upperville.

Judson Kilpatrick's cavalry would maintain its posts at Snickers' and Ashby's gaps. As soon as the I Corps reached White Plains, David Gregg would send part of his division to occupy Warrenton on the other side of the Bull Run Mountains. Buford, meanwhile, was ordered to hold Manassas Gap "as long as possible," and if practicable, until the III Corps arrived to

---

7 Ibid., 98.

assist him. Gamble's brigade was to watch Chester Gap and "report constantly [on the] movements of the enemy."[8]

At first blush, Meade's plan appears rather schizophrenic, for it divided the army between three separate missions in a situation that suggested the utility of concentration. In part this was because there was only so much space in the Loudoun Valley and only so many hours left before nightfall. Nonetheless, the general's own instructions made clear he was trying to accomplish multiple goals at the same time.

Two of the army's seven infantry corps, the II and the XII, had the defensive mission of protecting Snickers' and Ashby's gaps. Although they could march south or west from Snickersville and Paris to join any battle that might develop, the wording of Meade's circular made clear their primary task was to guard against the danger he had feared for several days: A Confederate offensive into the Loudoun Valley designed to cut his army off from Washington.

Dubious as that defensive mission might be, the orientation of the XI Corps and a third of the cavalry toward Warrenton was a logistical necessity. The army was eating its way through the rations it had carried south across the Potomac and would need to reestablish a railroad connection to the capital very soon. Warrenton, with its link to the Orange & Alexandria, was the only practicable point where this could be done. The town would have to be seized in the next few days, and it made sense to extend force in that direction preparatory to the inevitable move.

Placing Sedgwick's VI Corps and Hunt's Reserve Artillery at Rectors Crossroads served both defensive and offensive purposes. On the one hand, it was a measure of security for the army's center, guarding against any enemy strike northward through the Loudoun Valley. On the other hand, and perhaps more importantly, Sedgwick and Hunt could rush east or west to reinforce either wing of the army as circumstances dictated. The same could be said for Newton's I Corps. Although its principle mission was to support the thrust toward Manassas Gap, Newton's command would also be positioned to guard a temporary supply depot established at White Plains and could easily push east toward Warrenton if not called to the Blue Ridge.

Meade's two remaining corps were deployed with an offensive movement in mind. French's III Corps would advance toward the scene of

8 Ibid., 739-40.

yesterday's fighting at Manassas Gap. The V Corps under Sykes was stacked up behind French in the hope it could follow him through the pass and break out into the Shenandoah Valley. If need be, Sykes could reinforce the III Corps should it get into a serious fight for the pass. Practically speaking, however, he would be able to add little in the way of immediate offensive punch since the narrowness of the gap precluded the deployment of so large a force.

Because of the unavoidable late start there was no chance Union infantry could reach any of Buford's cavalrymen before dark. Merritt's troopers would have to do their best to hold onto Manassas Gap until French reinforced them, which at the earliest would probably be somewhere around midnight. As for Chester Gap, Meade had little choice but to let the Rebels do whatever they wanted there, with his cavalry merely observers of the scene.

*   *   *

The arrival of abrupt orders to move caught Meade's officers and soldiers by surprise. After laying in camp the previous day and receiving no orders to move that morning, most of the men had anticipated another day of rest. Those expectations were shattered when hurried instructions to pack up and get on the road spread through the bivouacs. Fortunately, the army was adept at rapid movement by this point in the war, and within an hour of being alerted the long blue columns were on their way.[9]

The II Corps left its bivouacs for Ashby's Gap at noon, while the V Corps headed toward Rectortown shortly thereafter and no later than 1:00. The VI Corps marched for Rectors Crossroads about the same time. For some reason, Meade's orders reached French later than the other corps commanders and it was 2:00 p.m. before his troops were on the move.[10]

9   Author Unknown, *History of 5th Massachusetts Battery* (Boston, MA,, 1902), 691.

10 Acken, *Inside the Army of the Potomac*, 319; J. L. Smith, *The History of the Corn Exchange Regiment, 118th Pennsylvania Volunteers, Antietam to Appomattox* (Philadelphia, PA, 1888), 286; *History of 5th Massachusetts Battery*, 691; Robert Westbrook, *History of the 49th Penn Vols.* (London, UK, 2013), 165-167; E. M. Woodward, *Our Campaigns* (Philadelphia, PA, 1865), 284; C. W. Bardeen, *A Little Fifer's War Diary* (Syracuse, NY, 1910), 252; Frank Moore, ed., *The Rebellion Record: A diary of American Events*, 8 vols. (New York, NY, 1864), vol. 7, 360; *OR* 27, pt. 1, 495-6.

Although the roads were generally good and the distances reasonable for the time allotted, the advance was not without its challenges. The sun beat down on the soldiers as they shuffled south in 80-degree heat, which made for what one private called a "hard, sultry trip" that taxed even the strongest of his comrades. The men had endured far worse in this campaign, however, and well before nightfall most had arrived at their destinations. The II Corps reached Paris and was going into bivouac by 5:00 p.m. The V Corps arrived at the tiny village of Rectortown around 4:30 p.m. Because of its later start, it was 7:00 p.m. before the III Corps marched into Piedmont Station.[11]

As Meade's troops neared the end of their day's march, evidence that Lee was pushing toward the Rappahannock became incontrovertible. At 6:00 p.m. Merritt reported Rebel cavalry columns "moving down the Valley" from Winchester to Front Royal alongside "large wagon trains" headed in the same direction. Sending word that he had been driven from Chester Gap, Gamble wrote Buford that there was "no doubt" the Confederates were advancing through the pass as "fast as [they] possibly can." Unable to impede that progress, Gamble could only add that he hoped the Army of the Potomac would "act accordingly."[12]

After hearing from Merritt and Gamble, Buford passed their dispatches on to Pleasonton, amplifying each by stating he was "convinced that Longstreet is marching direct to Culpeper or Gordonsville." Though he felt certain of the enemy's intentions, Buford confessed he knew nothing of the Union army's movements or what he was now "expected to do." Declaring that it would be pointless for his troopers to contend against a heavy force of Rebel infantry, the general decided to confine himself to observing and reporting on the Confederate movements.[13]

Absent alternate instructions, Buford told Pleasonton he was directing Gamble to stay where he was and ordering Merritt to retire to Orleans, about six miles southeast of Barbee's Crossroads and within striking distance of the route Longstreet was likely to follow. The 1st Cavalry Division's train of

11 Unknown, *History of the 5th Massachusetts Battery*, 691; J .L., Smith, *Corn Exchange Regiment*, 286; Acken, *Inside the Army of the Potomac*, 319; Bardeen, *A Little Fifer's War Diary*, 252; Ruth Silliker, ed., *The Rebel Yell & Yankee Hurrah: The Civil War Journal of A Maine Volunteer* (Camden, MI, 1985), 113-14, entry for July 22 misdated July 26.

12 *OR* 27, pt. 3, 741 -742. Time (2:00 p.m.) must be wrong as it is clearly written after 6:00 p.m.

13 *OR* 27, pt. 3, 741-2, mislabeled 2:30 p.m.

nearly empty wagons, together with part of Tom Devin's brigade, would be sent "half way to Warrenton" during the night in order to get it out of the way. The next morning, Buford would lead the remainder of Devin's command to reinforce Merritt at Orleans.[14]

Fast on the heels of Buford's news, additional intelligence arrived from Colonel McIntosh, whose cavalry brigade was still stationed around Hillsboro. At 7:00 p.m. he reported that some "intelligent young men" who had entered his lines to evade Confederate conscription agents claimed Longstreet had marched for Front Royal three days ago and that Fitz Lee had moved in the same direction during the morning of the 22nd. As far as McIntosh could tell, only a handful of Rebel cavalry regiments remained in the area around Charles Town and along the Shenandoah River opposite Snickers' Gap.[15]

All of this news added up to convincing evidence that Lee was evacuating the Valley. Two additional messages received at Meade's headquarters late that evening added further confirmation. One dispatch sent from the signal station at Ashby's Gap stated that the Valley Pike was "alive with wagons trains" and that several hundred vehicles and four batteries of artillery were moving on Front Royal. Additionally, "a goodly number of stragglers" were visible on the road between Millwood and Front Royal—a sure indication that a significant body of troops had passed that way recently. Rebel infantry columns and wagons had also been spotted on the Strasburg pike. Furthermore, there were no longer any sizable Confederate camps to be seen around Winchester, while "heavy bodies" of Southern cavalry had been sighted "at and beyond Berryville." A second dispatch, sent at 7:50 p.m. from Manassas Gap, reported "clouds of dust, evidently from the passage of heavy columns" drifting into the air above the pike connecting Winchester and Front Royal.[16]

His conclusion of the forenoon vindicated by these messages, Meade felt he finally had enough information to take the initiative. Despite numerous reports that the Confederates had been withdrawing through Front Royal and Chester Gap for two days, he thought it "probable that but a small

14 Ibid.

15 Ibid., 742-3.

16 Ibid., 743-4.

portion" of Lee's army had made its way beyond the Blue Ridge. Therefore, he perceived an opportunity to strike the Rebels by forcing his way through Manassas Gap and then slamming the Rebel escape hatch shut by capturing Front Royal. This done, five Federal corps would pour through the pass into the Valley and catch a sizable portion of Lee's army while it was on the move and weakened by whatever elements had managed to flee through the mountains.[17]

Having determined upon his plan, Meade issued orders that night which would put it into motion at 4:00 a.m. the next day. The Federal I and XI corps would march east, the former to secure Warrenton and the latter to occupy New Baltimore. Here, along with two of Gregg's cavalry brigades already in that region, they would protect the Orange & Alexandria Railroad, which would become the army's principle line of communication.[18]

The remainder of Meade's command would shift to Manassas Gap in hope of launching an attack on the Confederates "now moving through Front Royal and Chester Gap." General French, followed by General Sykes, was to advance into the gap. After leaving a brigade on guard at Ashby's Gap, the II Corps would march south to Markham Station just outside the entrance to Manassas Gap. Once there, it would hold itself in readiness to aid French and Sykes if and as needed. Slocum's XII Corps would advance to Paris, relieve the II Corps brigade holding Ashby's Gap (which would then move to rejoin its command) and stand by to "move at a moment's warning" to wherever it was directed.[19]

John Sedgwick was ordered to send a division to White Plains, where it could protect the Engineer Battalion and Reserve Artillery that were also directed to that spot. The rest of his VI Corps would move to Rectortown, where it was to "be prepared to move to Manassas Gap or [in any] other direction at a moment's notice." Both the III and V corps were instructed to leave their trains in the rear—the III parking its wagons at Piedmont Station and the V at Rectortown—in order to both speed their march and increase their maneuverability.[20]

17 Ibid., pt. 1, 98.

18 Ibid.

19 Ibid.

20 Ibid.

This plan would have been a good one 48 hours earlier, and might even have had a chance to accomplish something meaningful if it had been launched 24 hours before. But by the time it would be put in motion on the morning of July 23, it was hopelessly out of date. This was primarily because Meade seriously misunderstood the strategic situation and failed to wholly grasp what the Rebels had been doing over the last three days.

A great deal more than "a small portion" of Lee's command had slipped through the mountains. Daylight on the 23rd found Longstreet well past Chester Gap and all but a single brigade of A. P. Hill's corps moving through the pass close behind. Even as Meade prepared to lunge west with five of his seven corps, two-thirds of the Rebel army was rapidly marching eastward, already beyond his reach.[21]

Failing to understand this, Meade directed his blow at the wrong point. Instead of routing his troops southward through the Loudoun Valley in order to bring Longstreet's and Hill's columns to bay and jam up Ewell's probable course through the mountains, Meade chose to fight his way through the awful terrain of Manassas Gap—a battlefield so narrow he could deploy only a single corps, and that with great difficulty. What's more, the pass was reportedly occupied by an entire Rebel division, which all but ensured it would take considerable effort and time to get to Front Royal. Even if the Union army managed to seize that point, it would be fairly easy for whatever enemy formations remained in the Valley to make a rapid march southwest through Strasburg in order to cross the Blue Ridge, far from Meade's ability to interfere.

By heading in the wrong direction, the Union general risked missing his last opportunity to force Lee into battle before the Confederates were safely behind the Rappahannock. There was, however, a slight hope that Meade's misguided thrust could manage to inflict a serious wound. If French acted aggressively with his III Corps, it was possible he might take Manassas Gap and Front Royal so quickly that Ewell would be caught by surprise. Should that happen, the bulk of the Army of the Potomac could attack an isolated Rebel corps and perhaps, just perhaps, wreck a third of Lee's army.

Those were not the stakes Meade thought he was playing for, but they were the only ones actually within his grasp. Whatever the Federals thought they might accomplish, a great deal now depended on General French. If he

---

21 Ibid.

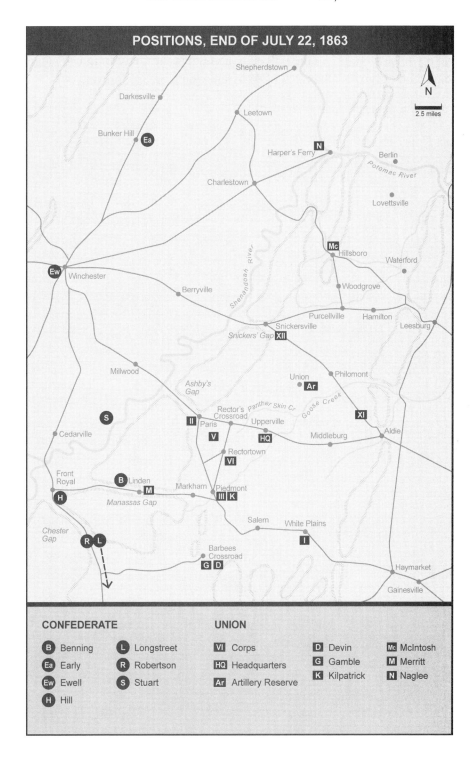

POSITIONS, END OF JULY 22, 1863

N

2.5 miles

Shepherdstown

Darkesville

Leetown

Bunker Hill   Ea

Harper's Ferry   N

Berlin

Potomac River

Charlestown

Lovettsville

Mc Hillsboro

Waterford

Ew Winchester

Shenandoah River

Berryville

Woodgrove

Purcellville   Hamilton

Leesburg

Snickersville

Snickers' Gap XII

Millwood

Union

Philomont

Ashby's Gap

Ar

Rector's Crossroad

Panther Skin Cr.

Goose Creek

XI

II Paris   Upperville

Middleburg

Aldie

S

V

HQ

Cedarville

VI Rectortown

Front Royal

B Linden

M

Markham   Piedmont

H

III K

Manassas Gap

Salem   White Plains

Chester Gap

R L

I

Barbees Crossroad

G D

Haymarket

Gainesville

CONFEDERATE

- B Benning
- Ea Early
- Ew Ewell
- H Hill
- L Longstreet
- R Robertson
- S Stuart

UNION

- VI Corps
- HQ Headquarters
- Ar Artillery Reserve
- D Devin
- G Gamble
- K Kilpatrick
- Mc McIntosh
- M Merritt
- N Naglee

handled the III Corps with skill and decisiveness there was an important victory to be won. If he failed, fleeting hopes that the Gettysburg campaign might end differently than that of Antietam would be lost forever.

CHAPTER 11

"This Was Precisely the Time to Attack"

Major General French—The Union III Corps Moves on Manassas Gap—Wright's Brigade Assumes a Blocking Position—Shock at the Arrival of So Many Yankees—A Plea for Help—Rebel Reinforcements Far Away

WILLIAM H. French was new to corps command. The 48-year-old general cut something less than the ideal military figure, with his portly visage, red-face, sleepy eyes, and bushy mustache. Still, he had a solid résumé. The general graduated from West Point in 1837, drew a commission in the artillery corps, earned two brevets for gallantry in Mexico, fought Seminoles in Florida, and co-authored an artillery manual. He was a captain in the 1st US Artillery in West Texas when the war broke out in 1861. Refusing to surrender his troops to secessionists, French instead marched his men down the Rio Grande to the Gulf of Mexico and sailed his command for Key West. That kind of grit got a lot of notice at the start of the war, as it should have, and shortly thereafter French was made a brigadier.

Promotion came quickly. He earned praise and a bump to major general for his actions during the Peninsula campaign. His future looked bright until the division he was tapped to lead drew difficult assignments that would include attacking the Sunken Road at Antietam, charging Marye's Heights at Fredericksburg, and forlornly attempting to hold a key position at Chancellorsville. French was in command of the Harpers Ferry garrison at the outset of the Gettysburg campaign, during which he dispatched the cavalry that destroyed the pontoon bridge Lee left over the Potomac when he

Major General William H. French
Library of Congress

invaded Maryland. When Meade assigned French's division to the shot-up III Corps after Gettysburg, French assumed its command on the basis of seniority.

The men of the III Corps did not take to their new general. French was a stranger who had done his fighting in the II Corps, and thus out of their sight. They compared him unfavorably with their previous commander, Dan Sickles. Although he was an infamous rogue of suspect competence, and practically without formal military training, the brave, dashing, and brash former politician lost a leg at Gettysburg and won the hearts of most of his men. When French was installed as his replacement, the corps' veterans resented the fact that one of their own generals had not received the assignment.

No one quite knew what to make of French. Maybe his bloody experiences at Antietam, Fredericksburg, and Chancellorsville had permanently ingrained caution into his makeup. Certainly, the physical comparison between him and Sickles was not to the former's credit. Still, it remained to be seen whether appearances deceived or all too clearly indicated the caliber of the man. Either way, Manassas Gap was going to be his first opportunity to prove himself at the head of a corps.

When French and his III Corps arrived at Piedmont Station around 7:00 p.m. on July 22, stark evidence of the ravages of war were all around to greet them. The village had come into existence as a stop on the Manassas Gap Railroad in 1852 and earned a footnote in history when Confederate forces massed there in 1861 to board trains that carried them to the battle of Bull Run—the first combat rail movement of troops in recorded history. The community gained further notoriety in late 1862 as the spot where George

McClellan relinquished command of the Army of the Potomac to Ambrose Burnside. Unfortunately, the railroad brought with it woe as well as fame.

During the Second Manassas campaign, Rebel troops tore up Piedmont's rails and destroyed its rolling stock to deny their use to Union forces. The totality of that destruction was still evident a year later. The once romantic little hamlet remained a scene of devastation. Wrecked locomotives rusted alongside twisted iron rails and half-burned railroad ties. Partially destroyed bridges and culverts littered the landscape, which was further disfigured by the remains of a dilapidated station house whose broken windows and smashed doors gave the place a slightly haunted air.[1]

It was a depressing prospect for a bivouac, but only part of the III Corps would spend the night amongst the railroad's ghosts. Obedient to Meade's orders, General French directed his 1st Division, temporarily commanded by Brigadier General John Henry Hobart Ward, to move on to Manassas Gap and reinforce Federal cavalry defending the important pass. Ward immediately ordered his brigades into motion and sent an officer riding ahead with instructions to ascertain the state of affairs in the gap from General Buford, who was supposed to be at Linden. The rider was also to inform the cavalryman that assistance was on the way.

When he reached Linden, Ward's messenger found a very worried Wesley Merritt instead of John Buford. The young general was on edge, as well he might be, after spending two days confronting Rebel infantrymen who had grown in number from a single regiment to a full division with alarming speed. Expecting to be attacked early the next morning, the cavalryman was anxious for any help he could obtain, and no doubt relieved to discover assistance was finally near at hand.[2]

Getting that assistance to Merritt would prove more difficult than commonly believed. Only an hour into Ward's march, dusk enveloped the countryside. Night fell quickly in the shadow of the mountains and the first quarter moon would not rise until after midnight. Nonetheless, Ward's men continued to move through the darkness, stumbling along rocky roads that became increasingly steep as they led up into Manassas Gap. It was 11:00 p.m. before Ward called a halt near the village of Petersburg—eight miles

1   Warren Cudworth, *History of the First Regiment Massachusetts Infantry* (Boston, MA, 1866), 413.

2   *OR* 27, pt. 1, 495-6.

west of Piedmont Station and just a mile and a half shy of Linden. Ward allowed his exhausted troops to catch a few hours' sleep prior to resuming their journey.[3]

Confederate regiments were also on the march that night. About dusk, Evander Law began shifting three of the four brigades in Hood's division to the Chester Gap road. They would camp there for the night prior to following the rest of Longstreet's corps through the mountains the next morning. Henry Benning's brigade of Georgians, reinforced with the 4th and 15th Alabama, was left behind to keep watch on Manassas Gap. Law ordered Benning to hold his position until relieved by units from A. P. Hill's corps, which should be on hand no later than daylight, and then move on to rejoin the division "as soon as possible."[4]

A little before dawn on July 23, Ward's Federal infantrymen were roused from their short slumber and put back into motion. By 5:00 a.m. they were at Linden. Riding over to confer with Merritt, Ward learned for the first time that the cavalry had been ordered to Orleans and would soon depart. In view of this news, the general quickly deployed his troops, dispatching infantry to replace the horsemen, ordering his artillery into position, and sending scouts forward to see what they could learn of the enemy. That done, he settled in to await events.[5]

The bulk of the III Corps began moving about the same time Ward's regiments started taking up their posts. General French allowed his troops a "swallow of coffee in lieu of breakfast," recalled one disgruntled soldier, and then ordered them on their way to Manassas Gap. The first rays of sunshine were breaking through the dark gloom when these Union soldiers picked their way past the wreckage of the railroad and began the long climb toward the enemy.[6]

Full daylight found the blue column tramping through a setting of breathtaking beauty. Wherever the mountain slope "was gradual and easy," wrote one, farmers had cleared away the underbrush to plant "grass, clover and grain." The black soil—"exceedingly rich"—produced vibrant green

---

3   Ibid.

4   *OR* 27, pt. 2, 417-18; Stocker, *From Huntsville to Appomattox*, 130.

5   *OR* 27, pt. 1, 496.

6   Haley, *Rebel Yell & Yankee Hurrah*, 114.

pastures whose encompassing stone or rail fences accented the bucolic scene.[7]

The countryside was idyllic, but the path along which the column traveled was "rougher than anything the Army of the Potomac had ever before experienced," grumbled a Massachusetts man. The ground was covered with "loose stones . . . of all sizes and shapes," some several feet high and just as wide. Tall grass camouflaged many of these treacherous obstacles, which often remained unseen until an unfortunate soldier or animal stumbled over them. The roadway was made more miserable by innumerable little creeks cutting across its path and often sharing its bed, creating washouts and potholes in addition to muddy sloughs. The route was so bad, men accustomed to the toils of battery horses and mule teams felt pangs of sympathy for the poor brutes as they watched the hard-working animals trip over small boulders or be "jerked and twitched about" to evade the rocks that could be avoided.[8]

Despite the poor road and uphill climb, by 9:00 a.m. the head of the corps reached Linden. French directed Ward to send a small battalion of skirmishers forward to "feel the enemy and compel him to show his pickets." Meanwhile, the Federal corps commander was determined to take every precaution to ensure his rear and flanks were as "well-guarded as the rugged nature of the country permitted."[9]

Companies were detached from regiments and regiments from brigades to watch side roads winding over the mountains. Batteries were sent to occupy high ground, and a signal station was established atop a peak north of the gap. Obtaining these vantage points was time-consuming, difficult, and exhausting work. In some spots it took a dozen horses to pull a single gun into position.[10]

Taxing though it was, the outfits detailed to such duty found compensation for their labors in the form of an "ocean of blackberries" covering the steep slopes. For hungry men such delights were not to be

7 Cudworth, *History of the First Regiment Massachusetts Infantry*, 413-4.

8 Ibid.

9 *OR* 27, pt., 1, 489.

10 Thomas Osborn, *Battery D, 1st New York Light Artillery, Winslow's Battery* (Albany, NY, Printers, 1902), 1207.

neglected, and the troops, wrote Private John Haley of the 17th Maine, were soon "diligently engaged in making blackberry jam."[11]

There were pleasures for the eyes as well as the stomach. The view from the heights was "soul-enchanting [and] exquisitely beautiful," thought Private Haley. Front Royal, nestled in the western foreground, stood in charming relief before the "swelling ranges" that gave the Valley its spectacular terrain. Distant massifs adorned the horizon "like mighty billows," while to left and right, the "abrupt spurs and towering peaks of the Blue Ridge" framed the scene. Turning around to look eastward, Union soldiers marveled at the "tranquil loveliness" of the Loudoun Valley. Regardless of the direction one gazed, the vista was, recorded an impressed Northerner, "well calculated to rivet the attention and awaken the admiration of the beholder."[12]

Closer examination, however, revealed more martial—and much less pleasant—visages. From hilltop perches, Northern soldiers watched in silence as Rebel troops crossed the Shenandoah River, their formations appearing to Private Haley like "long, gray serpents" slithering "through the wheat fields far below." A large body of enemy infantry, he continued, "moving in close column and most perfect order" was clearly visible, as were wagon trains "extending as far as could be seen." While the Federals watched, Confederate brigades massed in woods at the foot of the mountains, "as deliberate in their movements" as though the Union army was a "thousand miles away."[13]

Among those surveying the enemy was Lieutenant Colonel Julius Hayden, the III Corps' chief of staff, whom French had dispatched to make what was tantamount to an aerial reconnaissance. Completing this duty and returning to Linden, Hayden related what he had seen. His observations, and those of others, were taken as confirmation that the Rebels were fleeing the Valley through the Blue Ridge passes.

Everyone assumed that only a single enemy corps had made its escape thus far, and that the force seen approaching Front Royal was the advance of a second Rebel corps, while a third "must yet be in the rear." There was, of

---

11 Haley, *Rebel Yell & Yankee Hurrah*, 114.

12 Ibid.; Cudworth, *History of the First Regiment Massachusetts Infantry*, 415-16; Moore, *Rebellion Record*, vol. 7, 360.

13 Haley, *Rebel Yell & Yankee Hurrah*, 114.

course, no definitive proof of this conclusion, but neither was there evidence it was false. All the prisoners taken to date at either Manassas or Chester gaps had been from Longstreet's corps—a fact that tended to support the preferred analysis.[14]

Regardless, it was clear the Confederates were hurrying elsewhere, either farther up the Valley or through Chester Gap just beyond sight. General French guessed the force to his front was nothing more than a flank guard, put in place to delay any thrust that might interfere with the enemy's retreat. If true, there could be no doubt that the "situation was eminently favorable" for carrying out Meade's plan to "cut the Rebel column in two" and destroy half or more of Lee's army. This was, as one Northern reporter on the scene put it, "precisely the time to attack." A vigorous push on Front Royal would disrupt the foe's passage of the rivers and open the western exit of Manassas Gap, allowing the Union army to pour into the Valley and swamp whatever Confederates it found in its path. Here was the opportunity to reap the final harvest of the Gettysburg campaign. Aggressive action may well win the day, and might go far toward winning the war.[15]

General French, however, thought otherwise. The sight of multitudes of gray uniforms drew him up short, and made the new corps commander cautious rather than bold. Where some saw opportunity, French saw only danger. Where others saw the need for quick action, French came up with reasons to remain in place. With so many Rebels visible, how many remained unseen? Perhaps their presence was simply screened by the mountains hemming in the III Corps?

The appearance of 50 or so shadowy figures on a hillside near Linden exposed the general's sensitivity to that imagined possibility. When word of these soldiers reached the alarmed commander, French hurriedly deployed the 20th Indiana to confront this threat to his right flank, only to have the Hoosiers discover the supposed menace to be a party of Union stragglers stealing sheep from an abandoned Virginia homestead. The mistake did little to mollify the benign outcome of this encounter, and certain that rashness just now might cost the Union more than it could afford, French proceeded

14 Moore, *Rebellion Record*, vol. 7, 361.

15 *OR* 27, pt., 1, 489; Moore, *Rebellion Record*, vol. 7, 361.

with his protracted and muscle-bound steps to guard every byway and trail emerging into the gap, ignoring the waiting opportunity within his grasp.[16]

Indeed, French took so many precautions that some of his officers and many in the ranks spent the morning convinced they had come to defend Manassas Gap rather than attack through it. Others took a cynical view of the defensive preparations, believing the high command had no real desire for a battle whatsoever. Among them was Private Haley of the 17th Maine, who quipped that the "Rebel object was not to fight, but to escape; ours seemed to be the same."[17]

French was apparently as ignorant of such opinions as he was ill-disposed to take chances. For now, he was willing to poke at the Southerners along his front, but he would not push hard until he could advance with his entire force, armed with the confidence of victory.[18]

*   *   *

The enemy awaiting French's thrust was Ambrose Wright's brigade of Richard Anderson's division, A. P. Hill's corps. After marching from Front Royal that morning, Wright's command had relieved Benning's Georgians about 9:00 a.m., just as the main body of the III Corps reached Linden. Wright's four subordinate commands—the 3rd, 22nd, and 48th Georgia, and 2nd Georgia battalion—had seen heavy fighting at Gettysburg and could boast of making a deeper penetration of Meade's line than any other unit. That honor had come at a high price in casualties, and the brigade could muster just 600 men this day.[19]

One of those missing from the brigade's ranks that July 23 was its commander, Ambrose R. Wright. A prewar lawyer, Wright was an aggressive fighter who possessed a bit "too much dash" in the opinion of

---

16 Susan Gilbreath Lane, ed. *Dignity of Duty: The Journals of Erasmus Corwin Gilbreath, 1861-1898* (Chicago, IL, 2013), 104.

17 Regis De Trobriand, *Four Years with the Army of the Potomac*, (Boston, MA, 1889), 526; Haley, *Rebel Yell & Yankee Hurrah*, 114.

18 *OR* 27, pt., 1, 489-90.

19 Ibid., pt. 2, 626; Charles Andrews, *Condensed history of the 3rd Georgia Volunteer Infantry*, Georgia Archives, 1885, www.3gvi.org/ga3hist1.html; *OR* 27, pt. 2, 560; Stocker, *From Huntsville to Appomattox*, 130.

division commander Richard Anderson. In fact, Wright's superior felt the Georgian could benefit from "a little more coolness" both on and off the battlefield. Just now, the brigadier was still bitter over what he concluded was a lack of support at Gettysburg, where his troops had briefly made a lodgement atop Cemetery Ridge late on the afternoon of July 2 only to see their success wasted for want of reinforcements. Simmering discontent over that issue exacerbated Wright querulous disposition and produced a clash with Anderson over a routine question regarding the brigade's transportation. The argument led to his arrest for insubordination and removal from command.[20]

In Wright's absence, Colonel Edward J. Walker of the 3rd Georgia led the men. General Benning consulted with Walker—an 1851 graduate of the South Carolina Military Academy and the only surviving field officer in the brigade after Gettysburg—before leaving to rejoin Law, assuring the colonel there was little more than Yankee cavalry in Manassas Gap. Moreover, the blue horsemen appeared satisfied to stay at arm's length and thus posed little danger.[21]

For Walker and his men, Benning's report was comforting news. Nonetheless, to be on the safe side, Walker deployed his troops as though a much greater threat loomed. The 3rd Georgia, under Captain Charles H. Andrews—a 28-year-old pre-war druggist from Madison, Georgia—was stretched out as skirmishers and posted on the far south end of Wapping Heights. Its position was "somewhat in advance of and disconnected from the balance of the brigade," which was placed on a ridge several hundred yards to the rear.[22]

Because there was too much ground to cover with his under strength command, Walker spread his remaining two regiments out as skirmishers as well. The 48th Georgia under Captain Matthew R. Hall took the right of the line while Captain Benjamin C. McCurry's 22nd Georgia deployed on the left, its northern flank resting on the railroad. Two of the four companies in

20 Andrews, *Condensed history of the 3rd Georgia* www.3gvi.org/ga3hist1.html; Dorothy Herring, *Company C of the Twenty-Second Georgia Infantry Regiment in the Confederate Service* (Westminster, MD, 2000), 185.

21 Ibid; Krick, *Lee's Colonels*, 382; *OR* 27, pt. 2, 626. The South Carolina Military Academy became the Citadel Military College.

22 *OR* 27, pt. 2, 626; Charles H. Andrews papers, SHC/UNC http://finding-aids.lib.unc.edu/02849/.

Captain Charles J. Moffett's 2nd Georgia Battalion were deployed as skirmishers in front of McCurry and to the left of Andrews on Wapping Heights. The remaining pair was sent one and a half miles to the rear to defend the intersection of the main road and the lane leading to Wapping House.[23]

For almost an hour after stationing his men, Walker rested easy in Benning's assertion—mostly accurate when made—that there was nothing to fear in Manassas Gap other than Yankee cavalry. Then, at 10:00 a.m., to the horror and amazement of the colonel and his troops, large numbers of Federal infantry, apparently in corps strength, made its appearance.[24]

Just as the Federals moved into view, a signal corps detachment from General Ewell's headquarters arrived on Wapping Heights. The specialists had been sent to assure Colonel Walker that the Second Corps was "marching rapidly" for the pass and to request a careful estimate of how many enemy troops were nearby. That responsibility fell to Captain Andrews who used his field glasses to scan the surrounding countryside, which was rapidly filling with blue uniforms.[25]

No doubt relieved to learn help was on the way, Andrews surely must have felt growing alarm as he methodically examined the deploying III Corps through his binoculars. Noting the various corps, division, and brigade flags as he spotted them, the captain soon concluded there were anywhere from 10,000 to 20,000 Yankees in his front. Realizing the import of these observations, the signalmen quickly wigwagged a message to Ewell telling him that Wright's (Walker's) 600 men, aided by neither cavalry nor artillery, were confronting upwards of 20,000 Federals. The transmission ended with a somewhat superfluous plea for Ewell to "hasten to our support!"[26]

By the time this message was sent, there was no chance help could be obtained from anyone else. Longstreet's corps, except for Benning's brigade, was already well past the eastern exit of Chester Gap. Having marched all the previous night, it was moving relentlessly on Gaines

23 *OR* 27, pt. 2, 626; Herring, *Company C*, 185.

24 Ibid.

25 Ibid.

26 Ibid.

Crossroads and well beyond recall. Hill's corps, following Longstreet, was equally out of position to assist. Already working its way through the mountains, most of Hill's infantry was near or beyond the gap's entrance, while the rest of his column so clogged the pass that when Benning reached the western end of the gap he found the road "perfectly blockaded" by Hill's long wagon train.[27]

The only Confederates within supporting distance belonged to Stuart's cavalry, which had marched for Front Royal from near Millwood at 8:00 a.m. Crossing the Shenandoah below Berry's Ferry at Island Ford, the brigades under Fitz Lee, Jenkins, and Ferguson had ridden to Happy Creek Station, just a few miles east of Front Royal. Dismounting his men there for a time, Stuart learned that Wesley Merritt had beaten him to the punch and already occupied Manassas Gap.[28]

Since the Yankee cavalry around Linden appeared unlikely to cause trouble, and Wright's infantry already held a blocking position in the pass, Stuart decided there was no need for his troopers to linger in the area. Electing to move on to the Rappahannock, he began shifting his command toward Chester Gap. As the Rebel horsemen rode away, Walker sent a message asking the cavalrymen if they could spare a battery to strengthen his position. Unfortunately for the Georgian, Beckham's battalion of horse artillery had taken a different route toward Front Royal and the troopers had no guns to offer.[29]

This meant the only help available for Colonel Walker was Ewell's Second Corps, but it was still a good distance away. The night before, Ed Johnson's division and Ewell's headquarters had camped along Red Bud Run, about a mile north of Winchester. Robert Rodes' division had bivouacked that same night astride Abrams Creek, which flowed just east of the town. Early's command, a full day's march behind the other two divisions courtesy of its thrust against Kelley's Federals, had spent the night at Bunker Hill.[30]

---

27 *OR* 27, pt. 2, 418; Stocker, *From Huntsville to Appomattox*, 130-31.

28 Morrissett Diary, MOCW; Swank, *Sabres, Saddles and Spurs*, 85.

29 Trout, *Memoirs of Stuart Horse Artillery Battalion: Moorman's and Hart's Batteries*, 2010, 107; Morrissett Diary, MOCW, *Swank, Sabres, Saddles and Spurs*, 85; *OR* 27, pt. 2, 626.

30 McDonald, *Make Me a Map*, 162.

All three formations resumed their southward march early on the morning of the 23rd, but it would take most of the day for Rodes and Johnson to reach Front Royal, and longer still for them to get troops into Manassas Gap. That meant Walker would have to hold out against impossible odds for upwards of six or seven hours before any support could be expected. Nonetheless, there could be no thought of retreat, for to give up the pass was to allow what looked like Meade's entire army to come storming down on Ewell's strung-out corps.

The Georgians would have to fight for every inch of ground. Captain Andrews went along his line instructing his men "not to waste a shot," and to hold their fire until the enemy was close enough for each of them "to make sure of his man." Irrespective of Rebel marksmanship, he knew that when the Yankees launched any form of assault, the outcome could not be in doubt. Walker's men might be determined to buy every minute possible for Ewell, but watching more and more Federal flags crowd into the valley below, they suspected it would take something akin to a miracle for any of them to survive the day.[31]

31 Andrews, *Condensed History of the 3rd GA*, www.3gvi.org/ga3hist1.html.

Chapter 12

"We Resisted Them to the Utmost of Human Capacity"

The Fight for Manassas Gap Begins—The Stand of Wright's Brigade—French's Caution—Confederate Reinforcements Arrive—Assault of the Excelsior Brigade—Night Stops the Battle

ALTHOUGH their situation looked grim, Walker's 600 or so Confederates at Manassas Gap comprising the Gettysburg survivors of Wright's brigade were not totally devoid of advantages. Principle among these was geography. The narrow pass made it impossible for the enemy to deploy on a front longer than Walker's command, so the threat of being outflanked was minimal. The Rebels would also be defending high ground, and the approaches to their line were rugged and difficult. Furthermore, the gap's topography made it problematic for the Yankees to effectively deploy artillery.

Perhaps the most important advantage the Southerners enjoyed was not related to geography but character. The Federal general opposing them was in no hurry to strike, and appeared more concerned about being attacked from an unexpected direction than charging through the gap and disrupting Ewell's corps. French was not only determined to be careful, he was also deploying, for the first time, the largest formation he had ever commanded in battle—something that could be said for a significant number of his subordinates as well.

All three of French's division commanders had replaced men lost at Gettysburg or who had been promoted into new positions since the battle.

The same was true for two of the three brigades in French's 1st Division. Additionally, the corps had lost about one-third of its men in Pennsylvania, including a high percentage of its officers. The majority of its regiments were woefully under strength. Thanks to these factors, the Federals would move with sluggishness on a day when speed was all-important.

Rather than send a "small battalion" forward to discover the Confederate positions, as directed, General Hobart Ward deployed most of his own brigade to do the job. It was a logical choice, not only because he knew these troops best, but because the 1,400-man brigade was the largest in the division. By contrast, the other two brigades in the division mustered just 776 and 897 bayonets.[1]

Since Ward was running the division, his brigade was under Colonel Hiram Berdan, the leader of the renowned 1st US Sharpshooters. That regiment, along with the 20th Indiana, 63rd Pennsylvania, 3rd Maine, 2nd US Sharpshooters, and the 4th Maine spread out into skirmish formation and readied itself to move toward the Rebels. The 86th New York, 99th Pennsylvania, and 124th New York took position behind these regiments as their supports. So deployed, Berdan had roughly 900 men detailed as skirmishers and another 500 in reserve.[2]

About 11:00 a.m., the mile-wide Federal line extending from one side of the pass to the other moved to within a short distance of the Rebels and the firing began. For men who had seen the fury of Gettysburg, however, the struggle seemed to one participant "almost like opera bouffe." As they methodically loaded and fired, Union soldiers often paused to "eat a mouthful of blackberries" between shots. One soldier felt the combatants "seemed very good-natured" about the whole thing and "fought in the most leisurely way." The Northerners looked none too anxious to launch a serious attack and they did not. The Confederates appeared, thought a Federal, "equally apathetic."[3]

The fitful shooting went on for several hours to no noticeable effect other than to knock a few men out of the lines, including Colonel Walker who fell with a severe bullet wound in his right thigh. As senior captain,

1 Bradley Gottfried, *Brigades of Gettysburg* (Cambridge, MA, 2002), 187-194.

2 Noah Andre Trudeau, *Gettysburg: A Testing of Courage* (New York, NY, 2002), 571.

3 Andrews, *Condensed History of the 3rd GA* www.3gvi.org/ga3hist1.html; *OR* 27, pt. 2, 626; Bardeen, *A Little Fifer's War*, 255.

Benjamin McCurry of the 22nd Georgia should have taken command of the brigade, but being in feeble health, it was all he could do to manage his own regiment. The responsibility thus passed to the 3rd Georgia's Captain Charles Andrews, who sent word back for Captain Victor Jean Baptiste Girardey, the brigade's assistant adjutant general, to take charge of the left of the line while Andrews maintained direction of its right.[4]

Shortly after Walker went down, General Ewell appeared on the scene accompanied by General Rodes, whose divisional column was the leading element of the corps. Having received the distressing wigwag message from Wapping Heights a few hours earlier, Ewell and Rodes along with a few staff officers had ridden ahead to access the state of affairs for themselves. The paltry size of Andrews' force was readily apparent, while, across the way Ewell could see the "insignia of two corps" and indications a third was nearby. From what the Second Corps commander could tell, there were some 10,000 Yankees already in view and more on the way.[5]

No matter how heroic its resistance might be, Wright's diminished brigade could not stand for long against such overwhelming odds. Ewell, who had already directed Rodes to bring his division into the pass to block the Union advance, now sent word for Edward Johnson to hurry his command to Front Royal as well. Urging Andrews to maintain his position as long as possible, Ewell promised that "reinforcements were coming up," and then rode back to Front Royal with Rodes to hurry the latter's division onto the field.[6]

As Ewell dashed off, the rival skirmishers continued to bang away and French continued with his methodical preparations to make the assault every Confederate knew was coming. About noon, the Union general started forming his second and third divisions, commanded by Brigadier Generals Henry Prince and Washington Elliott, respectively, into a brigade column, closed in mass. This dense assemblage of troops, very much resembling a

---

4 Andrews, *Condensed History of the 3rd GA* www.3gvi.org/ga3hist1.html; *OR* 27, pt. 2, 626; Consolidated Service Records, 3rd Georgia, for Walker, www.fold3.com.

5 *OR* 27, pt. 2, 626; 449.

6 Ibid.

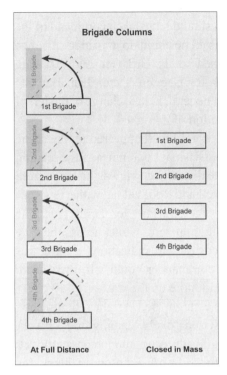

Brigade Columns: French formed his 2nd and 3rd Divisions in Brigade Columns Closed in Mass at Manassas Gap on the morning of July 23, 1863.

clinched fist, was brought up behind Ward, who was directed to deploy his division into line and prepare immediately to go forward.[7]

Since Colonel Berdan had already scattered skirmishers across the gap and placed his three supporting regiments athwart the railroad, the division's battle line was formed around the 1st Brigade. Colonel Andrew H. Tippin, temporarily leading the 2nd Brigade, moved up to take position on Berdan's left. The 3rd Brigade, under the French-born (and capable) Colonel Regis de Trobriand, deployed on Berdan's right.[8]

After the smoke settled at Gettysburg, de Trobriand was the only veteran brigade commander left standing in the division. Well-educated, sophisticated, and wealthy, he had settled in New York City in 1841 and two decades later became a naturalized citizen. Taking command of the 55th New York at the war's outset, the Frenchman had been with the army throughout all its campaigns. Somehow, his unit always seemed to wind up in reserve, and as a result he had seen little action. Despite this lack of combat experience, he was given command of a brigade after Chancellorsville and during the second day at Gettysburg (July 2) vindicated his appointment with a competent performance on the southern portion of

7 Each brigade was in line of battle, one behind the other, without leaving the necessary space required for them to wheel left or right. *OR* 27, pt. 1, 538; David Craft, *History of the One Hundred and Forty First Regiment Penns Vols 1862-1865* (Towanda, PA, 1886), 142.

8 de Trobriand, *Four Years With the Army of the Potomac*, 527; Craft, *One Hundred Forty-First Regiment Pennsylvania Volunteers*, 142.

Regis de Trobriand after his 1864 promotion to Brigadier General. *Library of Congress*

the field. As far as most were concerned, de Trobriand had a reputation as an officer who understood his business.

With specific instructions in hand to move straight ahead when the advance began, the colonel knew this meant his brigade would set the direction of march for the entire division. When the movement started about 2:00 p.m., he followed his orders faithfully. As he advanced, however, the rest of Ward's division obliqued left, crossed the railroad, and made for Wapping Heights.

It was soon clear to de Trobriand that something had gone awry. Either the other brigades were going astray, or he was. The colonel considered shifting his command left to maintain contact and close the widening gap created by Ward's divergent movement. However, his orders had been explicit, so he shrugged off that concern and continued pushing his men straight ahead.[9]

Traversing relatively flat ground at first, the 3rd Brigade soon found itself confronted by a deep ravine choked with a fine thicket. Although he began to doubt whether this was his proper avenue of advance, de Trobriand felt he had no choice but to plow through the obstacle. Demonstrating a thorough knowledge of the drill manual, the colonel astutely ordered his line to "break by the right of divisions to the front." His troops faced to the right as ordered and doubled their files to form a column. Once in order, the brigade divided itself into pairs of regiments, each of which executed a "by files left" so that what had been a long thin line of troops was now a line of three regimental columns moving forward parallel to one another. In this manner, de Trobriand's command could more easily plunge through the

---

9   de Trobriand, *Four Years With the Army of the Potomac*, 527.

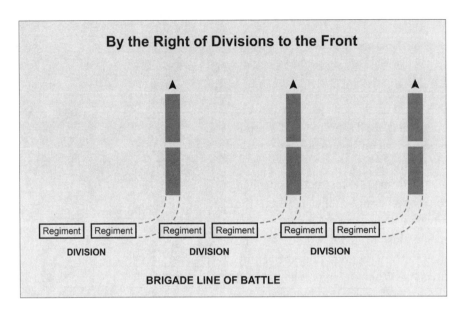

By the Right of Divisions to the Front

Regiment | Regiment | Regiment | Regiment | Regiment | Regiment

DIVISION   DIVISION   DIVISION

BRIGADE LINE OF BATTLE

underbrush by beating down three narrow paths rather than having to flatten the entire thicket, every man for himself.[10]

Once through the briar field, de Trobriand ordered his brigade back into line of battle before proceeding up the opposite side of the gorge and onto level ground, where he halted. Some distance in front, the pass and railroad made a sharp northward bend, and as far as he could tell there were no Rebel troops in that direction. Off to the left, the rest of Ward's command, followed by Prince's division, continued veering to the south, each step leaving the 3rd Brigade increasingly isolated. A concerned de Trobriand rode with his staff to what he described as the "most prominent point" he could find, the brigade's guidon fluttering in the breeze. The colonel hoped either Ward or French would see how far afield his orders had taken him, and then rectify the situation.[11]

From this vantage point, de Trobriand watched as Berdan's skirmishers, who had gone down into the valley in front of Wapping Heights, began to gradually ascend the high and steep face of the ridge, which was littered with boulders and covered in tall grass. The terrain made the approach to the

10 Ibid. Within a brigade a "division" is two regiments positioned in line next to one another.

11 Ibid.

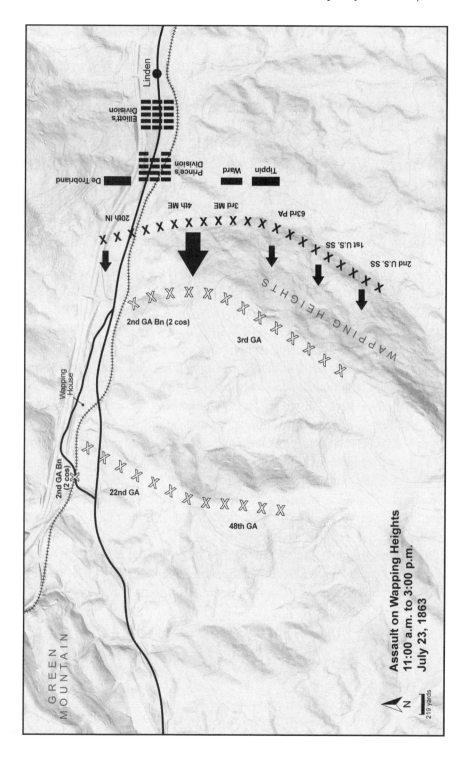

Assault on Wapping Heights
11:00 a.m. to 3:00 p.m.
July 23, 1863

This photo, circa 1954, looks from the southern portion of Green Hill east toward Linden. On July 23, 1863, Ward's division advanced from Linden against a Rebel skirmish line made up of the 3rd Georgia Infantry and two companies of the 2nd Georgia Battalion on Wapping Heights. *Western Heritage Society*

enemy slow and difficult but not without its advantages, for it offered considerable cover to the Union troops as they made their way upward. [12]

On the far left of the Federal advance, the 1st and 2nd US Sharpshooters were in their element. Despite being kept under a hot fire by the Georgians, they had the luxury of easily slipping cartridges into their breech-loading Sharp's rifles from a prone position. This not only gave them a higher rate of fire, it facilitated their ability to dart from boulder to boulder as they advanced. The Southerners, however, fighting from behind what Captain Andrews described as a "broken down rail fence overgrown with briars and grapevines," were giving as good as they got and putting up a "most stubborn resistance."[13]

To break the stalemate, Ward recalled the 3rd and 4th Maine from his skirmish line and ordered them to charge the Rebel left, which was held by two companies of the 2nd Georgia Battalion. The pair of New England regiments, together numbering just 230 men, reformed into line of battle, crept up the hill unobserved by the Confederates and, once at the summit,

12 Ibid; Martin Haynes , *History of Second Regiment New Hampshire Volunteer Infantry* (Lakeport, NH, 1896), 195.

13 Haynes, *Second Regiment New Hampshire Vol.*, 195; Andrews, *Condensed History of the 3rd GA* www.3gvi.org/ga3hist1.html; Stevens, *Berdan's US Sharpshooters*, 351.

"sprang to their feet and delivered a volley." In response, the woods to their front blossomed with puffs of white smoke made by the discharge of Confederate muskets.[14]

As Colonel de Trobriand watched from the other side of the pass, Colonel Moses Lakeman of the 3rd Maine rode the length of the two advancing regiments before returning to the center of their formation. From that point, he gave the command to charge and the entire Federal line, recalled a Federal, "burst forward on a run towards the woods." Surprised by the impetuosity of the attack, the outnumbered defenders gave way as the Yankees swept through the woods in a flash, leaving behind a few killed, wounded, and prisoners.[15]

With the left of the Confederate line broken, Captain Andrews had no choice but to order the 3rd Georgia to pull back. The withdrawal was well organized, and the Rebels retreated, as one Federal put it, at a "gentle cow trot over the hills and fields" to where the rest of Wright's brigade was posted. Despite having yielded his advance position, Andrews was proud of the prolonged resistance his men had put up, and credited them with giving the Federals a lesson that did much to deter a renewal of their advance for at least an hour.[16]

Just as the two Maine regiments attacked, a staff officer, sent by either Ward or French, reached de Trobriand to share with him what he already knew: His brigade was not where it was supposed to be. The order to advance straight ahead had been intended only to ensure there was no crowding when Ward's brigades also started moving. De Trobriand's superiors had forgotten to transmit instructions for his brigade to conform its movements to the rest of the advancing division. The colonel's immediate response passed unrecorded. Later, de Trobriand recalled that he believed the entire movement had been "badly arranged" and overly complicated

---

14 Moore, *Rebellion Record*, vol. 7, 361; de Trobriand, *Four Years With the Army of the Potomac*, 527-28.

15 Colonel de Trobriand did not identify the officer he saw leading the charge, but he was almost certainly Colonel Moses Lakeman of the 3rd Maine Infantry. The 4th Maine was led by Captain Edward Libby after Gettysburg. Moore, *Rebellion Record*, vol. 7, 361; Peter Dalton, *With Our Faces to the Foe: A History of the 4th Maine Infantry* (Union, ME, 1998), 285; de Trobriand, *Four Years With the Army of the Potomac*, 527-28.

16 Andrews, *Condensed history of the 3rd GA* www.3gvi.org/ga3hist1.html; Silliker, *Rebel Yell & Yankee Hurrah*, 114; *OR* 27, pt. 2, 626.

given the circumstances—a series of "useless evolutions" that were not even "executed correctly."[17]

However bungled the advance, at least de Trobriand now had orders to reconnect with Ward. By the time he got his brigade moving, the colonel found the entire 2nd Division on Ward's right flank, which made it impossible for him to link up as General French desired. This left the brigade north of the road while the rest of Ward's (and all of Prince's) division were south of it, save the 20th Indiana, which remained deployed as skirmishers. Accepting the situation for what it was, de Trobriand detached the 110th Pennsylvania to screen the buildings of Wapping, which lay a short distance ahead of his battle line, and placed the rest of his troops beside Prince's column of brigades.[18]

By the time he completed these maneuvers sometime around 3:00 p.m., de Trobriand discovered something else to puzzle over: The entire advance had come to a halt without anybody knowing why. Someone seemed to be shifting troops about, but to what end was unclear. A battery was brought up on the left side of the railroad, and de Trobriand was ordered to detach a regiment to support it. He dutifully sent the 17th Maine to do the job, all the while wondering why given that virtually two full divisions were already on that side of the pass. Ward's skirmish line was on the western slope of Wapping Heights and still exchanging fire with the Rebels, but other than that, the Union attack had sputtered to a stop shortly after it had begun.[19]

Confusion and uncertainty might have reigned in the Union ranks, but on the other side of the battlefield, the Confederates knew exactly what they were about. Andrews' Georgians, benefiting mightily from the manner in which French was running things, had managed to do what many of them thought was impossible that morning: hold out until help arrived.

*   *   *

Robert Rodes had marched his Rebel division out of its camp near Winchester between 5:00 and 6:00 a.m. that morning. Ed Johnson and Jubal

---

17 de Trobriand, *Four Years With the Army of the Potomac*, 528.

18 Ibid.

19 Ibid.

Early took to the road about the same time. Despite a steadily climbing thermometer that would register 86 degrees by mid-afternoon, the Southern commanders pushed their troops hard throughout the day. At roughly 2:00 p.m., after a fatiguing march of 23 miles, Rodes' column reached the Shenandoah and hurried across the river, some troops fording while others used the pontoon bridges.[20]

Swinging through Front Royal, weary soldiers anticipated being sent into bivouac at the end of their long and grueling hike. When word spread through the ranks that fighting was underway at Manassas Gap, however, the infantrymen began to doubt their day's work was done. Sure enough, instead of orders to make camp, the column was turned in the direction of the mountains and hustled off toward the distant sound of gunfire.[21]

Colonel Edward A. O'Neal's brigade of Alabamans, approximately 990 strong, was at the head of the division when it entered the western end of Manassas Gap around 3:00 p.m. Wright's brigade, which could be seen up ahead, looked like a thin line of skirmishers confronting what appeared to these veterans to be "most of Meade's army." Rodes immediately dispatched the sharpshooters of Stephen D. Ramseur's and O'Neal's brigades, together numbering about 250 men, to bolster the embattled Georgians. While they dashed ahead, O'Neal was directed to deploy the rest of his command as skirmishers on a ridge 600 yards behind Andrews's men. As the remaining brigades of the division came up, they were thrown into line on a spur of the mountain several hundred yards to the rear and northwest of O'Neal's position.[22]

The troops rushing to Andrews' assistance were some of the best in the Southern army, even if their organizations were relatively new. Although the North had enlisted sharpshooter regiments early in the conflict, the South had been slow to follow. The Confederate Congress authorized the formation of sharpshooter battalions in May of 1862, but a shortage of

20 Leon, *Diary of a Tar Heel*, UNC-CH, 31; Hubbs, *Voices From Company D*, 189; Krick, *Civil War Weather*, 104; *OR* 27, pt. 2, 593.

21 Leon, *Diary of a Tar Heel*, UNC-CH, 31; Hubbs, *Voices From Company D*, 189.

22 Colonel O'Neal was in command of Rodes' Brigade. Trudeau, *Gettysburg*, 588; Eugene Blackford, letter August 4, 1863, Army Heritage Center Foundation, Carlisle; *Jeremiah Tate, papers*, letter of Aug 6, 1863, Gilder Lehrman Institute of American History, New York, NY; *OR* 27, pt. 2, 560; 626; Hubbs, *Voices From Company D*, 189.

proper weapons and the speed of events had stymied the proposal for eight months.[23]

Nonetheless, commanders who liked the idea conducted a variety of battlefield experiments with the intriguing concept. Among the early advocates of such formations was division commander Daniel Harvey Hill, who ordered one of his brigadiers, Robert Rodes, to undertake the development of a sharpshooter unit. Rodes plunged enthusiastically into his task, and by early January 1863 had fashioned a unit of marksmen from hand-picked individuals in his brigade. The outfit was placed under the command of Major Eugene Blackford. These fine soldiers received rigorous training in skirmishing, scouting, and marksmanship that made them akin to elite troops.[24]

A few weeks later, Hill was transferred to North Carolina and his division went to Rodes, who immediately ordered the creation of sharpshooter battalions in the other four brigades of his newly inherited command. Always assigned to move at the head of their parent unit, these innovative formations proved invaluable at Chancellorsville and went on to render outstanding service at Gettysburg. During the retreat back to Virginia, Rodes used the sharpshooters as a rear guard for his division. By the time he approached Manassas Gap on July 23, the general was not only fully convinced of their utility, he had come to rely on them as something of a tactical trump card.[25]

O'Neal's and Ramseur's sharpshooters were well positioned at the front of their brigades and the first units to reach Andrews. Given their training, they were also uniquely capable of having a maximum impact on the tactical situation despite their modest numbers. Moving up the main road through the gap, Major Blackford, together with the sharpshooters of Colonel O'Neal's brigade, found Captain Girardey, who directed Blackford to extend the Confederate line to the left. This placed Blackford's men on the hillside north of the road, a spot that provided excellent cover and an elevated position from which to direct their fire. The sharpshooters from

23 Fred Ray, *Shock Troops of the Confederacy: The Sharpshooter Battalions of the Army of Northern Virginia* (Asheville, NC, 2006), 29.

24 Ibid., 45-49.

25 Ibid, 59.

Ramseur's brigade were sent off to the right to support Andrews' southern flank.[26]

While the reinforcements deployed and Wright's brigade gathered itself together on a single line, the rest of Rodes' division formed on Green Hill. This was the last ridge at the western end of Manassas Gap, and its mass forced the railroad to take a sharp curve around the hill's northeastern tip. The feature's 1,295-foot peak represented a prominent knoll from which a long, heavily wooded crest ran to the northeast at an elevation of more than 1,000 feet.[27]

It was an ideal position for a battle line, not only because it blocked the exit of the pass and the road to Front Royal, but also because it towered above the two smaller heights to the southeast along which Andrews and O'Neal had placed their regiments. Once the 3,800 infantry in George Doles', Junius Daniel's, Alfred Iverson's and Stephen Ramseur's brigades were on the ridge alongside the 16 cannon of Lieutenant Colonel Thomas H. Carter's artillery battalion, the Confederates were well situated to make any Union attempt to get into the Shenandoah Valley a troublesome affair.[28]

Still, Ewell was taking no chances. In the event Rodes might need assistance, he had summoned Edward Johnson to the scene hours earlier. His division had gone into camp at Cedarville, five miles north of Front Royal, about the same time Rodes had crossed the river. Johnson's soldiers had hardly commenced cooking dinner before couriers arrived with orders to hurry toward Manassas Gap. Abandoning their partially prepared meals, the Rebel troops fell in and resumed their march, moving through the afternoon heat with increased urgency as news of the fighting flowed down the column.[29]

On the ground where that fight was taking place, meanwhile, Ward's Federal skirmishers had swept onto the western slope of Wapping Heights, while his main line had paused near its crest. Off in the distance, the general and his men could see heavy columns of Confederates moving southward, while closer to hand the latest position taken up by Wright's brigade seemed

26 Eugene Blackford letter Aug 4, 1863, Army Heritage Center Foundation; *OR* 27, pt. 2, 626.

27 Moore, *Rebellion Record*, vol. 7, 361; *OR* 27, pt. 2, 560.

28 Trudeau, *Gettysburg*, 587-8.

29 *Richmond Daily Dispatch*, Aug 1, 1863.

more daunting than the one just captured. Sheltered behind scattered fences, boulders, and hastily stacked stone breastworks, the Southerners looked to be well entrenched. Rather than appear rattled by their recent withdrawal, wrote a Northerner reporter on the scene, the Rebels "seemed disposed to resist" and clearly "were not intimidated" by Federal numbers.[30]

Even though still warmly engaged with the enemy, practical necessity dictated that the Federal skirmishers pause to catch their breath. Given the length of time they had been dueling with the Confederates—more than three hours—and the steepness of the climb they had just made, Ward's men were tired and beginning to run low on ammunition. Indeed, two key units, the 1st and 2nd US Sharpshooter regiments, had fired 60 rounds per man and most now had empty cartridge boxes. Being practical fellows, the sharpshooters had slung their rifles and gone to picking blackberries with both hands as though the battle was over.[31]

Although cognizant of these facts, Ward wanted to press whatever advantage his recent success might still afford. A short time after 3:00 p.m., he ordered Tippin and de Trobriand to pass through Berdan and take the next ridge. Before either brigade could get going, however, French inexplicably directed Ward to suspend his advance.

From the vantage point of the front lines, that command made little sense. Union infantrymen could see the arrival of Rodes and the approach of Johnson. None of them doubted that every minute wasted would make the coming struggle harder and bloodier. Moreover, the Southerners had just lost one position and it seemed wise to keep them on the run if at all possible. In other words, now was the time to push things rather than slow them down.

French did not agree. He saw the enemy reinforcements as readily as anyone, but instead of inciting him to boldness, their arrival instilled within him greater deliberation. He had worried about the Rebels going over to the offensive since his arrival at Linden, and now French could not bring himself to plunge into a fight with increasing numbers of Confederates until he was certain—completely certain—that his enemy was not trying to lure him into trap.

George Meade was in a somewhat similar frame of mind, torn between a desire to press the offensive and a compulsion to guard against a sudden

30 Moore, *Rebellion Record*, vol. 7, 361.

31 *OR* 27, pt. 1, 538; Stevens, *Berdan's US Sharpshooters*, 348-49.

Rebel thrust. After taking to the road with his headquarters early that morning, the general had reached Markham Station around 10:30 a.m. From there, either in response to messages sent by French or because of his own concerns, Meade sent an order directing VI Corps commander General Sedgwick to immediately shift two of his three divisions from Rectortown to Barbee's Crossroads. Their mission would be to guard against any Confederate movement aimed at French's rear from Chester Gap. The two divisions were to take their ammunition and ambulance trains with them, but Sedgwick was to send all the rest of his wagons to White Plains, where they would be out of the way should Lee strike northward into the Loudoun Valley.[32]

While he took these steps to guard against trouble from the south, Meade also sought to strengthen his planned offensive beyond Front Royal. The V Corps and II Corps had already been directed to support the III Corps (French) in its effort to break through Manassas Gap. Now, at 11:20 a.m., Meade sent John Slocum an order to leave the protection of Ashby's Gap to the cavalry and hurry his XII Corps to Markham Station. Once there, Slocum had orders to be careful not to block the road into the pass. Meade wanted that route clear to facilitate the flow of reinforcements into the gap, or, if necessary, make a rapid withdrawal out of it. The XII Corps was to hold itself ready to move on "very short notice" and, although Meade did not say it, move in any direction as dictated by the fluid circumstances.[33] Slocum, however, was to disregard the ordered change of position if the enemy was "already moving to attack Ashby's Gap in force." In that case, the XII Corps should not "abandon the gap unless forced by the enemy to do so," in which event it would retreat toward Markham Station.[34]

That danger was illusionary, but Meade's response to it was indicative of the strategic fog into which he had thought himself. The decision to keep a close eye on Chester Gap, where there was undoubtedly much enemy activity, was prudent. But it was also a wholly defensive reaction to an improbable threat. Worse, the general still could not completely let go of the notion that the Rebels were about to strike into his rear and cut the Army of

---

the Potomac off from Washington. Even as he worried that Lee might attempt some grand double envelopment, Meade kept pushing more troops toward Manassas Gap—apparently without stopping to consider whether the Confederate army was acting in any way other than how he imagined or hoped for.

The Union commander steadfastly clung to the idea that only one Rebel corps had passed through the Blue Ridge. Yet he never seemed to consider attacking that portion of Lee's army instead of fighting his way through the mountains to take on the two enemy corps he believed remained in the Shenandoah Valley. Furthermore, it seems not to have occurred to Meade to disrupt the movement of enemy troops through Chester Gap in order to block its exit and ensure the Rebels west of the mountains stayed where he wanted them to be.

Whatever Meade's reasoning, lacking his knowledge of the army's movements, French continued to be haunted by the specter of a Southern offensive—specifically one designed to trap him inside Manassas Gap. At 2:45 p.m., after reaching Linden with Meade, General Humphreys replied to an earlier dispatch from the III Corps commander that elaborated on these fears. Seeking to belay French's concerns, the army's chief of staff reminded French that the V Corps was nearby, and the II Corps just five miles behind Sykes. Merritt's cavalry, then resting at Markham Station, had been ordered back to Linden, except for one regiment which was being sent to scout the road to Sandy Hook, which lay just outside the exit of Chester Gap. Gamble's brigade—soon to be reinforced by two of Sedgwick's divisions—was already at Barbee's Crossroad and guarding against any threat that might emerge from that same pass.[35]

As far as Meade was concerned, Humphreys wrote French, these dispositions meant there was "no probability" of the Rebels attempting to attack the III Corps without running into significant opposition and the alarm being sounded. Therefore, unless Confederate resistance in the gap became stiffer than had been previously reported, the general was to "continue pushing" the enemy and "to do so with more rapidity" once Merritt's horsemen arrived.[36]

---

35 *OR* 27, pt. 3, 752-3. Army headquarters stayed at Markham Station while Meade, Humphreys and others went forward.

36 Ibid.

It is important to note that Meade did not direct French to launch an all-out attack; nor did he order him to use his entire force, or stress the need to move with vigor and swiftness. "Continue pushing" the enemy was a vague directive—and one that allowed a commander to read into it what he wanted, and certainly one that implied no particular sense of urgency. Not until cavalry arrived at the front was French to move more rapidly, although one wonders just how Meade thought a few mounted regiments could produce a speedier advance in the confines of Manassas Gap.

It is hard to imagine French didn't view Humphreys' reassuring dispatch as vindication of his decision to await the arrival of the V Corps before pressing beyond Wapping Heights. In this regard, however, the communication proved to be rather beside the point. Even as the courier carrying that message rode off to French's command post, the first of Sykes' troops made their appearance.

Sykes' command had left Rectortown at 5:00 a.m. amid the "clear, fresh morning" air of Loudoun Valley. Before long, however, the pleasant dawn had given way to sweltering heat and the movement to Manassas Gap became increasingly difficult. Around noon, having already passed through Piedmont and Markham, Sykes' men had begun the long climb into the pass. The rocky and generally bad road made the going hard. The sounds of fighting up ahead, however, proved a stimulus to weary legs, and by 3:30 p.m. the head of the corps was at Linden. Forty-five minutes later, Sykes' brigades were forming into columns of battalions massed on the center, in rear of the III Corps.[37]

With the V Corps now on the field, French believed he finally had the necessary support to safely resume his attack. Supposing Ward's units near the end of their ammunition and endurance, and perhaps feeling fresh troops would be better able to assault the Rebel-held hills, French decided to use Prince's 2,800-man division to carry out the next phase of the assault. Lieutenant Colonel Hayden rode to Prince and conveyed an order for him to have a brigade "penetrate the ravine" along Ward's front, "cut the enemy's

---

37 Robert G. Carter, *Four Brothers in Blue* (Austin, TX, 1978), 338; Unknown, *History of the 5th Massachusetts Battery*, 691; Woodward, *Our Campaigns*, 285; Smith, *Corn Exchange Regiment*, 288. A column of battalions massed on the center means the brigade went from a line of regiments abreast into a column of regiments (each in line of battle) stacked one behind the other. The flank regiments took position to the front or rear of the regiment in the center of the brigade line of battle.

Wapping Heights: Forces Actually Engaged, July 23, 1863

Confederate	Union
Wright's Brigade	*Third Corps, Army of the Potomac*
Col. Edward Walker	Major General William French
Capt. Charles Andrews	*First Division*
(Anderson's Division, Third Corps)	Brig. Gen. J.H. Hobart Ward
3rd Georgia Infantry	*First Brigade*
22nd Georgia Infantry	Col. Andrew Tippin
48th Georgia Infantry	57th Pennsylvania Infantry
2nd Georgia Battalion	63rd Pennsylvania Infantry
	68th Pennsylvania Infantry
O'Neal's Brigade	105th Pennsylvania Infantry
Col. Edward O'Neal	114th Pennsylvania Infantry
(Rodes' Division, Second Corps)	141st Pennsylvania Infantry
2nd Alabama Infantry	
5th Alabama Infantry	*Second Brigade*
6th Alabama Infantry	Col. Hiram Berdan
6th Alabama Infantry (twice)	20th Indiana Infantry
6th Alabama Infantry	3rd Maine Infantry
	4th Maine Infantry
Sharpshooter Battalions	86th New York Infantry
Maj. Eugene Blackford	124th New York Infantry
Ramseur's Brigade	99th Pennsylvania Infantry
O'Neal's Brigade	1st United States Sharpshooters
	2nd United States Sharpshooters
Carter's Artillery Battalion	
Lt. Col. Thomas Carter	*Third Brigade*
Orange Artillery (Fry's Battery)	Col. Regis de Trobriand
Morris Artillery (Page's Battery)	17th Maine Infantry
	3rd Michigan Infantry
	5th Michigan Infantry
	40th New York Infantry
	120th New York Infantry

line," and "drive him away." In response, Prince asked for and received permission to use his division as he "saw best." With this flexibility in hand, Prince detailed Brigadier General Francis B. Spinola's brigade to undertake the assault, and issued instructions for his remaining two brigades to move onto Wapping Heights to support the attack.[38]

---

38 *OR* 27, pt. 1, 490; 538.

Wapping Heights: Forces Actually Engaged, July 23, 1863 (continued)

Union, continued

Second Division
Brig General Henry Prince
First Brigade
Brig. Gen. Joseph Carr
1st Massachusetts Infantry *
11th Massachusetts Infantry
16th Massachusetts Infantry
12th New Hampshire Infantry
26th Pennsylvania Infantry
11th New Jersey Infantry
84th Pennsylvania Infantry

Union, continued

Second (Excelsior) Brigade
Brig. Gen. Francis Spinola
Col. J. Egbert Farnum
70th New York Infantry
71st New York Infantry
72nd New York Infantry
73rd New York Infantry
74th New York Infantry
120th New York Infantry

Third Brigade
Col. George Burling
2nd New Hampshire Infantry
5th New Jersey Infantry
6th New Jersey Infantry *
7th New Jersey Infantry *
8th New Jersey Infantry
115th Pennsylvania Infantry

* Detached as flank guards or battery
supports on July 23rd.

Unfortunately for Prince, thanks to French's earlier insistence on robustly guarding his flanks, each of Prince's three brigades was now missing some portion of its strength. Brigadier General Joseph B. Carr's brigade, for example, had detailed two full regiments to guard roads and/or support batteries; as a result, Carr only had about 575 men available for action. Colonel George C. Burling's brigade was in similar straits, for two of the six regiments under his command were also on detached duty, leaving just 550 troops for other operations.

By comparison, Spinola had lost only one regiment (the 120th New York) in this fashion and still controlled roughly 880 men. Thus his command, better known as the Excelsior Brigade, was the strongest in the division and the logical choice to spearhead the assault. The soldiers in its five available New York regiments—the 70th, 71st, 72nd, 73rd, 74th—had been recruited by Dan Sickles himself at the start of the war. Although the

Brigadier General Henry Prince
Library of Congress

brigade had lost half its strength at Gettysburg, the men who remained in its ranks were veterans and could be counted on to perform well.[39]

Spinola, however, was less than an ideal candidate to lead a determined attack. The presence of he and Henry Prince on the field was the result of unlikely happenstance and ironic coincidence. Both men were brigadier generals, but they had come to their current positions in very different ways. Prince was career military, West Point Class of 1835. Wounded in the Second Seminole War, he went on to win two brevets in Mexico. At the battle of Molino Del Rey, Prince had suffered a desperate wound that required years of convalescence and would never heal properly. He was made a brigadier in August 1862, promptly captured at Cedar Mountain, and spent five months in Libby Prison before being paroled. After his release, and in less than stellar health, the 51-year old general was assigned to duty in coastal North Carolina. It was there that he met Spinola.

The son of Italian immigrants, Francis Spinola was a Democrat and lifetime member of the infamous Tammany Hall political machine that governed New York City. Although he blamed the Republican Party for starting the war, Spinola was willing to fight to preserve the Union. Hence, he was among that class of pro-war Democrats that Lincoln found necessary to indulge and promote for the good of the Northern cause.

In June 1862, Secretary of War Edwin M. Stanton pressured the Republican governor of New York to grant Spinola permission to raise a

---

39 The strength of units on a given day is almost impossible to determine with certainty. These figures are approximate and based on deducting their casualties suffered at Gttysburg from their reported strength in the battle. In all likelihood the units probably had fewer men on the field. The 120th New York was detached from the Excelsior Brigade on July 23, 1863.

brigade of infantry. That October, after recruiting four regiments, he was rewarded with a general's star. To his disappointment, these units were not kept together as a brigade, but sent elsewhere one at a time as needed. Spinola and his sole remaining regiment, the 132rd New York, were shipped off to North Carolina, where they were placed under Prince's command and brigaded with three Pennsylvania regiments made up of nine-month volunteers.

Both Prince and Spinola took part in the April 1863 effort to lift the Confederate siege of Washington, North Carolina—an endeavor in which neither man showered himself with glory. Several times Prince vetoed aggressive operations Spinola planned for the relief of the town; usually on the grounds they were foolhardy or suicidal. When superiors dictated another attempt to lift the siege, Prince claimed he was too ill to undertake the venture (which he considered doomed to failure at any rate) and ordered Spinola to assume command of the expedition.[40]

Shocked with the sudden responsibility for 7,400 men, and all too aware of his self-confessed "limited military experience," Spinola tried to beg off. Prince, however, insisted. Thus forced to lead the operation, Spinola performed poorly. His offensive encountered an enemy that was well-entrenched but vastly outnumbered. Spinola made only a feeble effort to dislodge them, and after suffering a mere 11 casualties in a two-hour skirmish, concluded his task was impossible and ordered a retreat—much to the "surprise and mortification" of his troops.[41]

Shortly thereafter Prince took medical leave and Spinola, with his three Pennsylvania regiments—whose enlistments were about to expire—was transferred to Fortress Monroe, Virginia, and a few weeks later to the District of Columbia. Arriving in the Federal capital just days after the battle of Gettysburg, the Pennsylvanians were asked by General Halleck to extend their enlistments and take part in the effort to trap Lee before he crossed the Potomac. The troops announced their willingness, but they also declared Spinola "worthless," and replied that they would continue to serve only if they had a new leader.

---

40 Frank W. Alduino and David J. Coles, *Sons of Garibaldi in Blue and Gray: Italians in the American Civil War* (Amherst, NY, 2007), 193-95.

41 Alduino, *Sons of Garibaldi*, 196.

Brigadier General Francis Spinola
Library of Congress

Unwilling to be dictated to, Halleck discharged the Pennsylvanians, which left Spinola without a command. That meant he was available to be sent to the Army of the Potomac as a replacement for one of the 21 division or brigade commanders lost at Gettysburg. Ironically, the same was true of Prince, who had recovered from his illness and reported himself fit for duty. Meade needed to fill the high-ranking vacancies within his army, so Halleck sent him every available unattached officer—including Prince and Spinola. No fan of political generals, however, Halleck told Meade about the latter's reputation and gave him permission to relieve Spinola and "send him away" if the general wished.[42]

Meade, however, had little regard for the opinions of nine-month volunteers and was in need of general officers. He not only declined to send Spinola away, but gave him the Excelsior Brigade, whose commander had been on sick leave since July 11. Prince was put in charge of Andrew Humphreys' division after the latter was elevated to be Meade's chief of staff. And so it was that Prince once again became Spinola's superior, even as he remained acutely aware of the New Yorker's inexperience and general incompetence.[43]

Nonetheless, Prince gave the Excelsior Brigade the job of breaking the Rebel line in Manassas Gap, albeit after giving the novice brigadier careful instructions. Spinola was to move by his left flank around the northeastern edge of Wapping Heights into the valley below. Cautioning him to keep "on the lowest ground" possible to avoid being seen, Prince told Spinola to put his brigade into position near Ward's skirmishers and approximately in the

42 *OR* 27, pt. 1, 91; Alduino, *Sons of Garibaldi*, 198.

43 *OR* 27, pt. 1, 562.

Brigadier General J. H. Hobart Ward
Library of Congress

center of their line. Once ready to advance, he was to attack vigorously and take the hill defended by Andrews' Georgians. The 1st and 3rd brigades would move forward in support once the assault was launched.[44]

General Ward knew nothing of this plan until one of Spinola's staff officers rode over to inform him that the Excelsior Brigade had orders to move through his line and attack the Rebels. More than an hour had gone by since Ward's men had stormed and taken Wapping Heights—time the enemy had used to bring up heavy reinforcements. Now there would be further delay while another division was deployed to do a job Ward's men were already in position to accomplish. Moreover, the responsibility for conducting such an important assignment was being put in the hands of a political general of dubious competence.[45]

To a soldier of Hobart Ward's experience, it must have seemed a vexing situation. Born into a family with a strong military tradition—his father had fought in the War of 1812 and his grandfather in the American Revolution—Ward seemed destined for a martial career. He joined the Army at 18, and worked his way through the ranks from private to sergeant major. After fighting in the Mexican War, he had left the Regular Army to become commissary general of the New York state militia, a position he held throughout the 1850s. After raising a regiment at the outbreak of the Civil War, Ward fought in every major battle of the Army of the Potomac from First Bull Run through Gettysburg. Despite Ward's wealth of combat experience, however, he was outranked by Spinola, whose commission as a

44 Ibid., 538; 572.

45 Ibid., 496.

brigadier general predated his own by two days. The fact that an amateur was higher on the military ladder than he was could only have irked a man with Ward's impressive combat record.

Given his long military resume, word that someone like Spinola would lead an attack through his lines may not have surprised Ward. Still, the general was a loyal Union man and so naturally worried that an important attack such as this would fail, and good men would be killed or maimed if it was not properly carried out. Although he would not "presume" to give orders to a superior officer, Ward did send the staff member back with what he called "suggestions" on how Spinola might go about striking the enemy line.[46]

While the general and the aide discussed upcoming tactics, the massed Excelsior Brigade uncoiled into a column and began making its way from the general area of the railroad down along the northern foot of Wapping Heights. Eventually it entered the swale that separated Ward's men from Andrews's Confederates and began working its way into position for an assault.[47]

*   *   *

The valley on the western side of Wapping Heights was an inhospitable place to wage war. Although the ground was by and large open, with only the occasional orchard or field of corn to block visibility, rocks and boulders were scattered everywhere. Most of them, explained one Union soldier, were "treacherously concealed" by a "wild tangle of dewberry vines." A rugged gulch about 10 feet wide and just as deep cut across part of the valley floor, while a local watercourse known as Manassas Run snaked its way among the stones. Hidden behind these rocks, Union and Confederate skirmishers fired at one another across this unpleasant expanse, mostly concealed from their opponents but clearly visible to the soldiers of both sides stationed on higher ground to the east and west.[48]

46 Ibid.

47 *OR* 51, pt. 1, 205-07.

48 Haynes, *Second Regiment New Hampshire Vol.*, 195; Moore, *Rebellion Record*, vol. 7, 361; *OR* 27, pt. 1, 538.

This image, taken circa 1954, shows the northern end of the ridge assaulted by the New York Excelsior Brigade on the afternoon of July 23, 1863. The area visible in the photo was held by the 22nd Georgia and part of the 48th Georgia Infantry. The Union attack hit the Confederate battle line just off the right edge of this photo.

Warren Heritage Society

It was nearly five in the afternoon before the Excelsior Brigade reached its jump-off point. The sun was sinking slowly into the western horizon and only a handful of hours remained before nightfall. The column of men, sweaty in their wool uniforms, halted and fronted to face the enemy. Seconds later the order to "load!" echoed along the ravine. The regimental colors were "unfurled and let to the breeze." When the order "fix bayonets!" was announced, no one had to be told what was coming and the effect on the men was palpable. Although he had "never doubted" the courage of his troops, Captain Lovell Purdy, Jr. of the 74th New York thought the enthusiasm provoked by those two words "surpassed" even his most hopeful expectations.[49]

With their men deployed and their weapons readied, company and battalion officers walked back and forth along their formations explaining what they had to do. That was fairly standard procedure prior to an attack, but for anxious men about to step into a metal maelstrom, it was behavior that could irritate more than it could enlighten. At least one private thought

---

49 Rick Barram, *The 72nd New York Infantry in the Civil War: A History and Roster* (Jefferson, N.C., 2014), 156; *OR* 51, pt. 1, 205-6.

the verbal exercise entirely pointless and redundant, since it was obvious to everyone in the ranks what was about to be required of them.[50]

As the New Yorkers nerved themselves to go forward, a dreadful tension hung over their lines. In moments like these, generals were expected to steel the resolve of their soldiers, and in this regard Spinola did not disappoint. Although he might not know his drill manual, he would show, as de Trobriand put it, "that if he were ignorant he was not a coward." Riding to the front of his brigade Spinola made it clear he intended to go forward with his men rather than remain in the rear. Although they had been under his command for just two weeks, this met with the approval of the troops, who appreciated his willingness to put himself on the firing line and share their risks.[51]

The Excelsiors also appreciated Spinola's brevity. When the moment to attack came, the general simply turned in his saddle and shouted: "Now boys of the Excelsior Brigade, give them Hell!" With those nine words the five New York regiments—the 70th and 73rd on the left, the 74th in the center, the 72nd and 71st on the right—moved out.

This was no wild charge. A distant Union observer was impressed with what he took as the "regular manner and orderly array" of the brigade as it started its advance at a "slow step." In reality, no such parade ground precision existed and the speed of the movement was dictated by terrain, not tactics. The hill, rocky and precipitous, was described by one tasked to ascend it as being "nearly perpendicular" in some places. The 71st and 72nd New York, on Spinola's right flank, lagged behind. After first advancing through a cornfield, the troops unexpectedly encountered a deep wide gully into which the line of men had to slide before clambering up the opposite side to resume the advance. As a result, the left flank gained ground faster than the right, meaning Spinola would unintentionally strike the enemy *en echelon* rather than head-on and all at once.[52]

Whichever wing of the brigade they belonged to, the Federals found the going tough. In places men had to crawl on their hands and knees to climb the 300-foot-high slope. Elsewhere, they grabbed bushes or small trees to

50 Barram, *The 72nd New York*, 156.

51 de Trobriand, *Four Years With the Army of the Potomac*, 529.

52 Cudworth, *History of the First Regiment Massachusetts Infantry*, 417; Moore, *Rebellion Record*, vol. 7, 361.

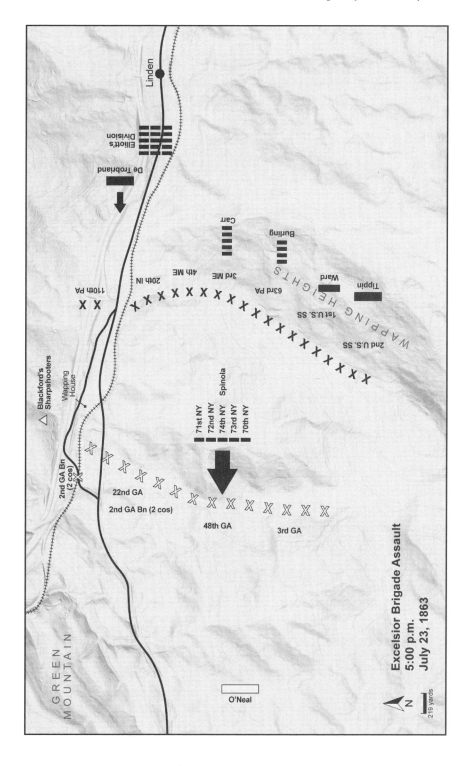

Linden

Elliott's Division

De Trobriand

Carr

Burling

4th ME 3rd ME

20th IN

110th PA

WAPPING HEIGHTS

Ward 63rd PA

Tippin

1st U.S. SS

2nd U.S. SS

Blackford's Sharpshooters

Wapping House

Spinola

71st NY
72nd NY
74th NY
73rd NY
70th NY

2nd GA Bn (2 cos)

22nd GA

2nd GA Bn (2 cos)

48th GA   3rd GA

GREEN MOUNTAIN

Excelsior Brigade Assault
5:00 p.m.
July 23, 1863

O'Neal

N

219 yards

pull themselves upward. Once the attackers became visible, the Georgians opened on them with what one New Yorker described as a "shower of bullets." Men went down quickly, some killed and wounded, and others slipping and falling on the steep slope. Nonetheless, the advance continued. Enemy fire fed the urge to get up the hill at an "accelerated pace" and the Yankee ascent began to pick up speed, with some men breaking into the double quick where the terrain proved favorable.[53]

Confederates along the crest, some sheltering behind piles of rocks stacked into small breastworks, were "pouring . . . a heavy . . . and very destructive" fire into the Union ranks. Struck by the Georgians in their front, the Yankees were also hit hard by the Alabamans on the Confederate left. Firing from "perfect protection" and high ground, Major Blackford's sharpshooters had plenty of easy targets. It seemed, he later recorded, as though every one of the bullets "took effect." With little return fire coming their way, it was as though they were in a shooting gallery, wrote Blackford, and his men enjoyed "the fun highly."[54]

The soldiers on the receiving end of that fire felt quite differently. For them, Southern marksmanship created a terrible ordeal. Private James Dean of the 72nd New York credited the sharpshooters with inflicting an unusually high number of fatal wounds. Hits to the legs were especially common and a significant number severe enough to cost men their limbs, and in some cases their lives. Most mounted Federal officers, who had experienced a difficult time ascending the hillside, were struck down, among them Captain Benjamin Price, acting major for the 70th New York. Price died quickly when a bullet tore through his neck and ripped apart his jugular vein. Spinola managed to stay in the saddle after being hit in the foot, but a second round struck his abdomen and unhorsed him. Falling leaders, however, did nothing to stop the momentum and the Yankees continued

---

53 Moore, *Rebellion Record*, vol. 7, 361; Cudworth, *History of the First Regiment Massachusetts Infantry*, 417; *OR* 51, pt. 1, 205-07; Mary Searing O'Shaughnessy, ed., *Alonzo's War: Letters From A Young Civil War Soldier* (Lanham, MD, 2012), 96; Christopher Ryan Oates, *Fighting For Home: The Story of Alfred K. Oates and the Fifth Regiment, Excelsior Brigade* (Charlotte, NC, 2006), 128-39; Barram, *The 72nd New York*, 156.

54 O'Shaughnessy, *Alonzo's War*, 96; Blackford letter of Aug 4, 1863, Army Heritage Center Foundation, Carlisle.

scrambling closer to the crest. The outnumbered defenders, after firing a few final shots, fell back.[55]

Although the winded New Yorkers swept onto the ridge in somewhat disorganized fashion, their attack seemed to have carried its objective. Within a short time, however, the Northerners discovered to their dismay that they had merely seized a lower plateau, not the actual summit. Ahead of them awaited a second elevation some 200 yards farther on. Worse, it was thick with Rebels who rose up from cover to deliver a solid volley. The Yankees were just beginning to return fire when the injured Spinola transferred command to Colonel John Egbert Farnum of the 70th New York, who, despite having been shot in the foot and having his horse badly wounded, refused to leave the field. Intensely aware that the brigade had to either keep going or risk being shot off the ridge man by man, Franum ordered the advance to halt for a few minutes so that he could align his regiments into some semblance of regular order. As soon as the officers and sergeants could shove and cajole most of their men into line, Farnum gave the order to resume the attack and make for the second hill.[56]

Standing in the path of that assault was Wright's brigade, which had been fighting with various levels of intensity since 11:000 a.m. The Georgians were in a tight spot. Ammunition was running low, and although more had been requested, no arsenal boxes were yet in sight. Andrews' men were reduced to taking rounds from the dead and wounded to keep shooting. Although near exhaustion from the physical strain of a day-long battle and the rigors of moving up and down the steep hillsides of Manassas Gap, somehow they still had fight left in them. Veterans to a man, they would not give ground until the enemy forced them to do so at bayonet point.[57]

That, of course, is exactly what the Federals intended to do. With Franum at their head, the Excelsiors sprang forward with a yell that "would have done credit to a band of demons." Making for the second crest, the Yankees endured the heaviest Rebel fire yet, and as the distance between the rival lines closed, more and more of them fell. Major Daniel Mahen of the 70th New York and Major Michael W. Burns of the 73rd had their horses

55 Barram, *The 72nd New York*, 157; O'Shaughnessy, *Alonzo's War*, 96; *OR* 27, pt. 1, 564; Alduino, *Sons of Garibaldi*, 200; Moore, *Rebellion Record*, vol. 7, 361.

56 Moore, *Rebellion Record*, vol. 7, 362; *OR* 27, pt. 1, 561.

57 *OR* 27, pt. 2, 626-27.

Colonel John E. Farnum
Library of Congress

shot from under them. The color sergeant of the 70th was severely wounded in the arm, but the brave solider merely switched the flagstaff to his other hand and kept going. Lieutenant James Short with the 74th and Captain Benjamin Price of the 70th were both killed during this part of the advance.[58] So too was Lieutenant Charles S. Preston. The Pittsburgh native had only recently rejoined the 74th regiment after being severely wounded at Chancellorsville. Despite a premonition of his impending death, the 21-year-old had gone into the battle willing to lay down his life for the Union and determined to do his duty. Somewhere amid the mass of blue uniforms charging the Rebel line he did both.[59]

The New Yorkers absorbed these losses and, despite growing disorganization, continued moving forward. Gaps opened in their ranks as breathless soldiers, unable to go farther, slowed down or dropped out of line. Among these was the color bearer of the 74th New York, who passed the regiment's flag to his mounted colonel, Thomas Holt. The officer, who had somehow made it this far uninjured, accepted the banner and continued on.

Leaking exhausted men at every step, the Federal line grew increasingly ragged. As stronger legs outpaced weaker ones, the Union formation eventually dissolved into scattered clusters of men rushing forward on their own. Those on the left hit the 3rd Georgia, which refused to yield despite three separate charges that carried the New Yorkers to within 15 paces of its position. In the center of Wright's brigade, however, the Yankees drove

58 Moore, *Rebellion Record*, vol. 7, 362; *OR* 51, pt. 1, 205-07.

59 *OR* 51, pt. 1, 205-07; Bruce Sutherland , "Pittsburg Volunteers with Sickle's Excelsior Brigade," *The Western Pennsylvania Historical Magazine*, Vol. 45 No. 4, December 1962, 321.

forward with what one described as the "fury of a hurricane" and engaged in hand-to-hand combat with those Georgians yet unwilling to flee.[60]

From a distance it was an inspiring and breathtaking scene. General French thought "nothing could be more brilliant" than the Excelsior Brigade's assault, which he felt displayed "fighting qualities of the highest order." Perhaps better appreciating the brutal reality of what they were seeing, soldiers in the V Corps marveled at the "rare opportunity of witnessing an engagement at long range." Like spectators at a sporting event, these onlookers raised cheer after cheer in a "prolonged shout of admiration and praise" for their attacking comrades.[61]

On the opposite side of the field, General Ewell was as impressed by the "great gallantry" displayed by his Georgians as French was by that of his New Yorkers. Like their V Corps counterparts, the men of Rodes' division, scrutinizing the battle from a safe distance, felt their hearts swelling with pride as they watched the "gallant fellows" under Andrews fighting obstinately against the attacking Federals. The stout conduct of Wright's brigade, which had only recently been torn apart at Gettysburg, was the subject of "much admiration" by men who well understood the sacrifice it was making.[62]

The accolades of their comrades meant nothing at that moment to the soldiers from New York and Georgia struggling for control of an unnamed Virginia hillside. Andrews' men resisted the attackers to the "utmost of human capacity," but it wasn't enough. Worn down, heavily outnumbered, virtually out of ammunition, and aware that the safety of Lee's Virginia army no longer rested solely upon their shoulders, the Georgians in the center of the line finally broke. Those Confederates who continued to stand and fight were either bayoneted or taken prisoner. Others turned and fled, tossing away weapons and accouterments in their desire to escape capture or death.[63]

60 Oates, *Fighting For Home*, 139; *OR* 27, pt. 1, 567; *OR* 27, pt. 2, 626-27; Moore, *Rebellion Record*, vol. 7, 361.

61 Carter, *Four Brothers in Blue*, 338; *OR* 27, pt. 1, 490; 539; Moore, *Rebellion Record*, vol. 7, 361.

62 *OR* 27, pt. 2, 560-61; 449.

63 *OR* 51, pt. 1, 205-07; Barram, *The 72nd New York*, 156; *OR* 27, pt. 2, 626-7; Moore, *Rebellion Record*, vol. 7, 361.

With the brigade's front pierced, Andrews had no choice but to order the 3rd Georgia to retreat. Captain Girardey was likewise compelled to pull back the Rebel left. As the Confederates withdrew, four 12-pounder Napoleons from Lieutenant Samuel Pendleton's Morris Artillery stationed on Green Hill opened fire on the pursuing Federals, as did the two 3-inch Ordnance Rifles and two 10-pounder Parrotts of Captain Charles W. Fry's Orange Artillery.[64]

For the weary Rebel infantrymen pulling back from their second sustained fight of the day, the sound of those guns was most reassuring. Private William Judkin of the 22nd Georgia thought it one of the few times during the war he found the "music of cannon" to his liking. He was certain that without the intervention of Carter's artillery the majority of Wright's brigade would have been taken prisoner.[65]

Though he had no way of knowing it, Judkin grossly overestimated the danger of falling into Union hands. The Excelsior Brigade was so exhausted by its two charges that it had lost most of its cohesion. The victorious New Yorkers were "breathless and exhausted with fatigue," recalled an Excelsior, and many simply slunk to the ground gasping for air. Anticipating that this might happen, General Prince had sent forward orders for the brigade to halt atop the second hill. Stopping all of the troops was more difficult than supposed. The left flank came to a halt on the crest rather easily, but on the right some men in the 71st New York and the 72nd tramped on for another 200 yards, their continued advance motivated by a desire to seize a large blackberry field.[66]

*   *   *

Although the Yankee advance had, at least for the moment, ceased, the success of Spinola's attack and the sudden enemy aggressiveness made Richard Ewell nervous. So much so that at 5:30 p.m. he sent a message informing Jubal Early that the situation inside Manassas Gap had worsened,

---

64 The commander of the Morris Artillery, Captain Richard Page, was wounded at Gettysburg. R. C .M. Page, *Sketch of Page's Battery or Morris Artillery, 2nd Corps, ANV* (New York, NY, 1885), 7.

65 *OR* 27, pt. 2, 603; Herring, *Company C*, 185.

66 Oates, *Fighting For Home*, 139; *OR* Vol. 27, pt. 1, 539.

and a "heavy force" of Federals was advancing in an effort to "get at the pontoon bridges" over the Shenandoah. Although Rodes was in position to resist, the corps commander wanted to know if Early's troops could get up in time to be of assistance. Anticipating a worst-case scenario, in which Rodes and Johnson were driven away and the bridges lost or destroyed, Ewell warned his Virginia subordinate that if his division could not reach Front Royal by nightfall, it would need to veer southwest toward Strasburg. Ewell wanted Early to send a "rapidly" riding courier to advise what hour his brigades would reach the battlefield, or if his column would head toward Strasburg instead.[67]

Ewell's dispatch had hardly left corps headquarters before other Federal units began to advance in the wake of Spinola's attack. Prince had directed Burling to bring up the 3rd Brigade in support of the Excelsiors, while Carr was told to move the 1st Brigade forward and protect their right flank. On the north side of the railroad, de Trobriand's regiments were also in motion, advancing straight ahead toward Green Mountain. The Confederates responded by shifting the fire of Carter's guns toward these mobile Yankee formations, while O'Neal's infantry aimed several volleys at the disorganized Excelsiors.[68]

Coming over the crest of Wapping Heights, Burling's brigade, deploying from a column of regiments into line of battle as it advanced, swept down into the valley below the western slope of the ridge and followed in the wake of the New Yorkers. Climbing the same difficult hillside Spinola had just assaulted, his men had the unwelcome experience of moving past the littered dead and wounded the Excelsiors had left behind. Struggling to the first plateau of the captured ridge, the brigade was met by Prince, who halted it there within easy supporting distance of the New Yorkers. The Rebels hurled a few shells into the area, but only managed to wound two of Burling's men.[69]

Luckily for Prince's 3rd Brigade, Carter's guns gave much more attention to Carr and de Trobriand. This was especially true of de Trobriand's troops, who had begun advancing at the same time Spinola

67 *OR* 27, pt. 3, 1035. Apparently Ewell also sent a message to R. E. Lee around this same time. See Chapter 14 page 246-247.

68 Ibid., pt. 1, 572-73; 589; ibid., pt. 2, 593, 603.

69 Ibid., pt. 1, 572-73.

Lieutenant General Richard S. Ewell
Library of Congress

launched his attack. "Still hoping to get in the dance," explained the aggressively minded Frenchman, de Trobriand pushed his men forward in an effort to engage the Rebel sharpshooters effectively tormenting Spinola's flank. This stratagem came to nothing, however, when de Trobriand's line was brought to a sudden halt by a deep and thickly wooded gorge that precluded advancing any farther.[70]

Faced with this obstacle, and with no instructions to launch an attack, de Trobriand ordered his troops to go prone on the eastern slope of the gorge. It was far from an ideal spot to halt a line of battle, for it was in full view of the Confederate guns across the way. His soldiers were forced to lay on the steep incline with their heads pointing down slope and their feet up. Worse, their blue uniforms showed "distinctly against a background of faded grass," making the long line of prostrate troops easy to see. In fact, there were so many Federals lying motionless on the ground a Southern newspaperman mistakenly thought the hillside was "literally *blue* with the killed and wounded."[71]

Not a few Union soldiers also worried about their exposed position. Left vulnerable to the enemy's "artillery and sharpshooters, without the least likelihood that they would err on the side of mercy," explained one of the unfortunates, wasn't a position any Northern infantryman relished. Carter's cannoneers accepted the opportunity thus presented and threw shot and shell into the Federal lines with "remarkable precision." The Rebel iron struck

---

70 Marie Caroline Post, *The Life and Memoirs of Comte Regis de Trobriand: Major General in the Army of the United States* (New York, NY, 1910), 303.

71 Silliker, *The Rebel Yell & Yankee Hurrah*, 114-15; *Richmond Daily Dispatch*, August 1, 1863.

several men and all the near-misses came much closer than the men in blue "deemed safe."[72]

From the vantage point of the common soldier it seemed criminal to stay where they were unless the Rebel guns moved off or ceased firing, neither of which seemed likely to happen. The only logical alternative to being "slaughtered as coolly as so many pigs" was for the foot soldiers to move elsewhere—and fast. To their growing dismay, no such order was given and the men remained where they were, hugging the ground in complete view of the enemy gunners.[73]

Few things were more difficult for a soldier than to remain still while being shelled. If a man was awaiting an attack, he could reassure himself that there was a reason for his ordeal. Being ordered to lay exposed to artillery fire for no discernible purpose, however, was a trial of a wholly different kind. Unable to move out from under the barrage or fight back, a man's mind was apt to start calculating the odds of being horribly maimed or killed by a random projectile.

Not everyone was capable of withstanding the resulting mental strain indefinitely, and thus it was no surprise that some of de Trobriand's men cracked under the pressure. After enduring the enemy's cannonade as long as he could, one Maine private decided he had had enough. Declaring "he didn't intend to be killed or maimed," the man jumped to his feet, called for his comrades to follow him to safety on the reverse slope of the hill, and headed for the rear.[74]

That invitation had a "startling" effect and about 50 other men "sprang to their feet" and started after their comrade. This was the type of moment every commander dreaded—when fear became a contagion and a man's instinct for self-preservation overwhelmed his sense of duty to produce panic and rout. Luckily, one of the regiment's officers was hiding behind a bush nearby and saw what was transpiring. Jumping to his feet, he confronted the frightened men and ordered them back into line. The habit of discipline, which the army worked so hard to instill, now made its value evident and the troops returned to their post after the officer promised to find

---

72 Post, *Life and Memoirs of Comte Regis de Trobriand*, 303; Haley, *Rebel Yell & Yankee Hurrah*, 114; *OR* 27, pt. 2, 449.

73 *OR* 27, pt. 2, 449.

74 Ibid.

The vantage point of this circa 1954 photo of Manassas Gap is slightly south of the position of Rodes' Division on Green Hill. The open ground where Colonel de Trobriand's brigade halted and was shelled by Rebel artillery is easily seen.

Warren Heritage Society

someone who would move them "to a safer place." The unnamed officer's quick action may have stayed a possible rout, but it did little to change the 1st Brigade's untenable situation.[75]

On the south side of the road, Federal soldiers found Confederate shells no more to their liking. Prince had directed his 1st Brigade to fill the void between those of de Trobriand and Spinola. Coming down from Wapping Heights, Joseph Carr led his men off to the right and eventually massed them in the woods near the road. His troops hugged the ground there to make "as little a mark as possible for the enemy's shot and shell." Their prone positions made it harder for the Rebels to see their targets, but it didn't keep the targets from seeing the cannoneers shooting at them.[76]

One private in the 11th New Jersey was especially fascinated by the work of a Southern gun directly in front of his regiment. It was, he recalled "interesting but not particularly pleasant" to watch the crew load their piece and then see the "flash of fire and smoke" when the gun was discharged. The sound of a shell whizzing overhead seconds later was much less intriguing. Fortunately, added the soldier, the Rebel gunners "mostly" missed the Union

75 Ibid.

76 O'Shaughnessy, *Alonzo's War*, 96.

infantrymen, and their ordnance exploded harmlessly in an orchard behind the brigade.[77]

The Confederates, who had no way of knowing that Burling, Carr, and de Trobriand were merely maneuvering to consolidate the ground Spinola had just captured, believed each Union brigade was endeavoring to launch a fresh attack. As General Rodes later reported, the enemy "attempted to make a father advance in line of battle," while a Rebel infantryman wrote home that the Yankees, "huzzaing at the top of their voices," attempted "several charges." Colonel O'Neal reported facing "three separate and distinct" assaults.[78]

None of the Federal units moved very far before coming to a sudden halt, so the Southerners credited their fire with breaking up the successive Yankee offensive forays. The apparent ease with which each of these "attacks" was stopped evoked deep contempt for the enemy among the Confederates. Samuel Pickens in the 5th Alabama, who had seen much of war and its many sides, remarked that it took the fire of only "one or two small pieces of artillery" to induce the Northerners to fall back. Louis Leon of the 53rd North Carolina put things more colorfully, claiming that Carter's guns "scattered [the Federals] like bluebirds." A Southern correspondent watching the bombardment reported (and likely exaggerated) that each discharge from Carter's guns "extorted loud cries of pain" from "wounded Yankees," to which Rebel soldiers "responded with cheers."[79]

Alabama Confederates admitted that the Federal officers "behaved very well" and "acted generally with great gallantry," but the Northern rank and file was another matter. When Union color bearers ran forward "waving their flags," recalled Samuel Pickens, only a few bluecoats fell into line to "fire off their guns" beside the colorful banners. The rest, he continued, seemed "not much inclined to follow" and remained "scattered" behind the battle line. General Rodes, who boasted that it took only a "few shots from Carter's artillery" and the fire of his skirmishers to break up the Yankee attacks, concurred with Pickens' assessment. In contrast to the courage

77 Ibid.

78 *OR* 27, pt. 2, 561; 593; Hubbs, *Voices From Company D*, 189.

79 Hubbs, *Voices from Company D*, 189; Leon, *Diary of a Tar Heel*, UNC-CH, 31; *Richmond Daily Dispatch*, August 1, 1863.

shown by his own troops, he thought the enemy infantry behaved in a "decidedly puerile [and] most cowardly manner."[80]

Some Union observers were also critical of the way French's III Corps was conducting its business. Few if any men wearing blue thought the Rebels had beaten back any attack or that their Northern comrades had displayed even a passing degree of cowardice. Still, there was a sense that the entire effort had been half-hearted. To the men of the 118th Pennsylvania, the tactics French employed seemed to indicate "no determined purpose" to push the enemy out of Manassas Gap.[81]

From a signal station on one of the peaks, Brigadier General Warren watched the fight unfold with growing unease. At 5:45 p.m. he sent a dispatch to Meade stating that as far as he could tell, there were "about 5,000" Confederate infantry and eight guns blocking the exit to Manassas Gap. Although he admitted the secessionists might have reserves nearby, Warren saw an opportunity to press the attack and added that the Rebel position was "a poor one." In a thinly veiled complaint, he stressed that "French's skirmishers only had been engaged," and that his troops "were not advancing" at all.[82]

Just how much of what was transpiring Meade himself could see is uncertain. The army commander reached Linden no later than 2:45 p.m. Since Spinola's attack didn't start until after 5:00 p.m., the general had plenty of time to ride forward and find a vantage point to observe the assault. According to a newspaper correspondent for the *New York Herald*, Meade and his staff witnessed the attack. If the general was in position to watch the Excelsior Brigade go forward, he was more than capable of assessing the robustness of the III Corps' offensive and directing that it be conducted with more energy, if he thought it necessary.[83]

There is no evidence, however, that Meade rode forward to confer with his subordinate commanders or that he sent them any instructions to press the attack. This may be because he was satisfied with French's performance, or, whatever he thought of the way the attack was being handled, Meade

---

80 Hubbs, *Voices From Company D*, 189; *OR* 27, pt. 2, 560-61.

81 Smith, *Corn Exchange Regiment*, 287.

82 *OR* 27, pt. 3, 753.

83 Ibid., 752; Moore, *Rebellion Record*, vol. 7, 361; *Detroit Advertiser and Tribune*, Aug. 4, 1863, 4.

This photo, taken circa 1954, looks due south from the northeastern tip of Green Mountain. Any Federal attack on Rodes' Division during the early evening of July 23, 1863 would have had to advance over this formidable terrain, known locally as Dismal Hollow.

Warren Heritage Society

realized circumstances rendered a renewal of the offensive impossible in short time (perhaps 90 minutes) of remaining daylight.

Prince's division—the only one within easy striking distance of the enemy—was in no condition to undertake an immediate advance and wouldn't be for some time. Spinola's brigade was spent. Although Carr's and Burling's commands were fresh, they now confronted O'Neal's brigade, in front of which Andrews had rallied his Georgians. Beyond this danger awaited Rodes' division and Carter's artillery on Green Hill. Further, a heavily wooded "very deep and wide hollow" yawned between the Union front and the Rebels. Given the difficulty that would attend negotiating that obstacle, and what his men would encounter on the other side of it, Prince felt "a farther advance without preparation would be irregular."[84]

84 *OR* 27, pt. 2, 560-61, ibid., pt. 1, 539.

In this regard he was not incorrect, and a pause to reorganize was essential if his division was to continue the assault with a hope of success. Such measures took time, and nothing mandated that Prince carry that burden. With so many other Union formations in Manassas Gap, French or Meade had it within their power to send reserves to the front and resume the attack with fresh troops. Practically speaking, however, this couldn't be done before nightfall.

Hobart Ward's division was still back on Wapping Heights at this time and it would be close to dark before it could be brought into position for an assault. French's 3rd Division under Washington Elliott was available and still massed in a column of brigades on the road near the heights. In theory, it might rapidly march forward and arrive in time to launch an attack from the general vicinity of Carr and de Trobriand. Although large, Elliott's division was new and most of its troops had never been in battle. No one seems to have considered trying to use it for such a daunting undertaking.

That left Sykes' V Corps. His men, however, were even farther back than Elliott's, and many of his regiments were awkwardly arrayed on the steep sides of the narrow pass. It would take time to assemble them and even more for them to elbow their way through the rear of the III Corps to get to the front. There was no possibility they could reach French's forward position in time to deploy, become familiar with the terrain or their objective, and launch an assault before dark.[85]

The disappointing reality was that nothing else of significance could be done before nightfall. This may have been a blessing in disguise, for the Rebel defenses, bolstered by the arrival of significant reinforcements, were not nearly as vulnerable as Warren supposed. Indeed, if the Union army had struck immediately it might have found itself in a bigger fight than anticipated, and certainly one that could not be brought to a successful conclusion before darkness arrived.

Since early afternoon the sound of musketry had been drifting back into Front Royal from the mountains. At Bel Air, the Buck family climbed onto the roof of their house to get a better view of the action transpiring just a few miles away. They could "distinctly see" Rebel gunners manning their pieces, the "flash of cannon," gun smoke rising into the air, and the explosion of

---

85 John Hennessy, *Fighting With the 18th Massachusetts: Civil War Memoir of Thomas H. Mann* (Baton Rouge, LA, 2000), 191.

Confederate shells in Union lines. While they watched this dramatic denouement to Spinola's attack, the Bucks also saw Edward Johnson's division arrive on the scene.[86]

In order to save time, Johnson's infantry had moved southeast from Cedarville to cross the Shenandoah at Morgan's Ford, about five and a half miles from Bel Air and only a mile or so behind Green Mountain. Meanwhile, Andrews' battalion of artillery (temporarily commanded by Captain Charles I. Raine) and Johnson's wagon train had followed the main road to the pontoon bridges. Not long after Rebel infantry began wading across the river, Raine's guns trundled past the Buck household on their way to the front.[87]

Johnson's appearance vastly decreased the odds of the Yankees reaching Front Royal, even if they had been able to orchestrate an attack before dusk. That meant French's failure to make an evening assault wasn't the missed chance it seemed to some. Moreover, what was true in a tactical sense seemed equally true in a strategic sense. Regardless of the III Corps' inability to land a final blow, the outcome of the day's fight appeared to have achieved the more important goal of compelling General Lee to abandon his withdrawal from the Valley and turn to offer battle on Federal terms.

This belief was substantiated by several pieces of evidence. One was the capture of prisoners from every corps in the Army of Northern Virginia, which clearly indicated Lee's entire command was close at hand. Second, Union scouts had spotted Confederate artillery hurrying back to Front Royal from Chester Gap, which made it look as though the Rebels moving through that pass were turning around. Finally, there was a report from Lieutenant Colonel Hayden of General French's staff that the "rebel corps that had moved down the valley was returning" to Front Royal.[88]

Any one of those pieces of intelligence, standing alone, would have been less than convincing. All three taken together, however, were mutually reinforcing and thus hard to refute. They also lent credence to the army commander's conception of the strategic situation, and thus set the foundation of the Union army's plans for the next day.

86 Baer, *Shadows on My Heart*, 238.

87 Ibid.

88 *OR* 27, pt. 1, 98; Moore, *Rebellion Record*, vol. 7, 362.

Unfortunately for the Federals, each one of these intelligence reports was either misleading or misinterpreted. While it was true that prisoners from all three enemy corps had been captured, it was an indication of how many Confederates had already slipped east of the mountains, not how many remained nearby. Union scouts had seen a battalion of artillery returning to Front Royal from Chester Gap, but those cannons belonged to Stuart's horse artillery, not to Longstreet's or Hill's commands. The guns had crossed the Shenandoah on the pontoon bridges early that morning. Major Richard Beckham, who commanded the battalion, had grown tired of the endless waiting for Hill's column to clear Chester Gap and decided to lead his batteries back through Front Royal in order to take an alternate route south.[89]

Hayden's claim proved just as misleading. The Yankees had known for 48 hours that Longstreet was near Front Royal and in Chester Gap. Over the last few days, however, they had managed to lose track of A. P. Hill's corps and assumed its men they had spotted were part of Longstreet's column. Ewell's abortive strike at Kelley three days earlier was now paying its ultimate dividend. Federal observers had mistaken Early's division for Hill's entire corps, and Rodes' and Johnson's divisions for Ewell's entire command. This intelligence blunder supported Meade's belief that two-thirds of Lee's army was trying to move up the Valley in order to cross the mountains farther south.

Operating on this assumption, Meade thought his thrust into Manassas Gap had taken the Rebels by surprise and threatened to cut off the enemy "corps" (in reality Early's division) that was still north of Winchester. In response, the Rebel "corps" headed south (in reality just Rodes' and Johnson's divisions) had been forced to backtrack and attempt a "desperate stand" in hopes of keeping the Army of the Potomac from breaking into the Valley to trap and destroy the rearmost Confederates. Despite the delay of a day and a half occasioned by Meade's uncertainty of Lee's intentions, the Federal high command now believed they were on the verge of drawing the enemy into a decisive battle.[90]

In fact, no such thing was about to happen. Perception being reality, however, Meade was certain his strategy was working according to plan.

89 Lewis T. Nunnelee postwar memoir/diary, Museum of the Civil War, Eleanor S. Brockenbrough Library.

90 Moore, *Rebellion Record*, vol. 7, 362.

That evening he wrote Halleck. Although information regarding the Rebels was "somewhat contradictory," he was reasonably certain that most of Lee's army was still in his front. The army commander assured the general-in-chief that he would attack at daylight. Meade may have been aware of the similarity of his current situation to that at Williamsport just ten days earlier. At that time, he had promised his superiors a battle only to see the enemy slip away just before he could strike.

Would history repeat itself on the morrow?

CHAPTER 13

"The Enemy Has Again Disappeared"

The Casualties at Manassas Gap—Preparations to Renew the Battle—Ewell's Withdrawal—Ordeal of Blackford's Sharpshooters—The Rebels Gone—Pursuit to Front Royal—Movement to Warrenton—French's Excuses

WHEN the sun set on July 23, Prince's and Rodes' divisions remained on the ragged edge of a fight yet unfinished. The most advanced Federal brigades deployed skirmishers after reaching what turned out to be their final positions. In some places the blue soldiers eased forward to within 20 yards of their Confederate counterparts. The result was a fitful exchange of fire until about 9:00 p.m. when darkness blanketed the field. No one had a firm idea what would happen when dawn arrived.[1]

Even before the noise of battle faded away with the sunset, many men turned to tending the dead and wounded scattered between Wapping Heights and Green Hill. Experienced officers like Warren and Rodes might think and report that the fighting hadn't amounted to much—and in the grand sense of things, it hadn't—but to the soldiers who actually struggled for the hillsides of Manassas Gap, it had been, in the opinion of a Rebel newspaperman who witnessed the fight, a "very serious business."[2]

1 Jeremiah Tate papers, letter Aug 6, 1863, Gilder Lehrman Institute of American History; Leon, *Diary of a Tar Heel*, UNC-CH, 31.

2 Munson, *Confederate Correspondent*, 91.

As the wounded were carried to the surgeons and the dead buried, the men of both sides began to grasp the toll of the day's battle. Wright's brigade had lost 168 of the 600 soldiers it took into action, or just over a quarter of its strength, with 19 dead, 83 wounded and 66 missing. Captain Andrews' 3rd Georgia suffered the most, losing 75 men (10 killed, 38 wounded, and 27 missing). The 22nd Georgia recorded 50 casualties (four dead, 25 injured, and 21 captured) while the 48th Georgia listed 32 (five killed, 17 wounded, and 10 missing). The 2nd Georgia Battalion sustained 11 casualties (one dead, three wounded, and eight captured). Rodes reported his division's losses at 14 men injured and one officer killed. Total Confederate casualties from all causes numbered 183.[3]

Northern figures were not quite as bad. The final tally of Union casualties was 93, of whom 20 were killed and 73 wounded—almost exactly the same number of dead and wounded as in Wright's brigade. All of the slain and 49 of the wounded were from Spinola's command. Ward's brigade (under Berdan) lost 18 men wounded, while de Trobriand had one man injured, and Carr and Burling each suffered two casualties. The 3rd Division under Elliott had a single soldier hurt.[4]

In all likelihood, casualty lists would increase before another day passed. For the moment, however, the addition of new names would have to wait until sunrise. French ordered Ward and Prince to cease operations "in consequence of the lateness of the hour" and "make dispositions for the night." Union infantryman were directed to "lay on their arms," which was martial terminology for resting in line of battle without removing accouterments.[5]

To keep the enemy uncertain of the Federal positions, no bugle or drum calls were permitted nor camp fires allowed. In fact, the troops were not even supposed to sleep, but instead remain ready all night to rise up in an instant if needed, form line, and resume fighting. Despite laying on ground so steep that in places the men had to place the heels of their shoes against sizeable

3   Cudworth, *History of the First Regiment Massachusetts Infantry*, 417; *OR* 27, pt. 2, 561; List of Casualties in Wright's Brigade, www.fold3.com/browse/249/hxF6FiBLibxa MQhEtYeHwikJcwq08GxUMUwsuIhGP.

4   *OR* 27, pt. 1, 192. Total Union losses in Manassas Gap on July 23 *and* 24 would equal 103 (20 dead, 83 wounded).

5   Ibid., 496; 490; 572; O'Shaughnessy, *Alonzo's War*, 96.

stones to keep from sliding downhill, French's tired soldiers quickly slipped into profound slumber.[6]

While the weary men of the III Corps tried to find rest, Meade urgently concentrated the rest of his army in anticipation of tomorrow's coming fight. The V Corps was already close behind French. During the night the II Corps was brought to Linden from Markham Station and placed behind Sykes. Slocum's XII Corps, marching on Markham since midday, had passed through Piedmont Station at sundown and would bivouac around 10:30 p.m. at a little spot called Somerset Mills. Slocum would have his men back on the road before dawn and was expected at the entrance to Manassas Gap by daybreak. In order to reinforce these four corps, Meade sent orders to Sedgwick to begin shifting his two VI Corps divisions at Rectortown toward Linden starting at 3:00 a.m.[7]

Unless something unexpected intervened to disrupt his plans, Meade would have five of the Army of the Potomac's seven corps stacked up on the road between Front Royal and Markham Station by mid-morning of July 24. That would give him roughly 60,000 infantry and artillerymen, supported by some 150 guns and most of General Merritt's brigade of cavalry to deal with whatever Rebels lay to his front.[8]

Assembling this mass was a fairly straightforward matter of giving and executing orders. Feeding these troops, however, was becoming problematic. The army had abandoned all railroad communication when it crossed the Potomac, and no supplies of any kind had been sent to it since July 19, when Meade's loss of telegraphic communication with Washington rendered quartermasters ignorant of his location. The lack of a supply line, however, had done nothing to keep the army from consuming food at a relentless rate. Consequently, many units would draw the last available

6 Woodward, *Our Campaigns*, 285; A. W. Bartlett, *History of the Twelfth Regiment New Hampshire Volunteers in the War of the Rebellion* (Concord, NH, 1897), 141.

7 *OR* 27, pt. 1, 149; *OR* 27, pt. 3, 754; M. Milo Quaife, ed., *From the Cannon's Mouth: The Civil War Letters of General Alpheus S. Williams* (Lincoln, NB, 1995), 241-42. Apparently Meade had forgotten that he had ordered General Sedgwick to send two divisions to Barbee's Crossroads earlier in the day. The VI Corps had no divisions at Rectortown that evening. It is presumed Sedgwick shifted his two divisions at Barbee's Crossroad, toward Manassas Gap, but there is no direct evidence that this in fact took place.

8 *OR* 27, pt. 1, 152.

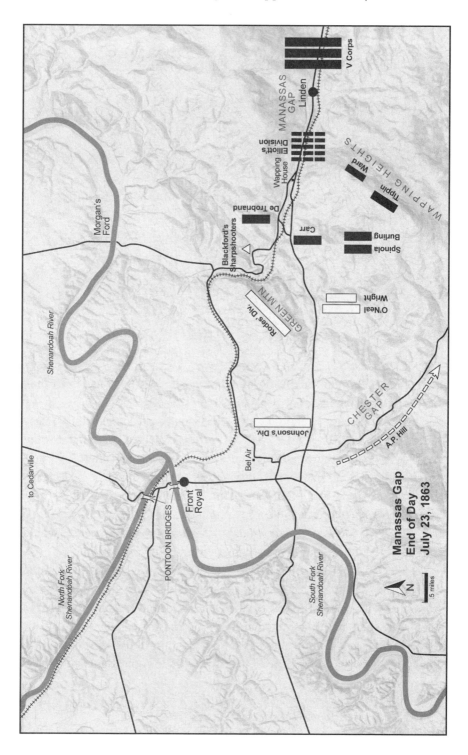

V Corps

MANASSAS GAP

Linden

Elliott's Division

Wapping House

WAPPING HEIGHTS

Ward

Tippin

De Trobriand

Carr

Burling

Spinola

Morgan's Ford

Blackford's Sharpshooters

Wright

O'Neal

GREEN MTN

Rodes' Div.

Shenandoah River

CHESTER GAP

A.P. Hill

Johnson's Div.

Bel Air

to Cedarville

PONTOON BRIDGES

Front Royal

North Fork Shenandoah River

South Fork Shenandoah River

Manassas Gap
End of Day
July 23, 1863

N

5 miles

The area around Linden where Meade massed 37,000 men on the night of July 23, 1863. Linden can be seen in the center of this circa 1950 photo. The area was probably more extensively forested during the war. *Warren Heritage Society*

rations from their trains on the morning of the 24th, and none had more than a day or two stockpiled.[9]

The looming supply shortage was a serious predicament with no easy solution. If the coming battle went as Meade expected, his army would smash its way into the Shenandoah Valley, defeat one or more of Lee's corps, and pursue the survivors. This success would require the Federals to move farther from Warrenton and their connection to the vital O&A Railroad. Once in the Valley, the army might be able to live off the land for a time, at least as long as it kept moving, but there was no guarantee this would meet its needs or even prove practicable.

Meade reported an "abundance of fresh beef [was] on hand," but he knew severe shortages of staples like hardtack, salt and coffee were inevitable. Uncertain when the army's subsistence supplies might be replenished, the general cautioned his troops to "husband" their food. Meade instructed his corps commanders that "the economical use of rations" was something "the occasion calls for," and expressed his hope they could make

9 *OR* 27, pt. 1, 99; Manley Stacey letter of July 24, 1863, http://martyhackl. net/staceyletters/2009/06/18/july-24-1863-manassas-gap-va/

the provisions on hand "hold out considerably beyond the time" for which they had been issued—perhaps as much as "one-third longer" than originally intended.[10]

For the troops inside Manassas Gap, thoughts of a pending fight were of far greater concern than worries about rations. During the evening, as more regiments reached the front, the pass became an increasingly uncomfortable place. By midnight, 37,000 men were clustered along the narrow road snaking through the defile. Officers found few viable campgrounds, which a correspondent from the *New York Herald* reported forced them to pack their soldiers into such "dense masses" they could "scarcely" find room to lie down. The concentration of so many troops in such a small space was virtually unprecedented, and it told all too clearly what the high command had in mind for the next day.[11]

The Confederates, however, had no desire to give Union generals the battle they sought. Positive that most of Meade's army was in front of him, Ewell recognized he could not fend off such a force indefinitely. Although certain Rodes would give the Yankees a "severe lesson" if they dared attack, Ewell had no intention of administering such punishment. The Second Corps commander had a far better grasp of the strategic situation than Meade, and knew that Longstreet and Hill had already passed through Chester Gap unmolested because of the day-long stand of Wright's brigade. With both the First and Third Corps on their way to Culpeper Court House, Ewell's goal now was not to fight, but to link up with the rest of the army as promptly as possible.[12]

Forewarned by General Lee that his command might need to take a more southerly route out of the Valley, Ewell had the option of choosing whatever course of action seemed most appropriate. With General Early still a day's march from Manassas Gap, there was no question of waiting to unite the Second Corps. Instead, Ewell decided to pull Rodes and Johnson back to Front Royal after dark and make an early march the next day up the Page Valley to Luray while Early altered his route from Winchester southward to Strasburg. From there, Early could move to New Market and traverse

---

10 *OR* 27, pt. 3, 754-55.

11 Ibid., pt. 1, 152; Moore, *Rebellion Record*, vol. 7, 362.

12 *OR* 27, pt. 2, 449-50.

Massanutten Mountain before veering eastward to cross the Blue Ridge at Fisher's Gap.[13]

With these decisions made, Ewell began extricating his divisions from Manassas Gap and the fight that Meade wanted. Shortly after nightfall, Colonel O'Neal pulled in his skirmishers and withdrew alongside Wright's brigade to the main Rebel line on Green Hill. Not long thereafter, Ewell directed Rodes to retire his men through Johnson's line and camp several miles south of Front Royal. Leaving Blackford's sharpshooter battalion behind as a rearguard, Rodes eased his men off the mountain as silently as possible. His troops, already exhausted by what Rodes called the "excitement of a threatened battle" and a 27-mile march on "one of the hottest of summer days," now had to trudge another four to five miles to ensure a head start on the enemy.[14]

This final hike was torturous. Lucy Buck watched as Rodes' Confederates moved past Bel Air that evening. Her heart ached as she watched the "poor fellows," whom she later described as "broken down soldiers." After marching through Front Royal, it was all the troops could do to keep going when their column turned south. Tracing a course along the east bank of the Shenandoah, the bone-tired Rebels made for Asbury Chapel, where they would finally halt for the night.[15]

By the time it went into bivouac, the division was "so thoroughly worn out," recalled one eyewitness, most of the men "could go no further." The cumulative strain of the last 24 hours, wrote a North Carolinian, was "positively more than we could bear." General Rodes agreed and admitted that this last effort "damaged [his] division severely." Even though the maneuver had been necessary, its ill-effects would linger for days. So many men were used up by the exertions of July 23 that straggling—which had

---

13 Ibid.; Jones, *Reminiscences of a Louisiana Tiger*, 82; McDonald, *Make Me A Map*, 163; *OR* 27, pt. 3, 1035.

14 *OR* 27, pt. 2, 594; Blackford, letter Aug 4, 1863, Army Heritage Center Foundation, Carlisle; Leon, *Diary of a Tar Heel*, UNC-CH, 31; *OR* 27, pt. 2, 561.

15 Baer, *Shadows on My Heart*, 238; E. B. Munson, ed., *Confederate Correspondent: The Civil War Reports of Jacob Nathaniel Raymer, Fourth North Carolina* (Jefferson, NC, 2009), 91-92; McDonald, *Make Me A Map*, 163.

been rare up to that point—became commonplace during the week that followed.[16]

Once Rodes cleared Front Royal, Johnson moved back two miles and went into camp on the southern edge of town. That left only the sharpshooters from Rodes' division in Manassas Gap. At midnight orders reached Blackford to pull his men off the line and follow the division into camp. The withdrawal was to be made quietly, which proved to be something of a challenge given the darkness and terrain. Stumbling at every step because of mud, rocks and underbrush, the major's men finally groped their way out of the pass. Assuming Ewell's corps would follow the same route as A. P. Hill, Blackford led his battalion onto the Chester Gap road and headed east. After traveling several miles, however, he bumped into a vedette who told him the Federals had cavalry just ahead and the Southern infantry had retreated toward Luray.[17]

Furious that his superiors had failed to relay this critical information, Blackford had no choice but to turn his deeply fatigued men around and head back toward Front Royal. It would be dawn before they reached Rodes' camp. Only then would the major learn that a pair of aides, sent to direct him onto the proper route, had fallen asleep at their post and failed to notice his battalion marching past in the wrong direction. When the negligent officers awoke, they assumed Blackford had been cut off and captured, and so hurried back to headquarters to report that erroneous assumption. It was a great relief to the entire division when the sharpshooters stumbled into camp at sunrise.[18]

The returning marksmen had covered nearly 35 miles the day before in addition to taking part in the fight at Manassas Gap. If the bulk of Rodes' command was nearly spent, these riflemen were completely exhausted. There would be little time for them to rest. As soon as the sun came up, Ewell's troops busied themselves with preparations for a quick march to Luray and beyond the reach of Meade's army. Everything moveable was evacuated from Front Royal and the pontoon bridges taken up. The latter would be sent down the Valley Turnpike on the west side of the river in order

16 Munson, *Confederate Correspondent*, 91-92; *OR* 27, pt. 2, 561.

17 Baer, *Shadows on My Heart*, 238; *OR* 27, pt. 2, 450; Blackford letter Aug 4, 1863, Army Heritage Center Foundation, Carlisle.

18 Blackford, letter Aug 4, 1863, Army Heritage Center Foundation, Carlisle.

to keep the slow-moving train from impeding Ewell's march. On the other side of the Shenandoah, the pontoons would not only be out of harm's way, but positioned to assist Early should he need them.[19]

While the Confederates maneuvered to deny Meade his anticipated battle, several miles away in Manassas Gap, the Federal army awakened with the expectation of a renewal of the fight. At daylight, Colonel Farnum deployed the 70th New York as skirmishers and sent it forward to scout the Rebel line. When they reached the position held by O'Neal at sunset the previous evening, Major William H. Hugo, commanding the regiment, found nothing but a few corpses to show where the Rebels had been. In an effort to discern how far the enemy had withdrawn, the major pushed his men forward for nearly three miles, but failed to see even a single straggler. Hugo realized the importance of this intelligence and hurried his regiment back to inform Farnum.[20]

Word of the New Yorker's discovery quickly reached Prince, who speedily dispatched it to French. III Corps headquarters passed it up the chain to Meade, who received it around 6:00 a.m. Upon reading French's message the Union commander immediately ordered his army into motion. Meade directed French to push his troops through the gap toward Front Royal while Sykes deployed his men into the mountains north of the pass to advance on the right flank of the III Corps.[21]

Although he hoped his troops might find that the Confederates had merely shifted position and were still vulnerable, Meade suspected the Rebels were gone. At 6:30 a.m. he had Humphreys send a dispatch to Slocum informing him that "the enemy appears to be withdrawing," and instructing the XII Corps to stop where it was and await further orders. Fifteen minutes later, a similar dispatch was sent to Sedgwick.[22]

Even as Meade was halting the flow of reinforcements into Manassas Gap, French was organizing a push toward its western exit. Since Prince was the corps' forward element he would lead the way, moving his division straight up the road toward Front Royal. Ward and Elliott, in that order,

19 Ibid; McDonald, *Make Me A Map*, 163.

20 Bartlett, *Twelfth Regiment New Hampshire Volunteers*, 141; *OR* 27, pt. 1, 564.

21 *OR* 27, pt. 1, 539; Woodward, *Our Campaigns*, 285.

22 *OR* 27, pt. 3, 761.

would follow in support. The Keystone Battery under Captain Matthew Hastings and a squadron from the 5th US Cavalry were sent to assist Prince, who gave his 3rd Brigade the advance.[23]

Charged with leading the way, but uncertain what trouble might lay ahead, Colonel Burling deployed the 2nd New Hampshire as skirmishers across the mouth of the gap, with the road bisecting its line. The remaining three regiments in the 3rd Brigade were formed in line of battle, the 115th Pennsylvania and 8th New Jersey on the right side of the road and the 5th New Jersey on the left. Carr's 1st Brigade, in column, followed Burling, while the Excelsior Brigade brought up the rear.[24]

It was 7:00 a.m. before these dispositions were made and the advance begun. Except for a scattering of enemy vedettes who fell back, Prince encountered no meaningful opposition. The 2nd New Hampshire, "sweeping a wide range on either side of the road," recorded the regiment's historian, captured "quite a number of footsore and discouraged Rebel stragglers." It quickly became apparent, however, there were no enemy soldiers willing to put up a fight.[25]

The real resistance, especially for Sykes' V Corps, came from the mountains. Sykes deployed his 1st Division, commanded by Brigadier General James Barnes, to lead the advance onto the highlands. With his 2nd and 3rd brigades in line of battle and the 1st Brigade following behind in column of divisions, Barnes' infantry began to climb the rugged northern face of Manassas Gap. The "toilsome ascent," recalled a member of the 118th Pennsylvania, was a hard slog the entire way. "The hill deflected but little from a perpendicular," he explained, "and was graced with "overhanging crags, huge boulders, a thick growth of stunted forest trees [and] dense underbrush [full of] sharp, protruding limbs" lining the mountainside to its summit.[26]

Brigadier General Samuel W. Crawford's 3rd Division found the climb just as challenging. Advancing in a column of divisions, its brigades struggled up the steep eastern side of one hill, only to find it necessary to

23 Ibid., pt. 1, 539.

24 Ibid., 572; 546; 564.

25 Ibid., 546; Smith, *Corn Exchange Regiment*, 288; Haynes, *Second Regiment New Hampshire Volunteer Infantry*, 196; Woodward, *Our Campaigns*, 284.

26 Smith, *Corn Exchange Regiment*, 288.

descend its western slope, which was so steep officers could not negotiate it on horseback and had to dismount and walk alongside their animals. Reaching the base of this hill, the men of the division discovered they had to scale what one Union soldier described as a "still steeper and higher mountain." The temperature, described as "excessively hot" (the morning low was 74 degrees) dropped several Northerners with sun stroke. One man fell and broke his neck, while another was "shot through the head" by a comrade whose weapon accidentally discharged while he struggled across the treacherous landscape.[27]

By the time Crawford's men reached the top of the second elevation, their formations had broken up, leaving companies and regiments mixed up and the troops so "completely fagged out" that more than one soldier believed even a small force of Rebels could have hurled them off the mountain. A captain in the 22nd Massachusetts concurred, writing home that "we got into an awful place and am afraid we should have been whipped if the Johnnies had fought." Luckily, the V Corps, like the III, encountered no Confederate resistance of any kind.[28]

Belatedly realizing there were no Rebels threatening his flank, at 8:00 a.m. Meade sent an order telling Sykes to bring his troops back down into the pass. Once there he was to put his men into column and move west on the road to Front Royal "immediately in rear" of the III Corps. It took so much time for the courier carrying this message to climb the mountain and find Sykes, however, that army headquarters grew impatient and resent the order at 8:30 a.m.[29]

Regardless of exactly when Meade's message threw the V Corps into reverse, the order received a mixed reception. Everyone was glad to stop clawing their way uphill, but so too were they frustrated to learn their ordeal had been unnecessary from its inception. Whether the sweat-soaked Yankee infantrymen cursed the leaders who initiated their pointless mountaineering expedition or not, they did appreciate the sea of blackberries encountered during their climb. With rations short or already gone, this agreeable treat

27 Woodward, *Our Campaigns*, 285; Krick, *Civil War Weather*, 104.

28 Ibid; Carter, *Four Brothers in Blue*, 340.

29 *OR* 27, pt. 3, 762.

was a welcome one. In the eyes of at least some Federal soldiers, the ensuing blackberry repast made their arduous hike worthwhile.[30]

Below the struggling soldiers of the V Corps, Prince's division eventually reached the foot of Green Hill, where Rodes' main line had waited for them the previous afternoon. Here, as elsewhere, there were no Confederates on hand to contest the Federal advance. The height was "lofty" and "thickly studded with undergrowth," reported General Carr, but once over it, the Yankees finally left Manassas Gap behind for the verdant Shenandoah Valley.[31]

Sometime after 10:00 a.m. and about a mile from Front Royal, the 2nd New Hampshire at last ran into a small Rebel rearguard. Under the command of Colonel Bradley Johnson, the paltry enemy force consisted of a battery of field pieces and some cavalry. The Rebel cannon fired a couple of shots in the direction of the advancing Federal skirmishers, which was enough to briefly halt the advance. Prince shifted Carr and Farnum into line and brought them up alongside Burling, with Carr taking position on his right and Franum on his left. Each officer threw out skirmishers and supports to their front. Captain Hastings' Keystone Battery galloped to the front and unlimbered on the left side of the road, its gunners, who had never been in combat, anxious to see some action.[32]

Once more, however, the enemy showed no inclination to fight. When the squadron from the 5th US Cavalry hurried to the front with orders to dash into Front Royal, the smattering of grey horsemen and enemy guns rapidly withdrew and headed south. Entering Front Royal, the Federal troopers found no sign of the enemy save some sick and wounded too ill to accompany Ewell's retreat. As Prince's infantry swept forward behind the cavalry, they could see the distant dust kicked up by Rebel columns, which were already beyond the reach of any possible pursuit.[33]

At 11:00 a.m., General Warren reported to army headquarters that he was "certain" the Rebels at Front Royal who had fled at Prince's approach were merely an "observing party." With Federal forces already in possession

---

30 Smith, *Corn Exchange Regiment*, 288.

31 *OR* 27, pt., 1, 546.

32 Ibid., pt. 2, 450, and pt. 3, 762; Haynes, *Second Regiment New Hampshire Volunteers*, 196; *OR* 27, pt., 1, 546.

33 Haynes, *Second Regiment New Hampshire Volunteers*, 196; *OR* 27, pt. 1, 539.

of the roads leading south from the village, Warren assured Meade that "no more troops are needed here."[34]

With Warren's message in hand, Meade was finally sure he had at last taken Front Royal. Unfortunately, capturing the town was no longer the prelude to destroying part of Lee's army. This was a disappointment for the embattled army commander, but hardly a surprise. After hearing the Rebels had evacuated Manassas Gap, virtually every Union commander expected to learn the Confederates had escaped. Indeed, French told Prince at the onset of his advance that, as soon as he was satisfied there was nothing in his front but cavalry and artillery, the division should retrace its steps back to Wapping Heights.[35]

When he discovered this was in fact the case, Prince rested his men at Front Royal for an hour and began his march back as ordered. Except for confirming that Lee had again slipped out of the Army of the Potomac's grasp, the Federals gained nothing from their four-day effort in Manassas Gap. Prince even left behind, as a food-consuming encumbrance, almost all of the 203 hospitalized Rebels he had found.[36]

There was nothing to do now but turn the army around and get it to Warrenton as quickly as possible. A circular issued during the afternoon set forth the route the various commands were to follow to that point. Although the movement was to begin immediately upon receipt of the order, Meade recognized that many of his units could not reach their destinations before nightfall. Therefore, each corps commander was instructed to get as far as he could before sunset and bivouac at whatever point he felt best adapted to speed his march the next day.[37]

Getting 37,000 men with their attendant guns, ambulances, and ammunition wagons out of Manassas Gap quickly and without mishap would not be easy. Meade eased the effort by ordering French's III Corps and Sykes' V Corps to march along the south side of the road while Hays' II Corps marched on the opposite shoulder, leaving the roadway clear for the guns and wagons. When the infantry arrived at the eastern entrance to the

34 *OR* 27, pt. 3, 762.

35 Ibid., 761, and pt. 1, 539.

36 Ibid., pt. 1, 539.

37 Ibid., pt. 3, 759.

Union troops coming out of the Blue Ridge, drawn by Alfred Waud.
Library of Congress

pass, the III Corps would take precedence in exiting, followed by the II and, finally, the V corps. Once beyond the gap, French was to make for Warrenton via Piedmont Station and Salem. Sykes would move through Barbee's Crossroads for the same location, while Hay's II Corps headed to Rectortown and on to White Plains, where it would obtain rations from the temporary depot established there some days ago. After filling its wagons, the corps would then make for Warrenton.[38]

Slocum's XII Corps was also directed to White Plains for resupply, after which it was to shift toward the railhead at Warrenton Junction. Sedgwick, meanwhile, would send one of the two VI Corps divisions he had marched toward Manassas Gap to Orleans and the other to Thumb Run, which flowed southwest from Warrenton. Sedgwick's remaining division, along with the Reserve Artillery and the Engineer Battalion, would march from White Plains to Warrenton. Newton's I Corps would sidle southward from Warrenton to guard the road leading to the Rappahannock River, while

38 Ibid.

Howard's XI Corps, moved east to Warrenton Junction. Army headquarters would camp for the night at Salem and go on to Warrenton next day.[39]

Meanwhile, General Buford, with Gamble's and Devin's cavalry brigades, would maintain his watchful position at Barbee's Crossroads, where Merritt's brigade would join him after leaving Manassas Gap. David Gregg received orders to move Huey's and Irvin Gregg's cavalry brigades into position to help protect Warrenton, while McIntosh's brigade shifted from Hillsboro to Snickersville. Judson Kilpatrick's division (still under Custer's command) was tasked with moving from Piedmont Station southwest to Amissville, where it could screen the army's advance on Warrenton and scout out whatever the Rebels were doing between Chester Gap and Culpeper.[40]

*   *   *

As the blue columns headed east, the weary and increasingly hungry men in the ranks had time to contemplate the miscarriage of yet another offensive effort. Coming on the heels of Meade's failure to prevent Lee's escape across the Potomac, his inability to bring the Rebels to bay at Manassas Gap proved especially frustrating. Although cries of disappointment from the ranks were not as numerous or vehement as they had been at Williamsport, there was still plenty of unhappy talk about this latest example of mismanagement by the high command.

French drew the most criticism. Unpopular with a large part of his own corps, it was little surprise that some Federal troops disapproved of their commander's performance. Private John Haley of the 17th Maine, writing in his diary, accused French of being drunk, hiding out in the rear and leaving his troops leaderless during the fighting on July 23. There is no evidence that those indictments were true. Charges of ineptness, however, were more easily supported.[41]

During the battle, for example, Warren had all but accused French of lacking aggressiveness. Months later, in testimony before the Joint

39 Ibid.

40 Ibid. and pt. 1, 149.

41 Haley, *Rebel Yell & Yankee Hurrah*, 115.

Committee on the Conduct of the War, Warren stated flatly that French had made only a "very feeble" attack and had cost the army a great opportunity. Other officers shared this assessment. According to Colonel de Trobriand French's "unskillfulness [was the] subject of comment not at all flattering."[42] A few days later, on business at headquarters, the transplanted Frenchman had a chance to meet the III Corps commander for the first time. Not surprisingly, the dapper sophisticate was unimpressed with the general's physical appearance. Even more distasteful, at least in de Trobriand's eyes, was a bottle of whiskey on French's desk, "which appeared to be on the table *en permanence*." Wishing to complete his business and depart as quickly as possible, the colonel instead found himself trapped "for a long time" as French tried to "justify" his conduct at Manassas Gap.[43]

De Trobriand found his superior's argument far from compelling and felt he made it even less so by repeating his case over and over, as though repetition would make it more believable. As the colonel put it, his "great argument" was that, except for the attack of Spinola's brigade, he had taken the pass using only skirmishers, thus keeping his main body out of sight and preventing the enemy from knowing its location. Given how easy it had been for both sides to observe one another in the mountainous terrain, the claim was patently absurd. French kept asking de Trobriand if he "understood the point." All the colonel could really see was that, through pure incompetence, "a very much confused" French had cost the army "precious time" and a chance to, at the very least, cut off General Lee's rearguard. Eventually, de Trobriand disentangled himself from the general's web of excuses and rode away in despair, worried that the "best days" of the III Corps were behind it.[44]

Whatever French's failings, there was no doubt that the strategy of pursuit and entrapment belonged to the Army of the Potomac's commander. Warren would later testify that since Lee's escape at Williamsport, Meade had "fully calculated to attack him at Manassas Gap or someplace similar to it." The general, he thought, was "more disappointed" by the outcome at

42 Warren's testimony, *The Reports of the Committees of the Senate of the United States for the Second Session, 38th Congress, 1864-1865*, 2 vols. (Washington, D.C., 1865), 381; De Trobriand, *Four Years With the Army of the Potomac*, vol. 2, 530.

43 De Trobriand, *Four Years With the Army of the Potomac*, 530-1.

44 Ibid.

Front Royal "than in anything else that happened" during the Gettysburg campaign.[45]

Given earlier complaints about his army being in no condition to fight, doubts about bringing Lee to battle once he was over the Potomac, and his belief that the proper strategy was to pause and reorganize rather than pursue the Rebels, just how deeply Meade's disappointment ran is open to speculation. Still, the powerful force he had concentrated at Manassas Gap demonstrated that he had been open to seizing opportunity and, having spotted one, had done all in his power to exploit it.

Unfortunately, Meade had based his strategy on a misreading of the situation, as he found out when General Pleasonton forwarded a dispatch from Merritt written at 9:30 a.m. on July 24. That message reported that a captured Rebel from the 13th Mississippi claimed both Generals Longstreet and A. P. Hill had moved through Chester Gap on their way to Culpeper throughout July 22 and 23. The captive Mississippian had no idea where Ewell's corps was, but by this time Meade knew he had been fighting Ewell at Manassas Gap, and so could answer that riddle himself.[46]

The fact that Meade had moved his army too late and in the wrong direction could not be denied, and to his credit, Meade didn't attempt to do so. At 8:00 p.m., he sent off a long telegram to Halleck explaining what the army had been doing during the last 24 hours, the logic behind its movements, and the intelligence upon which he had based his decision-making. Meade admitted his information had been wrong. By inference his strategy had been wrong as well and had allowed the Confederates to elude Meade's effort to bring them to battle. "I regret to inform you," he wrote the general-in-chief, that the "enemy has again disappeared."[47]

Despite Merritt's report, Meade could still not bring himself to believe that most of Lee's army had moved east through Chester Gap at almost the same instant his own men had tried to push west through Manassas Gap. The Rebels, he explained to Halleck, had been "for two days . . . retreating with great celerity" through Strasburg and Luray, sending only "sufficient force"

---

45 Warren's testimony in *The Report of the Committees of the Senate*, Vol. 2, 381.

46 *OR* 27, pt. 3, 761.

47 Ibid., pt. 1, 98-99.

into the gaps to cover Lee's flank and hold the Federal army in check. Those Rebels "disputed" control of the gap "so successfully," he continued, that the enemy rearguard had been able to safely withdraw through Strasburg.[48]

No matter how Meade tried to rationalize what had happened, the uncomfortable truth was that Lee had once more slipped beyond his reach. Press reports shied away from any comparison with Williamsport and, somewhat surprisingly, waxed sympathetic to the army commander. A story in the *New York Herald*, which was widely reprinted, contended that Meade had handled his army well, but was the victim of bad intelligence. Dubbing the fight on July 23 as the "Battle of Wapping Heights," the papers chose to emphasize the drama of the Excelsior Brigade's attack—which it called a "brilliant affair"—rather than the successful Confederate withdrawal to the Rappahannock line.[49]

The regimental historian of the 2nd New Hampshire in Burling's brigade, damned Meade with faint praise when he credited him for what the army had done—the general had "accomplished his purpose" by forcing his way through Manassas Gap and capturing Front Royal—while also noting that Lee had accomplished his purpose as well "by making Meade take a whole day to do it."[50]

Many in the ranks were not so kind. Private John Haley of the 17th Maine grasped that Meade's triumph had been tactical, while Lee's was strategic. Haley lamented that for "the second time this month Lee has evaded us," and while the Northern army had "fooled around," the Rebels "made track for Richmond with all speed." The private put the blame squarely at the feet of the Federal high command. "When we learned what fools the Rebs had made of us," he confided to his diary, "we were so mad our teeth hung out."

Regardless of who was to blame, and there was plenty of blame to go around, a most unpleasant reality remained: The last chance to follow up the defeat of Lee at Gettysburg with a potentially war-winning victory was now gone for good.[51]

---

48 Ibid., 98-99, 118.

49 *Detroit Advertiser and Tribune*, August 4, 1863.

50 Haynes, *Second Regiment New Hampshire Volunteers*, 196.

51 Silliker, *Rebel Yell & Yankee Hurrah*, 115.

CHAPTER 14

"I Have Had a Very Severe Engagement"

Ewell's Corps marches south—Longstreet moves on Culpeper—Fight of the 15th Alabama—Custer takes Amissville—Battle of Newby's Crossroads—Meade concentrates around Warrenton—The Army of Northern Virginia unites on the Rappahannock

W HILE General Meade shifted his troops east, the Confederates continued moving toward the Rappahannock River. On one side of the Blue Ridge, weather would dictate the pace of Rebel activity; on the other side, Federal cavalry would influence events.

Jubal Early camped his men three miles below Winchester on Opequon Creek on the July 23 and had them up early and on the road for Cedarville by dawn on the 24th. His short-term goal was to link up with the pontoon train retiring northward from Front Royal. Once that was achieved, he pushed his column west to Middletown on the Valley Turnpike and turned toward Strasburg. Baker's brigade of cavalry, still acting as the army's rearguard, dutifully followed along in the wake of the infantry.[1]

The weather remained hot and sticky. Early set a modest pace and halted his column once every hour for a 10-minute rest, but his troops were already tired and, admitted one, "despondent at times" from having to "bear up under the oppressive heat" of a seemingly interminable 25-mile hike. A reporter

---

1 Early, *Memoirs*, 284-85; *Richmond Daily Dispatch*, Aug. 1 and Aug 3, 1863.

marching with the column thought it "required all the energy and fortitude" the troops could muster to keep going. Little wonder that upon reaching Strasburg, the soldiers did not bother erecting tents or shelters of any kind, but simply threw themselves onto the ground and fell into a sleep "as sound and refreshing as an infant's slumber."[2]

Along the east bank of the Shenandoah River, Rodes' and Johnson's divisions were also heading south. As they made their way up the Page Valley toward Luray, the temperature rose steadily and reached the upper 80s by mid-afternoon. Suffering at the hands of a blazing sun and the dust cloud hanging over their column, the Rebels could at least be thankful the Yankees were not chasing after them. The lack of pursuit allowed General Ewell to set a leisurely pace, which was something of a necessity given the condition of his men. After covering just 12 miles, Rodes halted for the night at Milford. Johnson went into camp a little farther south after a march of only 15 miles.[3]

In contrast to what was happening in the Valley, the Confederates east of the Blue Ridge encountered more trouble from the enemy than the weather. After having been delayed for an entire day by Gamble's stout defense of Chester Gap, General Longstreet had marched throughout the night of July 22. Filtering out of the pass, his long column moved southeast through Sandy Hook and on to Flint Hill before swinging onto a more easterly path toward Gaines' Crossroads. There, at sunrise on the 23rd and about 10 miles from the mouth of Chester Gap, Longstreet halted to allow his troops a few hours to cook rations and sleep. A. P. Hill's divisions, meanwhile, came to a stop at Flint Hill, roughly three miles behind the First Corps. Longstreet resumed his march about noon on the road leading south through Newby's Crossroads toward Culpeper Court House.[4]

In between the tail of the First Corps and the head of Hill's column, Henry Benning's Georgians, accompanied by the 4th and 15th Alabama, were working hard to catch up with Evander Law's (formerly Hood's) division. The Georgians and Alabamans had been left behind to hold Manassas Gap until the arrival of Wright's brigade on the morning of July

---

2 Early, *Memoirs*, 284-85; *Richmond Daily Dispatch*, Aug. 1 and Aug 3, 1863.

3 Krick, *Civil War Weather*, 104; *OR* 27, pt. 2, 561; McDonald, *Make Me A Map*, 163.

4 Silver, *A Life for the Confederacy*, 138; *OR* 27, pt. 2, 418.

23, and had spent the rest of that day squirming through Chester Gap alongside Hill's trains. They did not pass his infantry until Hill's column stopped at Flint Hill.[5]

Once clear of the Third Corps bottleneck, Benning pushed his men two miles farther down the road in an effort to close up with Longstreet and put some distance between his brigade and Hill. Sometime around 5:00 p.m., he called a halt and put his men—who had been on the move for 20 hours—into camp. With the First Corps still many miles ahead and Hill's bivouac two miles to his rear, the Georgian knew he was on his own should trouble develop.[6]

If it arrived, danger would most likely come down the Warrenton Pike from the direction of Amissville, so Benning ordered Colonel William C. Oates to take his 15th Alabama a few miles toward Gaines' Crossroads, find a good defensive position, and keep an eye out for Yankee mischief. The 29-year old Oates, whose April 1863 commission as a colonel had not been officially confirmed by the war department, put his weary men on the road and headed east. About a quarter of a mile beyond the crossroads, he found a rail fence bisecting the road along a wooded bluff overlooking Battle Run. It was an ideal spot to make a stand. The elevation commanded the pike and a bridge spanning the creek, and the fence provided a light breastwork behind which the colonel could form a battle line.[7]

Although he took his mission seriously, Oates found the "beautiful creek of clear water" below the bluff too tempting to ignore at the end of a long, hot, and dusty march. The fiery Alabama officer ordered his men to stack arms and break ranks, and he allowed one battalion at a time to go swimming while the other kept watch. The peaceful interlude that ensued was enough to make everyone forget there was a war on, at least for a time. Unfortunately for the Rebel infantrymen, their repose would be brief. Benning had reason to fear trouble, and it was approaching in the form of Yankee cavalry.[8]

Judson Kilpatrick's division, still under George Custer's command, had ridden out of Piedmont Station that morning with orders to proceed to

---

5   *OR* 27, pt. 2, 418.

6   Ibid.

7   Krick, *Lee's Colonels*, 292; *OR* 27, pt. 2, 418; William C. Oates, *The War Between the Union and the Confederacy*, (New York, NY, 1905), 249.

8   Oates, *The War Between the Union and the Confederacy*, 249.

Amissville, which it reached at the end of a 15-mile journey around 5:00 p.m. The troopers occupied the town without resistance, after which Custer pushed an advance guard west down the Warrenton Pike toward Gaines' Crossroad. About a mile from Amissville, his troopers ran into a squad of a dozen Confederate cavalrymen herding 100 sheep and 25 head of cattle to Lee's commissary. The Southerners fled at the Federal approach, leaving the livestock behind to fill Federal bellies.[9]

Other tidbits of information picked up by Union troopers made it clear that Rebels were active in the area. Civilians claimed Confederates were "collecting and driving off" all the horses, sheep and cattle they could find. Two captured stragglers made reference to enemy forces at Culpeper and Gaines' Crossroads, while a black told Custer that Longstreet's corps had passed through the intersection early that morning. Custer found these reports intriguing, but the young brigadier wasn't quite sure what to make of them. The stragglers had been drunk, so it was hard to trust what they said, and for some reason, the general discounted the negro's information altogether.[10]

The only way to be sure of what was going on was to go see for himself, and that is what Custer intended to do. At 6:30 p.m. he wrote a dispatch to General Pleasonton relaying what he knew and promising to push "a considerable force" toward Culpeper in the morning. In the meantime, he sent Major Charles E. Capehart's 1st West Virginia Cavalry to Gaines' Crossroads to discover what Rebel troops, if any, might be there and to seize the road junction if possible.[11]

Capehart's West Virginians covered most of the four miles between Amissville and the crossroads without encountering any difficulties. A half-mile or so from Battle Run, however, they bumped into the Rebel troopers who had lost their herd to the Yankees a short time ago. The gray cavalrymen realized that enemy occupation of Amissville was potentially dangerous, so they had hovered just east of Gaines' Crossroad to see what the Northerners might be up to. Now they knew, and the lieutenant commanding the detachment courageously decided to slow the Federals

---

9   *OR* 27, pt. 3, 752-54; The regimental identity of the horsemen is not known.

10 Ibid., 752-54.

11 *OR* 27, pt. 3, 752-54, and pt. 1, 1020.

down as much as possible. After sending one man back toward Flint Hill for help, he deployed his little band across the path of the oncoming blue cavalry and fired a few rounds in their direction.

The echo of gunfire reached Colonel Oates while his second shift of Alabamans was enjoying its bath. Veterans all, the swimmers knew what the firing meant and clambered out of the creek to put on their uniforms. Minutes later a trooper Oates described as a "frightened cavalryman"— undoubtedly the courier sent back for help—galloped into the 15th's line at full speed.[12]

Oates helped to stop the horse and learned for the first time that a squad of Southern cavalry was up ahead and withdrawing from what the trooper claimed was an entire Federal brigade. After sending the courier back to his lieutenant with instructions to retreat toward the Alabamans, the colonel deployed his regiment behind the bluff-top fence. Hoping to lure the enemy into an ambush, Oates told everyone to remain out of sight until he gave the order to open fire. Shortly afterward, the Rebel cavalrymen appeared, retreated over the bridge spanning Battle Run, and hurried through Oates' line toward Gaines' Crossroad.[13]

The blue troopers were only a minute or two behind them. The enemy trotted out of a distant treeline and rode toward the bridge. It wasn't an entire brigade, but Capehart's single regiment of West Virginians. And it was riding right into Oates' trap. The colonel intended to let the enemy cross the bridge unopposed. Just before his main line would open fire, Oates planned to have Company A, which he had hidden face down behind a little hill near the bridge, rise up and rush the span to cut off the Federal retreat. Once his men delivered a surprise volley from behind the fence, the enemy would likely wheel about to withdraw over the creek. With their path obstructed, they would instead have to surrender or risk being shot to pieces from two directions.[14]

It was a clever scheme and it might have worked if Company A had let the enemy pass as ordered. Instead, its members opened fire when the head of the blue column trotted onto the bridge. A few Yankees were hit, and one

12 Oates, *The War Between the Union and the Confederacy*, 249.

13 Ibid.

14 Ibid.

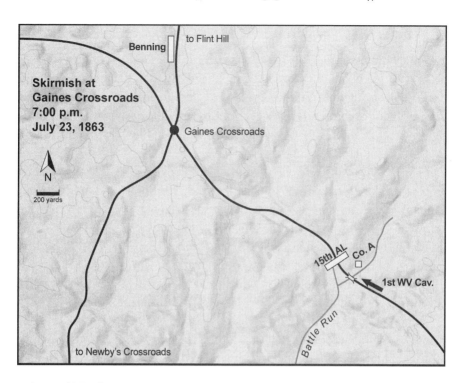

unhorsed Northerner was captured, but the rest fled before the trap could be sprung. Retreating back into some woods, the West Virginians dismounted and began exchanging fire with the Alabamans at long range. Neither side did any damage to the other. The skirmishing continued until dark, when the Federals finally withdrew to Amissville after losing one man wounded and five missing. The 15th Alabama suffered not a single casualty and maintained its post until daybreak, when the 2nd Virginia Cavalry arrived to take over its position.[15]

*   *   *

The appearance of Confederate horsemen on the field represented the end of a painful ordeal. In order to maintain an effective cavalry screen in the lower Valley, General Lee had kept Jeb Stuart with Jenkins', Fitz Lee's, and Chambliss' brigades at Leetown until July 22. When these Southern troopers rode south at dawn on the 22nd, they were a two-day march behind

15 Ibid; *OR* 27, pt. 1, 104, 1020.

Longstreet Corps and a full day's march behind Hill's troops. The Rebel horsemen did not arrived at Manassas Gap (the scene of a 48-hour standoff between Confederate infantry and Union cavalry) until the morning of July 23. After learning that Wright's brigade of Georgians held the pass and that most of Ewell's corps was due in Front Royal by the afternoon of the 23rd, Stuart concluded the situation was well in hand and he was free to follow Longstreet and Hill through Chester Gap.

The Rebel cavalry had emerged from Chester Gap late on July 23. When he reached Sandy Hook, just outside the pass, Jeb Stuart sent a dispatch to General Lee expressing his opinion that the Union presence in Manassas Gap didn't amount to much of a threat. Undoubtedly, that assessment was based on the situation that existed in the pass when Stuart left there that morning well before the appearance of French's III Corps. Still, the cavalry general's surmise was ironic, for while he was scribbling his words, General Ewell was confronting a crisis of potentially disastrous proportions.[16]

Ignorant of the Second Corps' distress, Stuart had ridden on to Flint Hill, where he swung his column a little south of town to avoid the mass of A. P. Hill's infantry before going into bivouac five miles west of Gaines' Crossroads. The ride from Leetown had taken a toll on the Southern troopers and their mounts. Rations had given out days ago, and following in the wake of two infantry corps had denied the troopers even a "chance to get a mouthful" of food, recalled one, as "every house [was] eat out along the road." As a result, Stuart's men had lived on blackberries while their horses subsisted on nothing but grass. By the time they went into camp, both men and beasts were hungry, weary, and in need of rest.[17]

Sleep would prove as difficult to find as food. Stuart's buglers sounded reveille well before dawn and by 3:00 a.m. his troopers were in the saddle and moving toward Gaines' Crossroads. En route, Stuart received a message from Lee in response to the early evening dispatch the Virginia cavalryman had sent from Sandy Hook on July 23. The army commander enclosed a note he had just received from Ewell and wrote Stuart, it "looks as if the presence of the enemy at Manassas Gap is of more importance than it appeared to

16 Ibid., pt. 3, 1037. Although the text of Stuart's 6:15 p.m. message has been lost, its content is fairly easy to discern from Lee's response on July 24.

17 Ibid.; Morissett diary, MOCW; Roger Harrell, *The 2nd North Carolina Cavalry* (Jefferson, NC, 2004), 187.

you." He went on to tell his subordinate that scouts had sent word of enemy movements toward Rappahannock Station, as well as reports of Federal trains running as far south as White Plains. The Yankees were not idle, and might still pose a serious threat if Meade was pushing troops toward Culpeper Court House.[18]

Lee did not yet know the exact position of Hill's corps. He hoped it was following Longstreet's path, but could not be certain because Hill had discretionary instructions to take an alternate route if he found fords on the Hazel River unusable. Regardless of the Third Corps' location, Lee directed Stuart to "do all in your power to cover the passage of the troops through the mountains and also gain what information you can as regards the advance of the enemy."[19]

Although the historical record leaves few clues as to how Stuart deployed his regiments on the morning of July 24, the general had clearly anticipated Lee's order—as he so often did—and led his command toward Gaines Crossroads. About a mile and a half from the road junction, Fitz Lee's brigade dismounted and Colonel Thomas T. Munford's 2nd Virginia was sent to relieve the 15th Alabama of outpost duty. Pushing beyond Battle Run, Munford's troopers ran into Federal cavalry and skirmished with it for a time. What other regiments Stuart deployed to fulfill similar tasks and where is uncertain. It appears most of his cavalry was thrown out to the north, or held near the crossroads to cover the movement of the Third Corps and its trains.[20]

As Stuart's horsemen took position near Gaines Crossroads on the morning of July 24, Longstreet's brigades, having camped along the Hazel

---

18 Morissett Diary, MOCW; *OR* 27, pt. 3, 1037. The note Lee refers to has never been found. Lee's comment—"[it] looks as if the presence of the enemy at Manassas Gap is of more importance than it appeared to you"—can be read as a rebuke of his cavalry commander and that he was displeased with Stuart's failure to secure the Blue Ridge passes, properly evaluate the situation at Manassas Gap, and support Ewell. Coming on the heels of Stuart's missteps during the Gettysburg campaign, Lee may have been especially sensitive to any potential mistakes by the cavalryman. However, it should be noted that Lee did not order Stuart to ride from Leetown until well after Longstreet's infantry was in Manassas Gap. The commanding general's order that Stuart hold Manassas Gap *and* cross the mountains to screen Longstreet and Hill may have been an unrealistic expectation for the Southern cavalry.

19 *OR* 27, pt. 3, 1037.

20 Ibid., pt. 2, 707, and pt. 3, 765; Swank, *Sabres, Saddles and Spurs*, 85.

River the previous evening (July 23), resumed their march southward for Culpeper Court House, where they arrived between 10:00 a.m. and noon on the 24th, passing through Rixeyville on the way. A. P. Hill's troops had marched away from Flint Hill at the same time the First Corps moved south from the Hazel river, following the same route toward Culpeper Court House as Longstreet. When Hill's column reached Gaines' Crossroads, however, he turned the Third Corps wagons southwest to take an alternate route to Culpeper via Sperryville and Washington. This allowed his infantry and Stuart's cavalry to stay between the slow moving trains and any potential enemy threat, as well as lessen congestion on the roads.[21]

Ahead of Hill's Third Corps, Benning's brigade and the 4th Alabama moved at daylight. After covering the last two miles to Gaines' Crossroads, they paused for a little more than an hour to wait for the 15th Alabama. Once this link up was complete, Benning put his entire command on the road for Newby's Crossroads, just 16 miles north of Culpeper Court House. Hill's corps trailed along, the head of its column not far behind the Georgians.[22]

Unbeknownst to the Confederates, George Custer was also heading for Newby's Crossroads with three regiments of Union cavalry—the 1st, 5th and 6th Michigan—accompanied by Battery M, 2nd US Artillery. Starting from Amissville, a little more than six miles away, the Federals eventually drew near the intersection along a road skirting the base of Battle Mountain, a heavily wooded 889-foot-tall elevation whose lower slopes ran right down to the crossroads. The tail of General Longstreet's First Corps cleared the area the previous afternoon. Benning's brigade, on the other hand, was just approaching Newby's about 9:00 a.m. when two Confederate troopers galloped toward the column shouting that the enemy was right behind them.[23]

Drawing rein, the pair explained to Benning they had been riding toward Amissville in hopes of getting their horses shod when they ran into a squad of Union cavalry and turned back to spread the alarm. Benning pondered the

21 *OR* 27, pt. 2, 362, 370; Mary E. Lewis, *The Life and Times of Thomas Bailey* (Courtesy Gettysburg NMP, 1994), 20. A captured Federal officer confirmed the route of Hill's train. *OR* 27, pt. 3, 766.

22 The 15th Alabama's connection with Benning was delayed because Oates' men, being out of rations, paused to breakfast in a large blackberry field. OR 27, pt. 2, 418; Stocker, *From Huntsville to Appomattox*, 131.

23 *OR* 27, pt. 1, 1004, and pt. 2, 418; Gallagher, *Fighting for the Confederacy*, 274.

Brigadier General Henry L. Benning.
Oil on canvas by Bjorn Egeli.
Special Collections Library
University of Georgia School of Law

troubling intelligence. The Yankees could be nothing more than a small scouting party, or they could be the advance guard of a much larger force. Either way, he had to confirm what was out there.[24]

When Colonel Oates volunteered to take his regiment forward to conduct a reconnaissance, General Benning accepted the offer. The Alabaman promptly shook out four of his companies onto a skirmish line, which left the other six to act as a reserve. Once all was ready, Oates advanced east to discover what enemy force was to his front. As he marched off, Benning deployed the rest of his regiments into line of battle.[25]

Approaching from the opposite direction, the 5th and 6th Michigan Cavalry regiments, followed by Battery M and the 1st Michigan Cavalry, were moving west through a dense wood on a road running along the southern end of Battle Mountain. About one mile from Newby's Crossroads, Custer ordered his two leading regiments to deploy skirmishers and probe toward the intersection. Obediently swinging from column into line, the troopers of the 5th and 6th Michigan dismounted 10 of their 12 companies for skirmish duty, keeping the remaining two as a ready mounted reserve. It took a several minutes for the horse holders to trot to the rear and the skirmishers to spread out, but once everything was ready, the Federals moved forward, the 5th Michigan holding the left flank and the 6th Michigan holding the right flank. A short time later the Midwesterners ran into Oates'

---

24 *OR* 27, pt. 2, 418.

25 Ibid; Oates, *The War Between the Union and the Confederacy*, 251. The 4th and 15th Alabama regiments were attached to Benning on July 22 to reinforce Benning's brigade and help defend Manassas Gap while the rest of Longstreet's corps moved through Chester Gap.

Alabama veterans and the two sides leveled their weapons and began trading fire.[26]

The rival lines industriously popped away at each other, but the engagement initially seemed anything but intense. The Yankee troopers moved ahead through a field of brush and timber overgrown with berries. Hungry Union soldiers, as they had the day before at Manassas Gap, couldn't ignore the ripe fruit and alternated between picking blueberries and shooting at Rebels as they advanced. After watching the action for a time, Benning concluded it was nothing more than a routine skirmish with a detachment of enemy cavalry out on a reconnaissance. When A. P. Hill sent word that he would detail a unit to relieve Oates, General Benning determined to leave the 15th Alabama behind for the moment and resume his march.[27]

As Benning moved off, Custer ordered Captain Alexander C. M. Pennington's Battery M, 2nd US Artillery into action. The captain placed three of his pieces in a clearing to the left of the road and the other three on the slope of Battle Mountain, about a quarter mile to the rear and on the roadway's opposite shoulder. As soon as his gunners were ready Pennington directed them to commence fire.[28]

The introduction of Federal cannon to the engagement surprised men on both sides of the skirmish line. Troopers in the 5th and 6th Michigan, who were still advancing but had no idea how strong the Rebels to their front might be, were delighted when they heard the whizzing shells fly overhead. The men cheered when Pennington's munitions burst above the enemy line.[29]

The Yankee artillery fire was an even bigger revelation for the Rebels. Benning's column had only marched about half a mile when, much to everyone's surprise, a shell streaked overhead, followed by several others in

26 *OR* 27, pt. 1, 1002-4; Eric Wittenberg, ed., *Under Custer's Command, Civil War Journal of James Henry Avery*, (Washington, 2000), 46; Major Crawley's report http://civilwarcavalry.com/?m=200701&paged=3

27 Wittenberg, *Under Custer's Command*, 46; *OR* 27, pt. 2, 418.

28 Janet Hewett, Noah Andrew Trudeau and Bryce A. Suderow, *Supplement to the Official Records of the Union and Confederate Armies*, 100 vols. (Wilmington, NC, 1994), Vol. 5, pt. 1, 287. Hereafter cited as *OR Supplement*.

29 Wittenberg, *Under Custer's Command*, 46; Pennington's report, *OR Supplement*, 5, pt. 1, 287.

rapid succession. Happily for the Confederates, no one was hurt by the offending projectiles, largely because an intervening hill shielded them from observation by Pennington's gunners. The unexpected barrage was not aimed at Benning's column at all, but the result of Federal guns overshooting Oates' skirmishers.[30]

Startling though the Federal fire was, Benning concluded it did not pose a serious threat and decided to push on toward Culpeper Court House. As he drew near the Thornton River, however, a message arrived from A. P. Hill asking the Georgian to pause at the ford so that the Third Corps' artillery could march behind his brigade. Benning called a halt and waited for the guns to arrive.[31]

The situation back at Newby's Crossroads, meanwhile, was becoming more ominous with each passing minute. Custer had thrown the 1st Michigan into the fight and Oates found himself in a nasty skirmish that had already cost him one lieutenant killed and three men wounded, one of them seriously. Seeing the arrival of the Third Corps column, the Alabaman rode back to the intersection in search of some help. Oates found A. P. Hill near a house, explained the state of affairs, and asked for a gun to counter the Yankee artillery. Concerned about what might lay behind the enemy's skirmish line, Hill decided it would be prudent to do a great deal more than detach a single gun.[32]

The corps commander halted his troops and deployed Henry Heth's and William Dorsey Pender's divisions into line of battle, and ordered Captain Ervin B. Brunson, commanding Pegram's battalion of artillery, to deploy enough field pieces to deal with the enemy guns. Brunson told Lieutenant William E. Zimmerman to take the four 3-inch Ordnance Rifles in his Pee Dee Artillery and silence the Union guns. At the same time, a pair of Napoleons from Captain Joseph McGraw's battery (the Purcell Artillery) was sent forward to take the Union cavalry under fire. Wright's brigade, still led by Captain Andrews, was detailed to support Brunson's guns.[33]

30 *OR* 27, pt. 2, 418.

31 Ibid.

32 Oates, *The War Between the Union and the Confederacy*, 251; *OR* 27, pt. 1, 997-1000.

33 *OR* 27, pt. 2, 615; 679. Both divisions were under Heth's leadership because Pender had fallen with a severe wound at Gettysburg. Although not considered life-threatening,

Battle of Newby's Crossroads: Forces Actually Engaged, July 24, 1863

Confederate	Union
Benning's Brigade	*3rd Brigade, 3rd Cavalry Division*
Brig. Gen. Henry Benning	Brig. Gen. George Custer
2nd Georgia Infantry	1st Michigan Cavalry
15th Georgia Infantry	5th Michigan Cavalry
17th Georgia Infantry	6th Michigan Cavalry
20th Georgia Infantry	Battery M, 2nd U.S. Artillery
	Lieut. Alexander Pennington
Law's Brigade	
(Detachment)	
4th Alabama Infantry	
15th Alabama Infantry	
Wright's Brigade	
Capt. Charles Andrews	
2nd Georgia Battalion	
3rd Georgia Infantry	
22nd Georgia Infantry	
48th Georgia Infantry	
Pegram's Artillery Battalion	
Capt. Ervin Brunson	
Pee Dee Artillery	
(Zimmerman's Battery)	
Purcell Artillery (McGraw's Battery)	

All of this took precious time—and more than anyone wished to squander. While General Hill's forces went about deploying, Benning's Georgians had little to do but loiter along the banks of the Thornton River and wonder what in the world was taking the Third Corps' artillery so long to reach them. Benning, who had been impatiently watching for Hill's artillery to roll up so that he could continue his southward march was instead surprised to see Lieutenant Robert Stanard gallop toward him from the direction of Newby's Crossroads.

The lieutenant pulled his horse up alongside Benning and explained that Pennington's Federal battery had become too troublesome for Hill to ignore.

Pender's wound proved fatal and the 29-year-old commander died on July 18 at Staunton, Virginia.

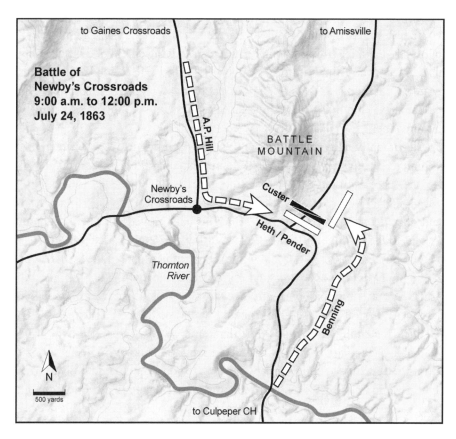

From their perch on Battle Mountain, the Yankee artillery pieces could throw shells at several points into any column marching from Newby's to the river, and in all probability could hit the ford as well. Unless those guns were silenced, they would "greatly annoy" the Third Corps' troops and trains, "if not stop their progress" altogether. Hill had decided it was necessary to drive Custer away before continuing southward.[34]

With Heth's and Pender's divisions already in line and Brunson's guns dueling with Pennington's effective battery, the Confederates were prepared to launch an assault to drive off the Yankee cavalry. The strength of the Federal position on the slopes of Battle Mountain, however, gave Hill pause. the general had plenty of experience with frontal attacks, and most of them— beginning with Beaver Dam Creek during the early stages of the Seven Days' Battles up through Gettysburg—had not gone well. An assault

34 Ibid., 419.

would be unduly risky and result in unnecessary casualties he could ill afford to lose. Instead, Hill told Benning to move around the enemy's flank, get into his rear, and cut him off from Amissville before Heth attacked with his infantry. Lieutenant Stanard knew a route by which the Georgians and Alabamans could maneuver into position unseen and would act as guide for the movement.[35]

Technically, Hill couldn't issue orders to Benning because the brigadier belonged to Longstreet's corps. But Benning, recognizing his command was the one "most conveniently situated to execute the suggested movement," and thinking "it right [to] accede" to the request, told Lieutenant Stanard to lead him where he needed to go. As the Rebels moved out, local civilians arrived to assist, including one "very willing and enthusiastic old citizen" who volunteered as an additional guide. Other inhabitants of the area offered reassurance that the only practical route between Newby's Crossroads and Amissville was the road currently occupied by Custer's cavalry. Once that road was cut, they suggested, the enemy would be trapped.[36]

While Benning undertook his flank march, Custer pushed the 15th Alabama back onto Heth's line and Pennington enjoyed a little success against Brunson's gunners by wounding three Rebels in the Pee Dee Artillery and knocking down Lieutenant Zimmerman with a shell fragment. Once close to the road linking Gaines' and Newby's crossroads, however, Custer realized he had bitten off far more than he could chew.[37]

To his front awaited an entire Confederate corps and three battalions of artillery. No matter how aggressively minded the 23-year-old brigadier might be, there would be no further advance. He also realized that if he hovered in the area too much longer, the enemy would come after him with what he described as "overwhelming force." The time had arrived to get back to Amissville before disaster struck.[38]

Custer ordered Pennington to retire four of his guns and directed the 1st Michigan Cavalry to fall back about half a mile to the east. Colonel George H. Gray would form a rearguard with his own 6th Michigan Cavalry and the

35 Ibid.

36 Ibid; Stocker, *From Huntsville to Appomattox*, 131.

37 *OR* 27, pt. 1, 1002-1004, and pt. 2, 679.

38 Ibid., pt. 1, 1002-1004.

troopers of the 5th Michigan under Major Crawley P. Dake, assisted by a section of Battery M under Lieutenant Carle A. Woodruff. After waiting long enough for the 1st Michigan and Pennington's four guns to retire, the skirmishers from the 5th and 6th withdrew to the road where their horses waited and remounted. The column still faced west toward the enemy. Colonel Gray ordered the two regiments to countermarch in order to place the 6th at the front of the column for the ride back toward Amissville. Just as the Federal troopers completed their U-turn and began trotting ahead, a sudden crash of musketry erupted from the woods on their right that sent the column retreating in the opposite direction.[39]

The volley was delivered by Benning's men, who had reached the edge of the road after a two-hour hike of several miles over rough ground and through thick woods. Despite its difficulty, the circuitous march succeeded brilliantly and carried the Rebels into a good attack position without the enemy having any idea they were nearby. By happenstance, the Southerners had come up on the road minutes after Custer withdrew part of his command, and Captain Joseph B. Newell, whose 2nd Georgia was deployed as skirmishers, sent back word that a Yankee battery (actually a two-gun section under Lieutenant Frank Hamilton) lay just beyond the brigade's right flank on the opposite side of the road.[40]

Benning wanted to capture these guns and spent considerable time shifting his flank through the heavy woods to take the pair of fieldpieces by surprise. Unfortunately, the rest of the line opened fire on Gray's column before the assault could be made. Forewarned, Hamilton's artillery beat a hasty retreat just seconds before the Rebels came storming out of the forest, pulling back a half-mile to link up with another two-gun section commanded by Lieutenant Robert Clarke.[41]

If Hamilton's withdrawal meant Pennington had managed to get most of his cannon away, the same could not be said for the section led by Lieutenant Woodruff or the 5th and 6th Michigan. The sudden enemy onset had struck with such surprise that Gray's column had been forced to quickly wheel

39 Wittenberg, *Under Custer's Command*, 46.

40 Stocker, *From Huntsville to Appomattox*, 131; *OR* 27, pt. 2, 418; *OR Supplement*, 5, pt. 1, 288.

41 Stocker, *From Huntsville to Appomattox*, 131; *OR* 27, pt. 2, 418; *OR Supplement*, 5, pt. 1, 288.

Brigadier General George A. Custer
Library of Congress

about and reverse course to avoid being cut to ribbons. In the ensuing dash, the colonel was thrown hard from his mount and, wrote one eyewitness, "run over . . . by about 40 horses." Badly hurt, Gray momentarily yielded command to Major Dake, who found himself and his men in what one Union trooper called "a pickle, sure."[42]

To the west lay an entire Rebel infantry corps supported by ample artillery. The woods to the south were full of enemy infantry, while more Confederates had cut the road to the east, which was the only known way back to Amissville. That left north as the sole means of escape, but there was nothing in that direction save the dense thickets and rocks of Battle Mountain. Back toward Amissville, Custer had Pennington open fire with his four guns to keep Benning at bay and directed the 1st Michigan Cavalry to support the captain's battery. That might keep the enemy honest for a time, but once the Southerners decided to press the issue, the Federals would have to flee or be overrun. Either option would spell doom for Gray and Woodruff.[43]

The young Michigan brigadier was in a desperate situation and, arguably, one of his own making. Not yet the famous cavalier he would become, Custer had risen through the ranks fast—some thought too fast. After graduating last in his class from West Point in June of 1861, he had been commissioned a 2nd lieutenant of cavalry and assigned to drilling recruits. Fortuitously, during the first year of the war Custer had the luck, between line assignments, to serve briefly on the staffs of several influential generals. Each was impressed with his daring. Eventually he earned

42 Wittenberg, *Under Custer's Command*, 46.

43 *OR Supplement*, 5, pt. 1, 288; *OR* 27, pt. 1, 1002-1004.

promotion to captain and an appointment as an aide to Brigadier General Alfred Pleasonton. Custer's career didn't really take off until June 22, 1863, when his new boss was promoted to major general and given command of the Army of the Potomac's cavalry corps. Just seven days later, in the hope of instilling dash into the army's struggling mounted arm, Pleasonton elevated three promising captains to brigadier general: George Custer, Wesley Merritt and Elon J. Farnsworth.

If aggressiveness was what Pleasonton was after, his selections did not let him down. Although Farnsworth was killed leading a foolhardy charge ordered by Judson Kilpatrick on the afternoon of July 3, both Merritt and Custer proved their fighting abilities throughout the Gettysburg campaign and during the pursuit of Lee's beaten army to the Potomac River and beyond. Still, there is no substitute for real experience, and having worn stars for just 25 days, Custer had not yet had a chance to acquire much of that precious commodity. In a move that perhaps foreshadowed his ultimate fate at Little Big Horn 13 years in the future, he made the mistake on July 24 of plunging into a fight without proper reconnaissance of what lay to his front.

Faced with the consequences of his error, Custer had to find a way to forestall catastrophe. Anxious to save the half of his command that was cut off, Custer sent messengers through the woods along the slope of Battle Mountain with orders for Gray to abandon his artillery and escape with his troopers and gunners through the forest. Major Dake and Lieutenant Woodruff had other ideas.

The moment Gray's regiment was forced to wheel about under Benning's attack, Woodruff had unlimbered his guns and opened fire. Sizing up the situation, Major Dake ordered Captain Smith H. Hastings to dismount M Troop from the 5th Michigan Cavalry and support the artillery. The rest of the regiment and the 6th Michigan Cavalry were ordered to move by the left flank—meaning their column faced left and undoubled its files to form a line facing Battle Mountain—and ride forward. The Union troopers found concealment by disappearing abruptly into the woods, and some additional time to look for a way through the trees back toward Custer.[44]

By this time Colonel Gray had shaken off his injury, and it didn't take him long to find an escape route for his horsemen. However, there was no

44 Wittenberg, *Under Custer's Command*, 46-7; *OR Supplement* 5, pt. 1, 288; *OR* 27, pt. 1, 1002-1004.

way the guns could roll through the dense woodland. On two occasions couriers arrived from Custer with instructions to abandon the artillery, but Woodruff and Hastings ignored the orders. The lieutenant kept firing until troopers with axes hacked just enough of a path for his cannons and caissons to make it through the brush and trees. Once a way was cleared, the Yankee gunners limbered and bumped their way first north and then east in a roundabout retreat that saved the guns from capture. The terrain was rough, rocky and choked with thick underbrush, which made dodging the freshly cut tree stumps along the ersatz road a slow and difficult process. Captain Hastings' dismounted troopers, however, fell back slowly to allow both the guns and themselves to get away, while the fire of the rest of Pennington's battery prevented Benning's men from intervening.[45]

To Custer's great relief, the nearly surrounded troops reunited with the rest of his brigade. The regiments and guns were extracted largely because of the cool-headed thinking of Gray and Dake, as well as the courage and determination of Woodruff and Hastings. A grateful Custer withdrew his command to Amissville. Fortunately for the Federals, the Confederates decided not to launch a vigorous pursuit, and by 2:00 p.m. the Union cavalry was back where it had started.[46]

*   *   *

A. P. Hill's stratagem to outflank Custer had worked admirably and at little cost, with only six Rebels wounded and one killed. Not everyone was pleased, however. As far as Henry Benning was concerned, Hill's plan could and should have accomplished much more. Surprised by the fire of Woodruff's guns, which he had not known were at the front, Benning had his troops take cover in the road, which not only offered excellent protection from the enemy's fire, but blocked the only Federal route of retreat. Or at least the general believed that was the case. He had been assured by Lieutenant Stanard and local citizens that there was "no practicable way to Amissville" other than the road occupied by his brigade, "all others being

45 Wittenberg, *Under Custer's Command*, 46-7; *OR Supplement* 5, pt. 1, 288; *OR* 27, pt. 1, 1002-1004; *OR* 27, pt. 2, 419.

46 *OR* 27, pt. 1, 1002-1004.

excluded by the mountain and its spurs." As far as the Georgian was concerned, he had the Federal "cannon and cavalry secured."[47]

In fact, the locals had been right: there was "no practicable way" out. No one gave serious consideration (or any thought, for that matter) to the possibility of the Federals cutting through timber and underbrush to escape in the least practicable manner possible. Whether Benning fully appreciated the length to which the enemy went to escape is unclear. The frustrated Georgians sent word back to Hill that the threat to Newby's Crossroads was gone. Hill returned orders for Benning to move back to the river and resume the march on Culpeper Court House.[48]

Other than achieving the primary goal of driving off Custer, Benning had few tangible rewards to show for what he described as a "brisk fight," or the four hours consumed in making a march of "at least 4 miles over very difficult ground." Nonetheless, the general bragged that his troops had defeated a "well-laid plan of the enemy, organized on rather a large scale, to impede the march and cut off the trains of a large part of our army." After magnifying somewhat the intent of the Federals at Newby's Crossroads, the Georgian went on to exaggerate their strength and later reported that he and Hill had faced "two, if not three, brigades of cavalry and two or three batteries of artillery."[49]

George Custer also expanded the scope of the fight and the effect of the battle. In a pair of messages to Pleasonton, he acknowledged having been involved in a "very severe engagement" that had cost him 30 casualties: four killed, 12 wounded, and 14 missing. After describing the course of the action, Custer admitted his brigade had been cut in two by a Rebel counterattack and gave "great credit" to Gray and Woodruff for extracting their commands—while conveniently leaving out that he had twice ordered that the guns be abandoned. He did claim credit, however, for "compelling" A. P. Hill's entire corps to halt and form line of battle, as well as sowing "great consternation through the entire rebel column." Repeating an account from a civilian living near the crossroads, Custer boasted that, although he

47 *OR* 27, pt. 2, 419.

48 Ibid.

49 Ibid.

had been unable to arrest Hill's progress, his attack had so rattled the Rebels they had "moved off hurriedly and in great disorder."[50]

Both Benning and Custer inflated the scale and impact of their fight. A. P. Hill's Third Corps had never been in any real danger. The Federal attack, reported Hill, was nothing more than a time-consuming "annoyance" quickly "put to flight." Once the Yankee cavalry was dispatched, Hill detailed William Mahone's brigade of infantry to guard the crossroads until the tail of the column had passed and renewed his southward march unmolested. That evening Hill's troops camped along the Hazel River. Benning's brigade rejoined Longstreet and the rest of the First Corps at Culpeper Court House. Hill's men would reach the same point the next day (July 25).[51]

*   *   *

That morning, as the Confederates finished their march into Culpeper, George Custer set out from Amissville on another reconnaissance, this time headed for Gaines' Crossroads. He arrived there sometime around 10:00 a.m., but did not find a trace of the enemy. The questioning of some civilians garnered the news that Albert Jenkins' cavalry brigade had remained in the area until the previous evening, but left during the night. Back at Amissville by 1:00 p.m., Custer wrote Pleasonton that whatever Rebels had been marching through the crossroads were by this time well to the south. Finding out just where they had gone was something the cavalryman was eager to do, but his men were out of rations and his horses had not had any forage for three days. My command, admitted Custer, is not "in serviceable condition," and he asked his superior to give the division "a little rest" until it could be resupplied.[52]

Custer was not in a condition to go looking for the enemy, and the rest of Meade's army was not in a position to do so. The same day that brought two Confederate corps together around Culpeper Court House found the Army of the Potomac consolidating around Warrenton, 23 miles to the north. The

---

50 Both Captain Hastings and Lieutenant Woodruff were awarded the Medal of Honor for their role in saving Woodruff's guns, although not until 1897 and 1893, respectively. *OR* 27, pt. 1, 194, 1002-3, and pt. 3, 765-6.

51 Ibid., pt. 2, 615; Oates, *War Between Union and Confederacy*, 251.

52 *OR* 27, pt. 3, 765-6.

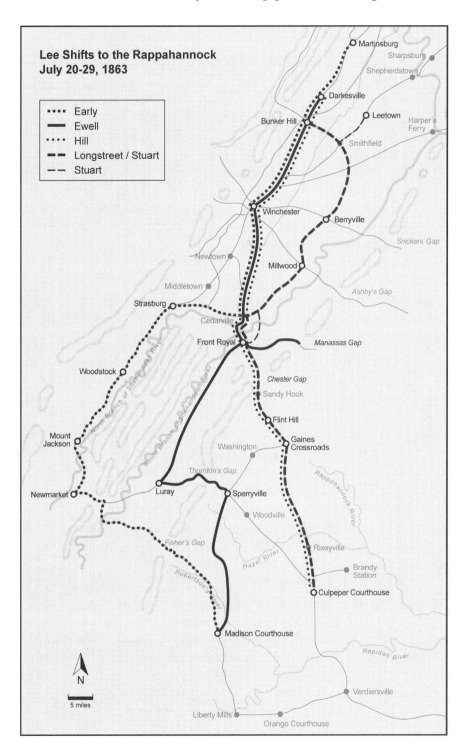

Lee Shifts to the Rappahannock
July 20-29, 1863

- ···· Early
- ——— Ewell
- ···· Hill
- — — Longstreet / Stuart
- – – Stuart

Martinsburg
Sharpsburg
Shepherdstown
Darkesville
Leetown
Bunker Hill
Harper's Ferry
Smithfield
Winchester
Berryville
Snickers' Gap
Newtown
Millwood
Middletown
Ashby's Gap
Strasburg
Cedarville
Front Royal
Manassas Gap
Woodstock
Chester Gap
Sandy Hook
Flint Hill
Mount Jackson
Gaines Crossroads
Washington
North Branch of Shenandoah River
South Branch of Shenandoah River
Rappahannock River
Thornton's Gap
Newmarket
Luray
Sperryville
Woodville
Fisher's Gap
Rixeyville
Hazel River
Brandy Station
Robertson's River
Culpeper Courthouse
Madison Courthouse
Rapidan River
N
5 miles
Verdiersville
Liberty Mills
Orange Courthouse

I Corps and XI Corps had been there for several days. Straggling into the neighborhood were the units that had been earmarked for the derailed offensive into the Shenandoah Valley.

Starting on the afternoon of July 25 and stretching well into the night, various Federal formations took up positions around Warrenton as they arrived from Manassas Gap. The III, II and XII Corps reached the area between 2:30 and 3:15 p.m. The VI Corps didn't appear until 10:30 that night, and it would be the same hour next morning before the V Corps was on hand. Uniting the army did not mean the Federals would be immediately setting out to pursue the retreating Confederates, however. Until the Orange & Alexandra Railroad could be opened to Warrenton Junction and his hungry army resupplied, Meade had no choice but to leave Robert E. Lee alone for a few days.[53]

While the Yankees gathered around Warrenton, A. P. Hill closed on Longstreet and Ewell's troops continued their southward trek on the western side of the Blue Ridge. On the same day that Hill's Third Corps arrived at Culpeper, the divisions under Rodes and Johnson reached Pass Run near Luray. Ewell's men found "excellent pasturage" for their animals in the area. Since the next day, July 26, was a Sunday, Ewell decided to give his men a well-deserved day of rest. Early on Monday morning he started them through Thornton's Gap in the Blue Ridge. The roads were in what was described as a "horrible condition" because they had been mostly neglected since the start of the war. Their poor shape, combined with the very warm day, made for a less than a pleasant march. The column trudged through the gap and reached the vicinity of Sperryville by the end of the day. The march was continued soon after sunrise on the 28th. After passing through Madison Court House, Johnson's division camped on the east bank of the Robertson River, which marked the western boundary of Culpeper County. Rodes bivouacked his men along the river's western shore.[54]

Jubal Early's division and Colonel Laurence Baker's cavalry brigade had been separated from the rest of Ewell's Second Corps since its July 21 thrust toward Hedgesville. Both started their final trek toward the Rappahannock from Strasburg on the morning of July 25. Marching for Mount Jackson, the troops endured heat, dust, and the melancholy sight of

53 *OR* 27, pt. 3, 766-768.

54 McDonald, *Make Me a Map*, 163.

scores of refugees fleeing southward with their household goods after abandoning their homes to what an accompanying reporter called "the desecration of the vandal Yankee." After covering nearly 20 miles, the Confederates had gone into camp just four miles shy of their destination. The next day, the two commands pushed on another 11 miles to New Market, where they halted for the night in the shadow of Massanutten Mountain.[55]

On the 27th, Early and Baker followed a winding road over the mountain to enter Page Valley. Heading east, they reached the South Fork of the Shenandoah around noon. There, Early brought forward the pontoon train he had shepherded south from Front Royal and directed the engineers to throw a bridge over the river. Three hours later, the span was complete and the column began crossing to the east bank. Once his and Baker's troops were on the opposite shore, the general directed that the bridge be taken up and moved to the railhead at Staunton. Early's column completed its eastward march across Page Valley by evening and camped near Hawksville, just outside the entrance to Fisher's Gap, fully prepared to cross the Blue Ridge Mountains the next day.[56]

The morning of July 28 found the Rebels beginning what would be a nearly day-long effort to pass through Fisher's Gap. Although they had the benefit of a macadamized pike, the trip was far from easy. The route was in disrepair and its "windings [were] like the convolutions of a huge serpent," recalled one Confederate. Twisting seven miles from the floor of Page Valley to the top of the pass, and then down six miles to its eastern exit, the road had so many curves that different parts of the column were often "within speaking distance" of each other, although they were several marching miles apart.[57]

The difficulties of the climb, however, were partially compensated for by the splendor of the scenery, which one witness described as "grand beyond description." As far as the troops could see there were "large smiling valleys" populated "here and there with beautiful farms, elegant residence[s] and little villages," while off in the distance the peaks of the Blue Ridge could be seen "lifting their heads above the clouds." Leaving such

55 Jones, *Reminiscences of a Louisiana Tiger*, 82; *Richmond Dispatch*, August 1863.

56 Jones, *Reminiscences of a Louisiana Tiger*, 82; *Richmond Dispatch*, August 3, 1863; Early, *Memoirs*, 285; Fisher's Gap was also known as Milam's Gap.

57 Jones, *Reminiscences of a Louisiana Tiger*, 82; *Richmond Dispatch*, August 3, 1863.

breathtaking vistas behind, the column wound its way down the eastern slope of the pass and onto flat ground to eventually camp along the banks of Robertson River. On July 29, Early and Baker reached Madison Court House, ending their five-day odyssey from Front Royal.[58]

*   *   *

The arrival of Early's division in Madison County brought an end to General Lee's strategic redeployment back to central Virginia. Against the odds—and undoubtedly against the hopes and expectations of President Lincoln, Generals Halleck and Meade, and the Northern public—he had managed to elude his pursuers after Gettysburg and make it safely back to the Rappahannock line. With the Army of Northern Virginia once more interposed between Washington and Richmond, the Confederate general and his troops had managed a significant feat. It remained to be seen if the return of the armies to the Rappahannock indicated a restoration of strategic equilibrium or presaged a renewed attempt by the Federals to capitalize on their recent success north of the Potomac.

One thing was certain. Lee had clearly outgeneraled Meade, and in doing so, had proven that he and his Virginia army were still an intact and dangerous foe despite their sharp defeat at Gettysburg. For the Federals, on the other hand, old problems persisted. Meade had demonstrated commendable strategic insight during the pursuit from Pennsylvania, but his innate caution hobbled the movements of the Army of the Potomac and allowed imagined fears to fatally influence its operations.

The pattern thus established by the rival generals during this, the final act of the Gettysburg campaign, would repeat itself throughout the coming months as Meade and Lee renewed their contest for the mastery of central Virginia and ultimate victory.

58 Jones, *Reminiscences of a Louisiana Tiger*, 82; *Richmond Dispatch*, August 3, 1863.

An Assessment of Command

ANOTHER pause in operations became apparent once the Army of the Potomac concentrated around Warrenton and the Army of Northern Virginia near Culpeper Court House. How long that hiatus might last was unknowable. What was clear then (and is obvious today) was that a significant phase of the campaign had come to an end. The Lincoln administration and the Northern public believed George Meade had fumbled a major opportunity to destroy the Army of Northern Virginia above the Potomac River. The fact that Meade had a second chance to trap the Confederate army in the northern reaches of the Shenandoah Valley was less obvious to the public at large. Both Meade's inability to bring about the destruction of Lee's army, and the ability of the Rebels to slip away under difficult circumstances, were the result of the generalship of respective commanders and the performance of their subordinates and troops.

Contrary to boastful proclamations by Union soldiers and their newspaper brethren, the final two weeks of the Gettysburg campaign proved beyond doubt the Army of Northern Virginia was neither shattered nor demoralized. Confederate troops had displayed discipline, professionalism, fortitude, and resilience throughout the withdrawal from Pennsylvania and during their trek from Falling Waters to Culpeper. Nothing more could have been asked of them, and they would have never entertained the idea of giving anything less. The same, of course, can be said of their counterparts in the Army of the Potomac. That equality of performance in the ranks is not as apparent when considering the leadership of the rival armies. Lee and his commanders clearly bested their opponents in the tactical, operational, and strategic sense.

As usual, Robert E. Lee had acted with decisiveness during the withdrawal from Gettysburg to the Potomac, and from there into central Virginia. Once across the Potomac he gave most of his troops a few days of rest, but Lee remained alert to the reality that the campaign was not over. Even though his cavalry could not tell him with certainty where Meade's army was or what it was doing, Lee assumed correctly that Meade would make his most dangerous move open to him and invade Loudoun Valley. Once he reached that conclusion, the Confederate general put his army in motion and did not second-guess that decision.

During the course of the movement to the Rappahannock River, Lee's subordinates turned in a creditable performance and the army marched with speed and agility. Both James Longstreet and A. P. Hill maneuvered their troops with the assured competence of veteran commanders who knew their business. With minimal force, they kept the Federals at bay in Manassas Gap while their two corps slipped eastward through Chester Gap. The Richard Ewell of Second Winchester appeared with demonstrable aggressiveness in the counterthrust north against Benjamin Kelley, and the expert handling of a threatening situation in Manassas Gap. All of this stood in marked contrast to the corps commanders' conduct at Gettysburg.

Lee's brigade and regimental commanders turned in an exemplary performance, which is altogether more impressive when one considers that many of them were assuming greater responsibilities than they had ever before shouldered. Brigadier Generals Montgomery Corse, William Wofford, Henry Benning, and Robert Simpson, Majors Joseph Cabell and Charles H. Andrews, in particular, fought with skill and tactical acumen despite depleted ranks and usually being outnumbered. They displayed cunning by successfully baffling or outmaneuvering their opponents rather than seeking to defeat them through brute force. The result was that vital objectives had been held or obtained without significant casualties, which was a commendable achievement.

Jeb Stuart's cavalry effectively screened Lee's army in the lower Valley and dealt decisively with threats from Union troopers under Kelley and David Gregg. Although more damage might have been done to the Federals at Shepherdstown, visions of surrounding Gregg's two brigades and destroying them on the banks of the Potomac were probably unrealistic.

Cavalry was simply too mobile to be pinned down in that fashion—a fact horsemen of both sides had proven time and again in many theaters of war, and would again that summer and fall.

The one blemish was the failure of Rebel cavalry to properly screen the Manassas and Chester gaps. This blunder might have had far more dire consequences if not for the foresight of Longstreet in deploying infantry into the passes before Yankee cavalry captured them, as well as Meade's lethargy in sending aid to his troopers. As it transpired, Southern foot soldiers barely beat the Federals to those critical points and had to do some superb fighting to hold them in check or, in the case of Chester Gap, knock the blue horsemen out of the way. Why these passes were left unguarded has never been properly explained. Perhaps it was a combination of factors, including the flooded state of the Shenandoah River, the concentration of force to screen the withdrawal of the infantry from the lower Valley, and the subsequent last-minute deployment of Stuart's troopers toward the mountains.

Despite the cavalry gaffe, Confederate operations during the two weeks between the army's reentry into Virginia and its arrival astride the Rappahannock demonstrate that Lee and his men had not lost their skill or their daring as a result of bloodletting at Gettysburg.

In contrast to the manner in which the Rebels had handled their business, the Army of the Potomac's performance left something to be desired. A *potential* (and it is important to stress that word) opportunity to destroy Lee at Williamsport had been squandered, and the chance to *potentially* cut off and wreck a portion of his army in the Valley was also missed. An even greater and more realistic chance to beat the Rebels to the Rappahannock or Rapidan was lost as well.

To be sure, the difficulties faced by Meade and his troops in trying to accomplish any of these goals were underappreciated by their government, the press, and the Northern public. In Meade's defense, he had been in command of the Army of the Potomac for less than a month by the time of the fight at Manassas Gap, and his army had suffered a serious body blow at Gettysburg and was nowhere near peak efficiency.

Once Lee got across the Potomac, George Meade displayed commendable strategic vision by entering Loudoun Valley rather than chasing Lee deeper into the Shenandoah. That move opened up the possibility of forcing Lee into battle at a disadvantage, cutting off part of his army as it tried to escape the Valley, or beating it to the old Rappahannock front. In the end, the Federals gained nothing from Meade's insight and the reason for that was the general himself.

In truth, Meade was reluctant to continue the campaign once Lee was across the Potomac, for he believed his army should stop to be reorganized and reinforced. He moved on because he was compelled follow the dictate of Lincoln and Halleck that he endeavor to cut up the Rebels wherever they may have gone. Forced into action, he pushed his army across the Potomac and continued his pursuit of his beaten enemy.

Once again on Southern soil Meade became cautious and advanced with hesitation. The army's halting movements were influenced by his serious concerns as to its condition and doubts about whether it was up to fighting another major battle so soon after Gettysburg. Whether he gave any serious consideration to the fact that the Confederate army was in the same basic shape as his own (or worse) is unknown. As a result, he essentially surrendered the initiative to the Rebels and thus always found himself one step behind Lee.

Meade's innate caution was magnified by his inability to learn anything about Lee's position west of the Blue Ridge, coupled with his fears that the Rebels were about to go over to the offensive. Although his concern was based on nothing more than a rumor in Southern newspapers that Lee was being reinforced, Meade's dread of being caught flat-footed colored everything the Army of the Potomac did for nearly a week. This apprehension led Meade to perceive Ewell's thrust toward Kelley as proof that such danger was imminent. His response was to bring the Union army's already cautious advance to a complete halt for 35 hours. That long pause proved fatal to any chance he may have had of trapping the Rebels in the Valley or beating them to the Rappahannock line.

Meade's pause of his infantry left cavalrymen Wesley Merritt and William Gamble unsupported at Manassas and Chester gaps, which enabled Longstreet and Hill to push their divisions through the mountains toward Culpeper. If Meade had advanced his infantry to support John Buford's troopers, who had seized what turned out to be the critical ground at those two mountain passes, the Federals might have been able to launch a dangerous attack though Manassas Gap or decisively block the exit to Chester Gap. Either event would have given Meade a chance to do Lee serious harm or force the Rebels farther up the Valley, opening the way for the Army of the Potomac to jump the Rappahannock and probably the

Rapidan. The consequences of that could have had a major impact on the future course of the war.

Meade, however, failed to take advantage of the accomplishments of his cavalry, which performed admirably throughout the campaign, and reacted slowly to the solid intelligence it produced. Even in the face of reports from Merritt and Gamble that Lee was withdrawing through the Blue Ridge, Meade delayed action until intelligence gathered from his signal stations made it unmistakably clear the Confederates were leaving the Valley. Only then did Meade act.

However, just as he had at Williamsport, he acted too late in northern Virginia. He only belatedly recognized the opportunity to strike the Rebels a hard blow as they tried to slide through the mountain passes, and then dispatched a single corps under William French to force Manassas Gap.

Although his performance there could hardly have been predicted (he had done well enough as a brigade and division commander), French performed poorly. To some extent French mirrored the caution of Meade and failed to use his massive preponderance of strength to push a single Rebel brigade out of his way. After wasting several hours making preparations to guard against the unlikely possibility of an enemy flank attack, French refused to make much of an offensive effort until the V Corps was on hand to support him. As a result, it was late in the day before the Excelsior Brigade drove Charles Andrews' Georgians back to the western exit of Manassas Gap, which left no time to make a follow-up assault toward Front Royal. Like Meade, French had taken one day too long to accomplish his objective and had squandered the accomplishments of his troops.

French's failures, however, were tactical in nature. Meade's mistakes were at the operational level. Despite his sound move into the Loudoun Valley and the possibilities it presented, Meade let his doubts and fears get the best of him. Notwithstanding the good work of Buford's division, which provided timely intelligence and kept possession of the critical ground for more than 24 hours, Meade badly misconstrued the strategic situation and delayed his hand just long enough to allow the Confederates to get a decisive head start. French might have redeemed Meade's error somewhat with a rapid thrust through Manassas Gap, but he failed to do so and Meade failed to press him.

The pattern set by the rival generals during this final act of the Gettysburg Campaign would repeat itself throughout the coming months as Meade and Lee renewed their contest for mastery of central Virginia.

Principle Engagements and Casualties

July 14 to July 31, 1863

Location	Date	Union Losses	Confederate Losses
Shepherdstown	July 16	135 (16 k, 64 w, 57 m)	100 (4 k, 35 w, 0 m, 61 unk)
Manassas Gap	July 21	39 (9 k, 12 w, 18 m)	26 (1 k, 3 w, 22 m)
Chester Gap	July 22	25 (1 k, 8 w, 16 m)	8 (0 k, 8 w, 0 m)
Wapping Heights	July 23	103 (20 k, 83 w, 0 m)	183 (20 k, 97 w, 66 m)
Newby's Crossroads	July 24	30 (4 k, 12 w, 14 m)	3 (0 k, 3 w, 0 m)
Total Losses		332 (50 k, 179 w, 105 m, 0 unk)	324 (26 k, 149 w, 88 m, 61 unk)

K = Killed; W = Wounded; M = Missing/Captured; Unk = Cause Unknown

Calculating precise casualty figures is impossible. The totals listed above are those reported or recorded from a variety of sources.

When commanders gave general statements on casualties (i.e. "our losses were 22 killed, wounded or missing"), I have indicated the number reported as cause unknown (unk). Whatever specific figures were given in those circumstances are included in the breakdown of killed, wounded, and missing. The number of Confederates casualties at Shepherdstown is very vague, the totals shown here represent an educated guess.

Primary Sources

Unpublished Manuscripts

Andrews, Charles. *Condensed history of the 3rd Georgia Volunteer Infantry*, Georgia Archives, 1885, http://www.3gvi.org/ga3hist1.html

Averell, William Woods, correspondence. New York State Library, Albany, NY

Bellamy, F. J., diary. Indiana State Library, Indianapolis, IN

Biddle, James Cornell. Letters, Historical Society of Pennsylvania.

Blackford, Eugene diary. *Civil War Miscellaneous Collection*, United States Army Center for Military History, Fort McNair, D.C.

Brown and Ewell Families, papers. Southern Historical Collection, University of North Carolina, Chapel Hill, NC

Carpenter, Thomas letters, Clerk Headquarters Army of the Potomac; Missouri Historical Society, Columbia, MO

Chapman, George, diary. William Henry Smith Memorial Library, Indiana Historical Society, Indianapolis, IN

Corn, A. P. to Shipman, Andrew, letter of July 20, 1863 and Shipman, J. K. P. to Shipman, Andrew, letter of Aug 27, 1863. www.rarebooks.nd.edu/digital/civil_war/letters/shipman/5043-17.shtml

Corse, Montgomery D. letters. Special Collections Branch, Alexandria Library, Alexandria, Virginia.

Crawford, George T., 5th U.S. Cavalry letter lot, www.ebay.com/itm/5th-US-Cavalry-Co-C-8-Civil-War-Letter-Lot-by-KIA-Corporal&_trksid=p2047675.m4100

Dake, Crawley P. Report on battle of Newby's Crossroads. http://civilwarcavalry.com/?m=200701&paged=3

Gregg, David McMurtrie, papers. Library of Congress, Washington, D.C.

Justice, Benjamin Wesley, papers (MSS386) Emory University, Atlanta, GA

Kirkpatrick, James; manuscript diary. Dolph Briscoe Center for American History, University of Texas at Austin, Austin, Tx.

Lane, Susan Gilbreath. *Dignity of Duty: The Journals of Erasmus Corwin Gilbreath, 1861-1898, A Personal Odyssey of Service from the Civil War to the Spanish-American War*. Chicago: Pritzker Military Museum & Library, 2013.

Lasswell, Mary. *Rags and Hope*. New York: Coward, McCann, 1961.

Lee, Robert E. General Order #82. Gilder Lehrman Institute of American History, New York, NY

Lewis, Mary E. "The Life and Times of Thomas Bailey: A Civil War Diary. Gettysburg National Military Park, Gettysburg, PA

Leon, Louis. *Diary of a Tar Heel Confederate Soldier*, electronic edition, University of North Carolina, Chapel Hill, 1998, http://docsouth.unc.edu/fpn/leon/leon.html

McVicar, Charles William, papers. Handley Regional Library, Winchester-Frederick County Historical Society, Winchester, VA

Morrisett, Algernon S., pocket diary. Eleanor S. Brockenbrough Library, Museum of the Civil War, Richmond, VA

Morissett, Lawson, pocket diary. Eleanor S. Brockenbrough Library, Museum of the Civil War, Richmond, VA

Nunnelee, Lewis T., postwar memoir/diary. Eleanor S. Brockenbrough Library, Museum of the Civil War, Richmond, VA

Smith, William Adolphus, 2nd Lt., Company J, 50th Virginia. Letters . Dolph Briscoe Center for American History, University of Texas at Austin, Austin, Tx

Sneden, Robert Knox, Diary, Volume 4. Virginia Historical Society, Richmond, VA

Soule, Pierre, letter of August 12, 1863. Gilder Lehrman Institute of American History, New York, NY

Tate, Jeremiah, letters. Gilder Lehrman Institute of American History, New York, NY

Wilber, Escek G. letters. Fondren Library, Rice University, Houston, TX

Materials Accessed On Line

Austin, Manning: 10th New York Cavalry, Letter of July 23, 1863. www.10thnycavalry.org/morrishistory.html Accessed 10/26/2015

Clapp, Alonzo, 1st Lt, Company A, 122nd New York, Diary, Onondaga, NY Historical Association, www.122ndnewyork.com/clapp1.html Accessed 7.24.2007

Consolidated Service Records, 1st North Carolina Cavalry. www.fold3.com

Consolidated Service Records, 1st Texas Infantry. www.fold3.com

Consolidated Service Records, 3rd Georgia Infantry. www.fold3.com

Consolidated Service Records, 5th North Carolina Cavalry. www.fold3.com

Douglass, Robert T. War Diary, Company F, 47th Virginia. www.localhistory.morrisville.edu/sites/letters/owen10.html Accessed 6/5/2011

Engle, Charles; Corporal, Company B, 137th New York; Letters of Aug. 23; Sept. 1, 5, 6, 13, 20, 21, 27; Oct. 1, 1863. www.members.aol.com/jocy13/ Accessed 7/24/2007

English, John J. Letter of July 9, 1863. http://www.mindspring.com/~nixnox/english.html Accessed 6/13/2011//

Hotchkiss, Jedediah, Major; 2nd Corps Staff; Letters of Aug. 21; Sept. 6; Oct. 9, 19, 22; Nov. 9, 11, 28, 30; Dec. 3, 1863; The Valley of the Shadow, Two Communities in the American Civil War, Virginia Center for Digital History, University of Virginia http://etext.lib.virginia.edu/etcbin/civwarlett-browsemod?id=A2590 Accessed 7/18/2007

Joskins, Joe; A Sketch of Hood's Texas Brigade of the Army of Virginia, 1865.

http://digital.utsa.edu/cdm/compoundobject/collection/p15125coll10/id/8440/rec/1 Accessed 3/15/2016.

Peel, A.L., War Diary of A.L. Peel. http://freepages.family.rootsweb.com/~peel.html Accessed 7/19/2007

Ricksecker, Rufus, Commissary Sergeant, 126th Ohio, Letters of Aug. 26; Sept. 10, 22, 25; Nov. 1, 15; Dec. 9-13, 1863. www.frontierfamilies.net/Family/Rufus.htm Accessed 7/24/2007

Roster of 10th New York Cavalry http://dmna.ny.gov/historic/reghist/civil/rosters/rosterscavalry.htm

Weist, Edwin B.; Company A, 20th Indiana, Diary. www.civilwarhome.com/weistdiary.htm Accessed 7/19/2007

White, William, Letters; Vermont Historical Society, Misc. File 0249; Letter of Aug. 23, 1863. www.vermonthistory.org/educate/cwletter/whitelet.htm, Accessed 7/18/2007

Winkler, Fredrick, Civil War Letters of Major Fredrick C. Winkler, Major, 26th Wisconsin; Letters of Aug. 2, 6, 10, 23; Sept. 1, 11, 17, 20, 22, 30, 1863. www.russscott.com/~rscott/25thwis/26pgwk63.htm Accessed 7/18/2007.

Wright's Brigade casualty list for Manassas Gap https://www.fold3.com/browse/249/hxF6FiBLibxaMQhEtYeHwikJcwq08GxUMUwsuIhGP Accessed 11/23/2015.

Published Memoirs and Regimental Histories

Acken, J. Gregory, ed. *Inside the Army of the Potomac: The Civil War Experience of Captain Francis Adams Donaldson*. Mechanicsburg: Stackpole Books, 1998.

Baer, Elizabeth R., ed. *Shadows on My Heart, the Civil War Diary of Lucy Rebecca Buck of Virginia*. Athens: University of Georgia Press, 1997.

Bardeen, Charles W. *A Little Fifer's War Diary*. Syracuse: C. W. Bardeen, 1910.

Bartlett, A.W. *History of the Twelfth Regiment New Hampshire Volunteers in the War of the Rebellion*. Concord: Ira C. Evans, Printer, 1897.

Baylor, George. *From Bull Run to Bull Run; or, Four Years in the Army of Northern Virginia*. Richmond: B.F. Johnson Publishing Company, 1900.

Beale, George W. *A Lieutenant of Cavalry in Lee's Army*. Boston: The Gorham Press, 1918.

Beale, R. *History of the Ninth Virginia Cavalry in the War Between the States*. Richmond: B.F. Johnson Publishing Co., 1899.

Boudrye, Louis. *Historic Records of the Fifth New York Cavalry: First Ira Harris Guard*. Albany: S.R. Gray, 1865.

Carter, Robert G. *Four Brothers in Blue*. Austin: University of Texas Press, 1978.

Cassedy, Edward K. *Dear Friends at Home: The Civil War Letters of Sergeant Charles T. Bowen, Twelfth United States Infantry, First Battalion, 1861-1865*. Baltimore: Butternut & Blue, 2001.

Coles, R. T. and Stocker, Jeffrey. *From Huntsville to Appomattox*. Knoxville: University of Tennessee Press, 1996.

Cowles, L. E. *History of the 5th Massachusetts Battery*. Boston: L. E. Cowles, Publisher, 1902.

Cowtan, Charles W. *Services of the Tenth New York Volunteers (National Zouaves) in the War of the Rebellion*. New York: Charles H. Ludwig Publisher, 1882.

Craft, David. *History of the One Hundred Forty-First Regiment Pennsylvania Volunteers, 1862-1865*. Towanda: Reporter-Journal Printing Company, 1885.

Cudworth, Warren. *History of the First Regiment Massachusetts Infantry*. Boston: Walker, Fuller Co., 1866.

De Trobriand, Regis. *Four Years with the Army of the Potomac*. Gaithersburg: Ron R. Van Sickle Military Books, 1988.

Dobbins, Austin, ed. *Grandfather's Journal*. Dayton: Morningside Press, 1988.

Early, Jubal. *Lieutenant General Jubal Anderson Early, C.S.A. Autobiographical Sketch and Narrative of the War Between the States*. New York: Konecy & Konecy, 1994.

Elwood, John. *Elwood's Stories of the Old Ringgold Cavalry: 1847-1865 The First Three Years of the Civil War*. Coal Center, PA: Morgantown Printing & Binding Co., 1914.

Farrar, Samuel C. *The Twenty-second Pennsylvania Cavalry and The Ringgold Battalion, 1861–1865*. Pittsburg: The New Werner Company, 1911.

Gallagher, Gary, ed. *Fighting for the Confederacy, The Personal Recollections of General Edward Porter Alexander*. Chapel Hill: University of North Carolina Press, 1989.

Harrison, Walter. *Pickett's Men: A Fragment of War History*. (New York, NY: D Van Nostrand, 1870.

Haupt, Herman. *Reminiscences of General Herman Haupt*. Milwaukee: Wright & Joys Co., 1901.

Haynes, E.M. *A History of the Tenth Regiment Vermont Volunteers*. Lewiston: Journal Steam Press, 1870.

Haynes, Martin, *A History of Second Regiment New Hampshire Volunteer Infantry in the War of the Rebellion*. Lakeport, NH, 1896.

Hennessy, John, ed. *Fighting With the 18th Massachusetts: The Civil War Memoir of Thomas H. Mann*. Baton Rouge: Louisiana State University Press, 2000.

Hodam, James H. *Sketches and Personal Reminiscences of the Civil War as Experienced by a Confederate Soldier Together with Incidents of Boyhood Life of Fifty Years Ago*. Eugene, OR: R. P. Hodam, 1996.

Hubbs, G. Ward. *Voices from Company D: Diaries by the Greensboro Guards, Fifth Alabama Infantry Regiment, Army of Northern Virginia*. Athens, GA: University of Georgia Press, 2003.

Humphreys, Andrew. *From Gettysburg to the Rapidan–The Army of the Potomac, July, 1863 to April, 1864*. New York: Charles Scribner's Sons, 1883.

Humphreys, Andrew. *The Virginia Campaign of 1864 and 1865*. Edison: Castle Books, 2002.

Hyndman, William. *History of a Cavalry Company: A Complete Record of Company A, 4th Penn'a Cavalry*. Philadelphia: Jas. B. Rodgers Co, Printers, 1870.

Jones, Terry, ed. *Campbell Brown's Civil War: With Ewell and The Army of Northern Virginia*. Baton Rouge: Louisiana State University Press, 2001.

——*The Civil War Memoirs of Captain William J. Seymour: Reminiscences of a Louisiana Tiger*. Baton Rouge: Louisiana State University Press, 1991.

Kohl, Lawrence F., Richard, Margaret C. ed. *Irish Green and Union Blue: The Civil War Letters of Peter Welsh: Color Sergeant 28th Massachusetts Volunteers*. New York: Fordham University Press, 1986.

Lloyd, William. *History of the First Regiment Pennsylvania Reserve Cavalry*. Philadelphia: King & Baird, 1864.

Longstreet, James. *From Manassas to Appomattox*. Secaucus, NJ: Blue & Gray Press, 1984.

Longstreet, James. "Lee in Pennsylvania," *Annals of the War*. New York: De Capo Press, 1994.

Lusk, William Thompson. *War Letters of William Thompson Lusk*. New York: Privately printed by William Chittenden Lusk, 1911

Malles, Ed, ed. *Bridge Building in Wartime: Colonel Wesley Brainerd's Memoir of the 5oth New York Volunteer Engineers*. Knoxville, University of Tennessee Press, 1997.

McDonald, Archie P., ed, *Jedediah Hotchkiss: Make Me a Map of the Valley: The Civil War Journal of Stonewall Jackson's Topographer*. Dallas: Southern Methodist University Press, 1973.

Meade, George. *Life and Letters of George Gordon Meade*. 2 volumes. New York: Charles Scribner's Sons, 1913.

Merrington, Marguerite, ed. *The Custer Story, The Life and Intimate Letters of General George A. Custer and His Wife Elizabeth*. New York: Devin-Adair, 1950.

Meyer, Henry C. *Civil War Experiences under Bayard, Gregg, Kilpatrick, Custer, Raulston, and Newberry: 1862, 1863, 1864*. New York: The Knickersocker Press, 1911.

Meyers, Frank M. *The Comanches: A History of White's Battalion, Virginia Cavalry, Laurel Brig., Hampton Div., A.N.V., C.S.A.* Marietta: Continental Book Company, 1956 reprint of 1871 edition.

Mohr, James C., ed. *The Cormany Diaries: A Northern Family in the Civil War*. Pittsburg: University of Pittsburg Press, 1982.

Moore, Frank, ed. *The Rebellion Record: A Diary of American Events with Documents, Narratives, Illustrative Incidents, Poetry, Etc., Seventh Volume*. New York: D. Van Nostrand, Publisher, 1864.

Munson, E.B., ed. *Confederate Correspondent: The Civil War Reports of Jacob Nathaniel Raymer, Fourth North Carolina*. Jefferson: McFarland & Company, Inc. Publishers, 2009.

Nanzig, Thomas P. ed. *The Civil War Memoirs of a Virginia Cavalryman: Lt. Robert T. Hubard, Jr.* Tuscaloosa: The University of Alabama Press, 2007.

Neese, George M. *Three Years in the Confederate Horse Artillery*. New York: The Neale Publishing Company, 1911.

Nevins, Allan and Thomas, Milton, eds. *The Diary of George Templeton Strong, The Civil War, 1860-1865*. 4 volumes. New York: MacMillan Co., 1952.

——*A Diary of Battle: The Personal Journals of Colonel Charles S. Wainwright,1861-1865*. New York: Da Capo Press, 1998.

Osborn, Thomas. *Battery D, 1st New York Light Artillery, Winslow's Battery*. Albany: No publisher listed, 1902.

O'Shaughnessy, Mary Searing, ed. *Alonzo's War: Letters From A Young Civil War Soldier*. Lanham, MD: Fairleigh Dickinson University Press, 2012.

Page, R. C .M. *Sketch of Page's Battery or Morris Artillery, 2nd Corps, ANV.* New York: T. Smeltzer, 1885.

Phisterer, Frederick. *New York in the War of the Rebellion*, 3rd edition. Albany: J.B. Lyon Company, 1912.

Post, Marie Caroline. *The Life and Memoirs of Comte Regis de Trobriand: Major General in the Army of the United States.* New York: E. P. Dutton, 1910.

Pyne, Henry. *History of the First New Jersey Cavalry.* Trenton: J.A. Beecher, 1871.

Quaife, Milo M. *From the Cannon's Mouth: The Civil War Letters of General Alpheus S. Williams.* Lincoln: University of Nebraska Press, 1995.

Rawle, William Brooke et al. *History of the Third Pennsylvania Cavalry 1861-1865.* Philadelphia: Franklin Printing Co., 1905.

Redding, Nicholas. *A History and Guide to Civil War Shepherdstown: Victory and Defeat in West Virginia's Oldest Town.* Lynchburg: Schroeder Publications, 2012.

Regimental Association Publication Committee. *History of the Eighteenth Regiment of Cavalry Pennsylvania Volunteers, 1862-1865.* New York: Winkoop, Hallenbeck, Crawford Co., 1909.

Regimental History Committee. *History of the Third Pennsylvania Cavalry, Sixtieth Regiment Pennsylvania Volunteers in the American Civil War, 1861-1865.* Philadelphia: Franklin Printing Company, 1905.

Rodenbough, Theophilus. *From Everglade to Canyon with the Second United States Cavalry.* Norman: University of Oklahoma Press, 2000.

Scott, Robert Garth, ed. *Fallen Leaves: The Civil War Letters of Major Henry Livermore Abbott.* Kent: The Kent State University Press, 1991.

Silliker, Ruth, ed. *The Rebel Yell & Yankee Hurrah: The Civil War Journal of A Maine Volunteer.* Camden: Down East Books, 1985.

Silver, James W., ed. *A Life for The Confederacy From The War Diary of Robert A. Moore, Pvt., CSA.* Wilmington: Broadfoot, 1987.

Sparks, David. *Inside Lincoln's Army: The Diary of Marsena Rudolph Patrick, Provost Marshal General, Army of the Potomac.* New York: Thomas Yoseloff, 1964.

Stevens, Charles. *Berdan's United States Sharpshooters in the Army of the Potomac.* St. Paul: Price-McGill Co., 1892.

Stewart, Robert L. *History of the One Hundred Fortieth Regiment Pennsylvania Volunteers.* Published by the Regimental Association, 1912.

Swank, Walbrook D., ed. *Sabres, Saddles and Spurs: Lieutenant Colonel William R. Carter, CSA.* Shippensburg: Burd Street Press, 1998.

Tobie, Edward. *History of the First Maine Cavalry, 1861-1865.* Boston: Press of Emery & Hughes, 1887.

Unknown. *History of the 16th Regiment Pennsylvania Cavalry, For the Year Ending October 31, 1863.* Ithaca: Cornell University Library, 1864.

Walker, Francis. *History of the Second Army Corps.* New York: Charles Scribner's Sons, 1887.

Ward, Joseph R.C. *History of the One Hundred Sixth Regiment Pennsylvania Volunteers 2nd Brigade, 2nd Division, 2nd Corps.* Philadelphia: Grant, Faires and Rodgers, 1883.

Warfield, Edgar. *A Confederate Soldier's Memoirs*. Richmond: Masonic Home Press, Inc., 1936

White, Russel C., ed. *The Civil War Diary of Wyman S. White: First Sergeant, Company F, 2nd United States Sharpshooters*. Baltimore: Butternut & Blue, 1991.

Williamson, James. *Mosby's Rangers*. New York: Ralph B. Kenyon, Publisher, 1896.

Wise, George. *History of the Seventeenth Virginia Infantry, C.S.A.* Baltimore: Kelly, Piet & Company, 1870.

Wittenberg, Eric, ed. *One of Custer's Wolverines: The Civil War Letters of Brevet Brigadier General James H. Kidd, 6th Michigan Cavalry*. Kent: Kent State University Press, 2000.

Wittenberg, Eric, ed. *Under Custer's Command: The Civil War Journal of James Henry Avery*. Compiled by Karla Jean Husby. Washington: Brassey's, 2000.

Woodward, E.M., *Our Campaigns; or the Marches, Bivouacs, Battles, Incidents of Camp Life and History of Our Regiment During Its Three Years Term of Service*. Philadelphia: John E. Potter, 1865.

War of the Rebellion: Official Records of the Union and Confederate Armies. Volume 27, parts 1, 2 & 3, series 1; Volume 29 parts 1 and 2, series 1; Volume 30 parts 2, 3 & 4; Volume 32 part 1; Volume 36 part 1; Volume 51, part 2, series 1. Washington, D.C.: Government Printing Office, 1890.

Hewett, Janet; Suderow, Bryce and Trudeau, Noah Andre, ed. *Supplement to the Official Records of the Union and Confederate Armies*. 100 volumes. Wilmington: Broadfoot Publishing Co., 1995.

Atlas to Accompany the Official Records of the Union and Confederate Armies. Washington, D.C.: Government Printing Office, 1890.

Newspapers

Alexandria Gazette (Alexandria, VA)

Brookville Republican (Brookville, PA)

Daily Morning Chronicle (Washington, D.C.)

Daily National Republican (Washington, D.C.)

Fayetteville Observer (Fayetteville, NC)

Harper's Weekly (New York, NY)

Illustrated London News (London, England)

National Intelligencer (Washington, D.C.)

Philadelphia Evening Bulletin (Philadelphia, PA)

Republican & Sentinel

Richmond Dispatch (Richmond, VA)

Richmond Whig (Richmond, VA)

Southern Watchman (Athens, GA)

The Abingdon Virginian (Abingdon, VA)

The Evening Star (Washington, D.C.)

The National Tribune (Washington, D.C.)

The New York Daily Tribune (New York, NY)

The New York Herald (New York, NY)
The New York Times (New York, NY)
The Philadelphia Inquirer (Philadelphia, PA)
The Press (Philadelphia, PA)
The Richmond Enquirer (Richmond, VA)
The Richmond Examiner (Richmond, VA)
The Washington Republican (Washington, DC)
The Sun (New York, NY)
The World (New York, NY)
Troy Weekly News (Troy, NY)
Wyoming Mirror (Warsaw, NY)

Secondary Sources

Alduino, Frank W. & Coles, David J. *Sons of Garibaldi in Blue and Gray: Italians in the American Civil War*. Amherst: Cambria Press, 2007.

Bache, Richard Meade. *Life of General George Gordon Meade Commander of the Army of the Potomac*. Philadelphia: Henry T. Coates and Company, 1897.

Barram, Rick. *The 72nd New York Infantry in the Civil War: A History and Roster*. Jefferson, N.C.: McFarland & Company, 2014.

Boatner, Mark III. *The Civil War Dictionary*. New York: David McKay Company, Inc., 1959.

Brown, Kent Masterson. *Retreat from Gettysburg*. Chapel Hill: University of North Carolina Press, 2005.

Caughey, Donald C. and Jones, Jimmy J. *The 6th United States Cavalry in the Civil War*. Jefferson: McFarland, 2013.

Clark, Camp. *Gettysburg–the Confederate High Tide*. Alexandria: Time-Life Books, 1985.

Clark, Walter, ed. *Histories of the Several Regiments and Battalions from North Carolina in the Great War 1861-1865*. 5 volumes. Goldsboro: Nash Brothers, 1901.

Clark, William B. *Maryland Geological Survey, Volume Two*. Baltimore: Johns Hopkins University Press, 1898.

Cleaves, Freeman. *Meade of Gettysburg*. Norman: University of Oklahoma Press, 1960.

Clemmer, Gregg. *Old Alleghany: The Life and Wars of General Ed Johnson*. Staunton: The Hearthside Publishing Company, 2004.

Coddington, Edwin B. *The Gettysburg Campaign: A Study in Command*. New York: Simon and Shuster, 1968.

Dalton, Peter. *With Our Faces to the Foe: A History of the 4th Maine Infantry*. Union: Union Publishing Co., 1998.

Dawson, John. *Wildcat Cavalry: A Synoptic History of the Seventeenth Virginia Cavalry Regiment of The Jenkins-McCausland Brigade in the War Between the States*. Dayton: Morningside House, Inc. 1982.

Divine, John. *The Thirty-fifth Battalion Virginia Cavalry*. Lynchburg: H.E. Howard, 1985.

Farnsworth, Charles E. *Whirlwind and Storm: A Connecticut Cavalry Officer in the Civil War and Reconstruction*. Bloomington: iUniverse, 2014.

Faust, Patricia, ed. Historical Times Illustrated Encyclopedia of the Civil War. New York: Harper & Row, 1986.

Freeman, Douglas Southall. R.E. Lee. 4 volumes. New York: Charles Scribner's Sons, 1935.

——Lee's Lieutenants. 3 volumes. New York: Charles Scribner's Sons, 1944.

Fyre, Dennis. The Twelfth Virginia Cavalry. Lynchburg: H.E. Howard, 1988.

——The Second Virginia Cavalry. Lynchburg: H.E. Howard, 1984.

Gallagher, Gary. Lee & His Army in Confederate History. Chapel Hill: University of North Carolina Press, 2001.

Gottfried, Bradley M. Stopping Pickett: The History of the Philadelphia Brigade. Shippensburg: White Mane Books, 1999.

Harrell, Roger. The Second North Carolina Cavalry. Jefferson: McFarland & Company Inc., Publisher, 2004.

Hartley, Chris. Stuart's Tarheels: James B. Gordon and His North Carolina Cavalry in the Civil War. Jefferson, NC: McFarland & Company, Inc., 2011.

Hattaway, Herman and Jones, Archer. How the North Won. Chicago: University of Illinois Press, 1983.

Herring, Dorothy. Company C of the Twenty-Second Georgia Infantry Regiment in the Confederate Service. Westminster, MD: Willow Bend Books, 2000.

Holland, Lynwood. Pierce M. B. Young: The Warwick of the South. Athens: University of Georgia Press, 1964.

Humphreys, Henry. Andrew Atkinson Humphreys–A Biography. Gaithersburg: Ron R. Van Sickle Military Books, 1988.

Jordon, David M. Happiness Is Not My Companion: The Life of General G.K. Warren. Bloomington: Indiana University Press. 2001.

Kesterson, Brian Stuart. Campaigning With the 17th Virginia Cavalry Nighthawks at Monocacy. Washington, WV: Night Hawk Press, 2005.

Krick, Robert. Civil War Weather in Virginia. Tuscaloosa: The University of Alabama Press, 2007.

——Ninth Virginia Cavalry. Virginia Regimental Series. Lynchburg: H.E. Howard, 1982.

——Staff Officers in Gray: A Biographical Register of the Staff Officers in the Army of Northern Virginia. Chapel Hill: University of North Carolina Press, 2003.

——30th Virginia Infantry. Virginia Regimental Series. Lynchburg: H.E. Howard, Inc. 1983.

Longacre, Edward G. Lee's Cavalrymen: A History of the Mounted Forces of the Army of Northern Virginia. Mechanicsburg: Stackpole Books, 2002.

——Lincoln's Cavalrymen: A History of the Mounted Forces of the Army of the Potomac. Mechanicsburg: Stackpole Books, 2000.

Marshall, Michael. Gallant Creoles: A History of the Donaldsonville Canonniers. Lafayette: University of Louisiana at Lafayette Press, 2013.

Matteson, Ron. Civil War Campaigns of the 10th New York Cavalry, With One Soldier's Personal Correspondence. Publisher: Lulu.com, 2007.

McGrath, Thomas. Shepherdstown: Last Clash of the Antietam Campaign. Lynchburg: Schroeder Publications, 2013.

McLean, James. *California Sabers: The 2nd Massachusetts Cavalry in the Civil War*. Bloomington: Indiana University Press, 2000.

Mesic, Harriet Bey. *Cobb's Legion: A History and Roster of the 9th Georgia Volunteers in the Civil War*. Jefferson, NC: McFarland & Co, Inc., 2011.

Meyers, Frank. *The Comanches: A History of White's Battalion, Virginia Cavalry, Laurel Brigade, Hampton Division, Army of Northern Virginia, C.S.A.* Baltimore: Kelly, Piet & Co., 1871.

Oates, Christopher Ryan. *Fighting For Home: The Story of Alfred K. Oates and the Fifth Regiment, Excelsior Brigade*. Charlotte: Warren Publishing, 2006.

Palmer, Michael. *Lee Moves North: Robert E. Lee on the Offensive from Antietam to Gettysburg to Bristoe Station*. New York: John Wiley & Sons, Inc, 1998.

Pfanz, Donald. *Richard S. Ewell: A Soldier's Life*. Chapel Hill: University of North Carolina Press, 1998.

Ray, Fred. *Shock Troops of the Confederacy: The Sharpshooter Battalions of the Army of Northern Virginia*. Asheville: CFS Press, 2006.

Rogers, Larry and Rogers, Keith. *Their Horses Climbed Trees: A Chronicle of the California 100 and Battalion in the Civil War from San Francisco to Appomattox*. Atglen: Schiffer Publishing, LTD, 2001.

Sifakis, Stewart. *Compendium of the Confederate Armies: Virginia*. Berwyn Heights: Heritage Books, 2003.

Smith, J.L. *The History of the Corn Exchange Regiment 118th Pennsylvania Volunteers. Antietam to Appomattox*. Philadelphia: J.L. Smith Pub., 1888.

Snell, Mark. *West Virginia and the Civil War: Mountaineers Are Always Free*. Charleston, S.C.: The History Press, 2011.

Staats, Richard. *History of the Sixty Ohio Volunteer Cavalry*, 2 vols. Westminster, MD: Heritage Books, 2012.

Trudeau, Noah Andre. *Gettysburg: A Testing of Courage*. New York: Harper Collins Publishers, 2002.

Trout, Robert. *After Gettysburg: Cavalry Operations in the Eastern Theater, July 14, 1863 to December 31, 1863*. Hamilton, MT: Eagle Editions Ltd, 2012

——*Galloping Thunder: The Stuart Horse Artillery Battalion*. Mechanicsburg: Stackpole Books, 2002.

——*Memoirs of the Stuart Horse Artillery Battalion: Moorman's and Hart's Batteries*. Knoxville: University of Tennessee Press, 1998.

——*Memoirs of the Stuart Horse Artillery Battalion, Volume 2: Breathed's and McGregor's Batteries*. Knoxville: University of Tennessee Press, 2010.

Urwin, Gregory. *Custer Victorious: The Civil War Battles of General George Armstrong Custer*. Edison: The Blue & Gray Press, 1983.

Warner, Ezra. *Generals in Blue*. Baton Rouge: Louisiana State University Press, 1964.

Westbrook, Robert. *History of the 49th Penn Vols*. Baltimore: Butternut and Blue, 1999.

Wittenberg, Eric J, Petruzzi, J. David, and Nugent, Michael F. *One Continuous Fight: The Retreat from Gettysburg and the Pursuit of Lee's Army of Northern Virginia, July 4-14, 1863*. New York, NY, 2008.

Wise, Jennings. *The Long Arm of Lee*. New York: Oxford University Press, 1915.

Articles

Poe, Rebecca. "Wapping or Dismal Hollow?" *Warren County Historical Society*, no date.

Polk, Leonidas L. The 43rd North Carolina Regiment during the War: "Whiffs from My Old Camp Pipe" in *Weekly Ansonian* (Polkton, NC), 1876.

Sullivan, Jack, ed. "The Dark Clouds of War" The Civil War Diary of John Zimmerman of Alexandria, Part II: The Journey Toward Appomattox." *The Alexandria Chronicle*. Alexandria: Alexandria Historical Society, Fall 2014.

Sutherland, Bruce. Pittsburgh Volunteers With Sickles' Excelsior Brigade Part 4 Gettysburg to Petersburg." *The Western Pennsylvania Historical Magazine*. Volume 45, Number 4. December 1962.

Government Documents

Report of the Joint Committee on the Conduct of the War at the Second Session of the Thirty-eighth Congress, Volume I. Washington: Government Printing Office, 1865.

Tomahawk Spring WV application for National Register of Historic Places www.wvculture.org/shpo/nr/pdf/berkeley/94001344.pdf

U.S. Census records, 1860, www.fold3.com.

Index

Jeffrey William Hunt is Director of the Texas Military Forces Museum, the official museum of the Texas National Guard, located at Camp Mabry in Austin, Texas, and an Adjunct Professor of History at Austin Community College, where he has taught since 1988. Prior to taking the post at the Texas Military Forces Museum, he was the Curator of Collections and Director of the Living History Program at the Admiral Nimitz National Museum of the Pacific War in Fredericksburg, Texas for 11 years.

Jeff holds a Bachelors Degree in Government and a Masters Degree in History, both from the University of Texas at Austin. In 2013, he was appointed an honorary Admiral in the Texas Navy by Governor Rick Perry, in recognition of his efforts to tell the story of the Texas naval forces at the Texas Military Forces Museum. Jeff is a frequent speaker for a wide variety of organizations as well as documentaries and news programs, and the author of *The Last Battle of the Civil War: Palmetto Ranch*, and has contributed to *Essential Civil War Curriculum*, the *Revised Handbook of Texas*, and the *Gale Library of Daily Life: American Civil War*.